Chicken Soup
for the Soul.

The
Dog
Really
Did
That?

Chicken Soup for the Soul: The Dog Really Did That?
101 Stories of Miracles, Mischief, and Magical Moments
Amy Newmark. Foreword by Dr. Robin Ganzert

Published by Chicken Soup for the Soul, LLC www.chickensoup.com
Copyright ©2017 by Chicken Soup for the Soul, LLC. All Rights Reserved.

Front cover photo courtesy of iStockphoto.com/LexiTheMonster (©LexiTheMonster)
Back cover photo of Riley the rescue pug by Amanda Romaniello
Interior photo courtesy of iStockphoto.com/adogslifephoto (©adogslifephoto)
Photo of Amy Newmark courtesy of Susan Morrow at SwickPix
Photo of Robin Ganzert courtesy of American Humane

Cover and Interior by Daniel Zaccari

Distributed to the booktrade by Simon & Schuster. SAN: 200-2442

Publisher's Cataloging-In-Publication Data
(Prepared by The Donohue Group, Inc.)

Names: Newmark, Amy, compiler. | Ganzert, Robin, writer of
    supplementary textual content.
Title: Chicken soup for the soul : the dog really did that? : 101
    stories of miracles, mischief, and magical moments / [compiled by]
    Amy Newmark ; foreword by Dr. Robin Ganzert, President and CEO,
    American Humane.
Other Titles: Dog really did that? : 101 stories of miracles,
    mischief, and magical moments
Description: [Cos Cob, Connecticut] : Chicken Soup for the Soul, LLC,
    [2017]
Identifiers: LCCN 2017942299 | ISBN 978-1-61159-969-5 (print) | ISBN
  978-1-61159-269-6 (ebook)
Subjects: LCSH: Dogs--Behavior--Literary collections. | Dogs--
    Behavior--Anecdotes. | Dog owners--Literary collections. | Dog
    owners--Anecdotes. | Human-animal relationships--Literary
    collections. | Human-animal relationships--Anecdotes. | LCGFT:
    Anecdotes.
Classification: LCC SF426.2 .C453 2017 (print) | LCC SF426.2 (ebook)
  | DDC 636.7/002--dc23

PRINTED IN THE UNITED STATES OF AMERICA
on acid∞free paper

25 24 23 22 21 20 19 18 17   01 02 03 04 05 06 07 08 09 10 11

101 Stories of Miracles, Mischief, and Magical Moments

Amy Newmark

Foreword by Dr. Robin Ganzert
President and CEO, American Humane

Chicken Soup for the Soul, LLC
Cos Cob, CT

Changing the world one story at a time®
www.chickensoup.com

Table of Contents

Foreword, *Dr. Robin Ganzert*..xi

❶
~One of a Kind~

1. Geometry Dog, *Jeanne R. Kraus*..................................1
2. Pal, a Working Dog, *Marie Latta*...............................5
3. My Dog Sees Dead People, *Sallie A. Rodman* 8
4. Simba's Friend, *Dawn Hendricks*..............................12
5. The Cycle of Life, *James Michael Dorsey*.......................15
6. Tough Love, *Cynthia Briggs*.................................18
7. Mandy's Story, *Carol Bromby* 22
8. The Three-Legged Wonder, *Paula W. Millet* 24
9. Disappearing Dave, *Gwen Hart* 27
10. Detective Carlos, *Carole Brody Fleet*.........................30

❷
~Dog-Gone Silly~

11. I Saved a Dog, *Julie Theel*.................................37
12. Rosy and the Wildebeest, *Joei Carlton Hossack* 40
13. Bubbalicious, *Alice Klies* 42
14. A Lick and a Promise, *Michelle Preen* 45
15. A Dog's Prayer, *Harriet E. Michael*..........................48
16. Murray and the Three Dachshunds, *Leigh Anne Jasheway*.....51
17. The Critic, *Linda Zallen*...................................54
18. Making a Splash, *Kathleen Gerard* 57
19. He Wouldn't Hurt a Fly, *Mark Rickerby* 60

❸
~So Smart!~

20. What a Buddy, *Gwen Cooper* 67
21. The Sting, *Anna Scates* 70
22. Locked Out, *Ava Pennington* 72
23. An Unexpected Angel, *Maria Atlan* 75
24. Ding Dong, *Debbie Robertson* 77
25. Willy, the Ecumenical Dog, *Doris Schoon* 80
26. Staying True to the Red, White, and Blue, *Gwen Cooper* 82
27. Good Things Come to Those Who Wait, *Dorann Weber* 85
28. Frisby Loves Bacon, *Gayle Fraser* 88
29. All in a Day's Work, *Alice M. McGhee* 90
30. Wonder Dog, *David Hull* 93
31. The Fire Marshal, *Susan A. Hoffert* 97

❹
~Crazy Canines~

32. The Battle for the Sheep Pillow, *Sally A. Breslin* 105
33. Stupid Dog Love, *Barbara Clarke* 108
34. A New Leash on Life, *Adrienne A. Aguirre* 113
35. Canines and Car Washes, *Sherri Goodall* 117
36. Down by the Bayou, *Janice R. Edwards* 119
37. Maddie and the Invisible Raccoons, *Leslie A. Wibberley* 122
38. Say Goodnight, Gracie, *Kathy McGovern* 126
39. Hyper Ready, *Tammy Allison* 130
40. Do-It-Yourself Dog Wash, *Richard Matturro* 133
41. A Bittersweet Victory, *Becky Lewellen Povich* 136

❺
~We Are Family~

42. The Housewarming Gift, *Cathi LaMarche* 143

43. Andy, *Monica Agnew-Kinnaman* 147

44. Jazmine's Journey, *Gayle M. Irwin* 151

45. The M&M Twins, *Jennifer R. Land* 154

46. Our Daisy, *Debby K. Simon* 156

47. Pierre, the Gentle Giant, *Phyllis Wheeler* 160

48. Bob and Becky, *Saralee Perel* 163

49. Megan's Mia, *Sharon Dunn* 166

50. By My Side, *Jeanie Jacobson* 169

51. Murphy, *Lisa Leshaw* 173

❻
~Who Me?~

52. On Walkabout, *Jennifer Quasha* 179

53. The Pet Collector, *Joyce Laird* 181

54. Brains Versus Brawn, *Bonnie Sargent* 184

55. What a Card! *Mason K. Brown* 186

56. I Loved Lucy, *Jeffree Wyn Itrich* 189

57. Old Shep Becomes a Mom, *William C. Gibson* 193

58. Third Home a Charm! *Deb Biechler* 196

59. Chester's Bath, *Marianne L. Davis* 199

60. Sassy, *Barbara LoMonaco* 202

61. The Dog Thief, *Eva Carter* 206

62. Hidden in Plain Sight, *Jeanne Blandford* 210

❼
~My Best Friend~

63. Keeping Friends Together, *Dr. Robin Ganzert* 217

64. Little Nike, *Charlie Ess* 220

65. A Fluffy, White Angel with Paws, *Amy Catlin Wozniak* 224

66. Perimeter Girls, *Kathleen Gerard* 228

67. A Loyal Companion, *Shelley Skuster* 231

68. The Rescued One, *Joe Petersen* 233

69. Harry, My Firstborn, *Stephen Rusiniak*............................237
70. Saint Barklee, *Alice Klies* 240
71. Saving August, *Debra Zemke* 242

❽

~My Heroic Dog~

72. Rescue Dog, *Linda Morefield*....................................249
73. One Season, *Marya Morin* 254
74. Pitch Protection, *Roslyn McFarland*............................258
75. Hunting Down My Heart, *Caurie Putnam* 262
76. Rattled, *Phillip Merrill* 265
77. Our Two Marines, *Connie K. Pombo* 269
78. My Comical Security System, *Dalia Gesser*....................272
79. My Little Heroine, *Ellyn Horn Zarek*...........................276
80. Gulliver's Heart, *C.M. LaChance* 279
81. Teacher in a Fur Coat, *Jenny Pavlovic* 282

❾

~Meant to Be~

82. Roji, the Syrian Refugee, *Brett Roberson* 289
83. Saving Blake, *Paula Sparrow*.....................................292
84. Made for Each Other, *Anna M. Lowther*........................299
85. The Love of a Little Dog, *Tammi Kelly*...........................302
86. Paying It Forward, *Joyce Laird*...................................305
87. Runaway, *Joanne Moore* 309
88. When Hootie Met Roxie, *Lynn Sunday* 313
89. A Ticket Home, *Robin L. Reynolds* 315
90. A Boy and His Dog, *Marybeth Mitcham* 318

❿
~Four-Legged Therapist~

91. The Forecast Is Sunny Today, *Suzanne D. Cook* 325
92. Animal Magnetism, *Deborah Shouse* 329
93. Sadie, the Miracle Worker, *Lorraine Lush* 332
94. Therapy for the Therapist, *Patricia Boyer* 336
95. The Big, Black Dog that Stole My Heart,
    Dori Hillestad Butler 340
96. Rex to the Rescue, *Donna L. Roberts* 344
97. It's Mutual, *Lori Hufty* 347
98. What the Little Dog Knew, *Louise Canfield* 349
99. Dialysis and the Doberman, *Caroline Brown* 353
100. Are You in There? *Joyce Becker Lee* 355
101. Mission Accomplished, *Wendy Hobday Haugh* 358

Meet Our Contributors 361
Meet Amy Newmark 377
About Robin Ganzert and American Humane 379
Thank You 381

Foreword

Many dog lovers, including myself, have asked the proverbial question: The dog really did that? As pet parents, we marvel at the miracles, the mischief and the mayhem caused by dogs we love so much.

Our best friends are a bundle of personality traits. They can be dog-gone silly; they can be *so* smart; and they can be our therapists, and often, our heroes. Sometimes they're naughty but we love them anyway. And sometimes they can be so kind and protective and intuitive that they make us want to be better people. They're one-of-a-kind and they're family as much as anyone else is family.

How did humans get so lucky to have dogs as our best friends?

Dogs throughout history have gone above and beyond the call of duty for us, saving lives on the battlefield and here at home, comforting the ill, aged and afflicted, and bringing hope to those who have lost it. That powerful, age-old bond between dogs and people is so deep, and so profoundly important to so many of us, that it's hard to imagine mankind without our canine companions.

This new Chicken Soup for the Soul collection includes such a variety of amazing tales that I couldn't put it down. Many of them made me laugh out loud, a few made me tear up, and all of them made me nod my head in recognition, agreeing that there's nothing better than adding a dog to your family. I hope the stories will encourage you to open your heart and home to adopt a new best friend from your local animal shelter or rescue group. There are millions of animals right now waiting for a forever loving home and a second chance at life.

And if you can't adopt a new best friend right now, please consider volunteering at an area shelter. Dog walkers are always needed!

You'll read all about the miracles and lovable mischief of rescue dogs in this new collection from Chicken Soup for the Soul. When I think of miracles and mischief, I remember fondly my very special Weimaraner, Ashley. She was rescued from the streets of Ashland, Kentucky, and had a heart two sizes too big for her body. One day, I was defrosting hamburger meat in the kitchen. When I came back to the kitchen, nothing was left of the frozen meat, including the foil and plastic wrap it was in, but there was one happy Weimaraner! It was a miracle she didn't get sick. Despite her heart defect, I had some glorious years with Ashley, and I fondly recall the mischief she caused, not only with hamburger meat, but with sofas and shoes too!

Sometimes it seems that our favorite stories about our dogs involve mayhem. Have you ever taken your dog through the car wash? I am not that brave! If you are ready for a laugh, you will so enjoy the mayhem in "Canines and Car Washes!" in the chapter called "Crazy Canines." Heading into a car wash with Westies turned into seven long minutes of crazy, hyperactive madness for Sherri Goodall, who vowed to never bring her dogs to the car wash again! While the outside of the car sparkled, the inside looked like a tornado had hit.

Our family has a Daisy, so I got a kick out of the fact that five of the stories in the book feature a dog named Daisy. Debby Simon's story called "Our Daisy" really hit home for me. She tells us that when her family goes to check out a rescue dog, the woman fostering her warns that she may not warm up to them right away. However, that supposedly aloof dog, Daisy, runs to Debby's daughter and makes it clear that she has found her forever family. My Daisy did the same thing!

Then there are the dogs who exhibit such empathy and intuition that it makes you wonder how anyone lives without one. Gwen Cooper's story, "What a Buddy," is about how her little Terrier walks on only three legs the whole time that Gwen is recovering from foot surgery. He doesn't resume walking on four legs until Gwen is off crutches. He also acts as a service dog for her the whole time she is recuperating, knowing just what to do without any training.

It is remarkable how dogs gravitate toward the role of therapist. You'll read countless stories in this collection about dogs intuitively helping children and adults with autism, epilepsy, cancer, and other medical conditions. Amazingly, most of these dogs were rescued from shelters, some on the verge of being "euthanized" because they were senior dogs or large, black dogs, and thus considered undesirable.

My friends at Chicken Soup for the Soul share my passion for saving these dogs, and the millions of others who are in shelters right now, waiting to go home with humans whose lives will be immeasurably enhanced by these new family members. At American Humane, we care deeply about these family bonds. I hope you enjoy my story, "Keeping Friends Together," about how we help to make a difference, one animal at a time. I tell you about a beautiful Golden Retriever who was found shot amid a major flood disaster. The dog was rushed to American Humane Rescue's mobile veterinary clinic where our veterinarian and first responders saved his life, at no charge to his human family! Even though that family lost everything they owned in the flood, the *only* thing that mattered to them was their dog.

We have had a long and fruitful partnership with Chicken Soup for the Soul, and they are generously donating a percentage of proceeds from your purchase of this book to American Humane, allowing us to save more lives of our animal friends. Thank you for making a difference and for helping us to build a more humane world!

While this book features 101 heartwarming and hilarious stories about our best friends, there are at least a million more good reasons to consider adopting a dog. If you're thinking about getting a dog, be a hero and consider adopting a dog from your local shelter or rescue group. You'll be saving a life and greatly improving yours! Dogs are amazing, supportive, and heroic companions who can make a huge difference in your world as a best friend, an exercise buddy, or simply a furry face ready to greet you when you come home after a hard day at work.

Your local shelter is the perfect place to find dogs of every type, size, age and personality — all waiting for a loving home. Or if you prefer a particular breed that isn't at your local shelter, go online to find a legitimate breed-specific rescue group in need of adopters like you.

If you're thinking about bringing an adopted dog into your family, here are some things to consider:

- Like children, dogs are completely dependent on their owners for all their needs — food, water, medical attention, exercise, shelter, and most important… companionship.
- But unlike children, dogs will never learn to pour themselves a drink, fix breakfast, or clean up after themselves.
- Dogs never learn to look both ways before crossing a street and they can't stop and ask for directions.

Opening your home to a dog can be highly rewarding, as long as you understand and accept the daily responsibilities and routines that come with owning a dog.

And remember that the qualities and personality you want in a dog are more important than size and appearance. For example, an older Shepherd mix might do better in an apartment than an energetic Terrier.

For many, the years of companionship and unconditional love and devotion they receive from their dog far outweigh the daily responsibilities.

And you may be the perfect dog owner if you…

- Believe caring for a dog for fifteen years does not seem like a lifetime.
- Look forward to big wet kisses when you come home each day.
- Like sharing your house with someone who sheds, tracks dirt occasionally and possibly drools.
- Don't mind sharing your house with someone who will never clean up after him or herself.
- Want to take care of someone every day.
- Love a playmate who likes to chase balls and drag off shoes.
- Don't mind a playmate who likes to slobber on balls and toys.
- Would like to spend your extra money on pet food, toys, veterinary care, chew bones and more chew bones.
- Want someone to adore you even on a bad hair day.

- Believe that spaying and neutering pets will help solve the pet overpopulation problem.
- Can't imagine leaving your devoted pet behind when you move.
- Want to keep an ID tag on your pets, so they can always get back to you no matter what.
- Enjoy unconditional love and constant companionship.

What a good deal for us humans — unconditional love and constant companionship! If inspiration strikes after enjoying these stories, please visit your local shelter to adopt a new best friend. Remember, there is no greater love than that of a dog.

~Dr. Robin Ganzert
President and CEO, American Humane

Chapter 1

The Dog Really Did That?

One of a Kind

Geometry Dog

I think dogs are the most amazing creatures; they
give unconditional love. For me, they are the
role model for being alive.
~Gilda Radner

Our miniature Dachshund, Maggie, was a people magnet. Cute as a button, she weighed only eight pounds. Everywhere she went, she was the center of attention, especially with children. Her love for the limelight came in handy the year she became a local celebrity known as Geometry Dog.

As Curriculum Specialist at Margate Elementary, I taught a short math review every morning on closed circuit TV for the students at Margate. I used creative props, charts and on-air activities to focus the attention of 1,000+ children, ages six to eleven, as I taught about number sense, measurement and problem-solving.

One day, as I played with Maggie I noted that her long nose resembled a cone shape. And her long body appeared to be somewhat of a cylinder shape... well, Geometry Dog was born. On mornings when I would demonstrate topics related to Geometry, my husband would bring Maggie to the TV studio.

"What are some things you can think of that have a cone shape?" I would ask the audience-at-large.

"Cone shapes are a flat circle at one end, and the opposite side comes to a point." I would demonstrate this on an ice-cream cone, a funnel, a birthday-party hat, and... Maggie, as I pointed her cone-shaped nose toward the camera.

And cylinders? "A cylinder has long, straight sides with a circle at each end." I would hold up a can of tomato soup, a can of tennis balls, a paper-towel roll and... Maggie, modeling her sleek cylindrical body at all angles as though she were a canine Cindy Crawford.

Maggie helped demonstrate "sphere" with her favorite red rubber ball. And chewy sticks lined up next to each other became examples of parallel lines. (Chewy sticks were also effective for perpendicular lines and angles.)

Soon, I discovered Maggie could be utilized effectively for measurement study as well. On the air, we used a tape measure to measure the length of a wiener dog (with and without her tail), the length of her conical nose and her short, stubby legs. Her weight could be measured on a portable scale. Measurement could be done in standard units as well as metric. Teachers assured me that the children were mesmerized when Maggie came on camera. Even the wiggle-worm kids could sit still and watch the entire Geometry Dog broadcast.

It was no wonder that Maggie became somewhat of a Dog Diva. After the broadcast, it was not unusual for Maggie's appearance to be requested. A couple of students would hurry to the studio to plead for Maggie to visit their classroom before she left for the day.

Maggie's popularity made her very useful as a reward. "The first class that gets ten behavior points in the cafeteria gets a visit from Geometry Dog." Or, "Children who read more than fifteen books this semester get to have lunch with Geometry Dog."

Geometry Dog was also called in, on occasion, to help support a child who had recently lost a family member. It seemed that holding Maggie and petting her helped those children who were experiencing sadness or loneliness. Maggie was glad to be there for them.

Geometry Dog became somewhat of a local legend. Because she was so portable, we took her with us to places like Home Depot and outdoor flea markets. We consistently ran into children from Margate Elementary School who wanted to pet Maggie and show their parents the famous "Geometry Dog." One afternoon, we had her riding in our shopping cart in a garden shop. Two children from my school noticed her immediately and got terribly excited. The next thing I knew, they were belting out the school song, feeling a burst of school pride, I guess, at seeing Geometry Dog right there in the flesh, er... fur.

She even lent a paw in school and community events. It was not unusual to find Geometry Dog at school events, such as the Character Parade and the Holiday Shoppe. ("Take your picture with Santa and Geometry Dog!")

Maggie also played a starring role in the faculty-and-staff talent show. She performed in several acts, including the role of Chastity Bono in "Sonny and Cher" and her own "Oscar Mayer Commercial" complete with a Wienermobile.

That year, the PTA had a number of extra yearbooks that had not sold. They wanted to sell the rest of them before summer vacation. Maggie "volunteered" to assist with the sales.

Yearbooks were once again advertised on TV, along with Geometry Dog. "Get your Margate yearbook and meet Geometry Dog! As a special treat, when you purchase your yearbook, Geometry Dog will 'sign' your yearbook free of charge."

A table was set up in the center of the school. The next morning, a line of waiting students stretched around the courtyard. Of course, Maggie could not really sign the yearbooks, so I signed them: *Woof — With Love From Maggie*, along with a stamped paw print. But the best part was that the kids each got to pet Maggie and have their pictures taken with her, a lasting keepsake for them to have along with their yearbook. Every yearbook was sold, and Maggie had a great day!

The year of Geometry Dog was also the year I had the honor of being Teacher of the Year for my school. Traditionally, the Teacher of the Year was asked to ride in a car in the city's Fourth of July parade. This year, Maggie was included as a celebrity to ride in the parade. We arrived at the parade site to see a Hummer limo decked out with a huge banner proclaiming:

Jeanne Krauf — Teacher of the Year
Featuring Maggie as "Geometry Dog"

Yes, my name was spelled wrong. Maggie's name, however, was spelled correctly.

Once the children saw Geometry Dog's cone-shaped nose sticking out the window of the limo, they got excited and called to her, raising quite a ruckus in the crowd. No one noticed me, the Teacher of the Year, holding her. One parent walked alongside the window and chatted a bit with me.

"So, this is the famous Geometry Dog we have heard so much about! My daughter loves that dog. It's all she talks about!" the parent said.

"Yes, this is Maggie."

The parent looked at me curiously at that point. "Do you work in the school, too?"

~Jeanne R. Kraus

Pal, a Working Dog

There is no faith which has never yet been
broken except that of a truly faithful dog.
~Konrad Lorenz

"Better to shoot him and be done with it," Gramps said. He hadn't much use for dogs, and even less for people who dropped them off on country roads. This dog had just come to their farm from nowhere, apparently. Whoever abandoned him must have done it Saturday night because the next morning, Sunday, he was there by the back door, wagging his tail, letting Gram know he'd be pleased to have any breakfast scraps she might wish to toss his way.

As far as Gramps was concerned, an animal had to earn its keep by producing meat, milk, or eggs, or by pulling a plow or killing mice. A dog did none of those.

We grandchildren who came to visit that day were delighted with the new playmate and named him Pal. He looked like a Pal. A black-and-white Shepherd, big enough to withstand our roughhousing, but gentle enough to play with the smaller children, he romped with us all day until he disappeared at 5 p.m.

We ran to the house. "Pal's gone. We can't find him anywhere."

"Good," Gramps said.

"Hey, look what's coming down there!" My little cousin Don pointed to the pasture behind the barn.

We all looked. Daisy, the ornery old Guernsey, was running toward the barn with her tail in the air. Following her at a more leisurely pace were Betsy, Brownie, and all the others. A few yards behind the last cow, Pal trotted back and forth, ready to nip the heels of any laggard.

"Why, that's a trained stock dog," Gram exclaimed.

"Should have trained him not to bring a milk cow to the barn on the run," Gramps muttered.

In the days that followed, Pal proved his usefulness around the farm in many ways. On Tuesday, Gramps sold Daisy to Mr. Anderson, but when they tried to load her into the trailer, she refused to go up the ramp.

"Put her in, Pal," Gramps ordered. Pal barked and snapped at Daisy's hind leg. She lowered her head and started toward him menacingly, but he moved too fast for her and nipped the other leg. After a minute or two, Daisy charged up the ramp and out of range of her yapping assailant.

Then on Thursday, Gram looked out the kitchen window and saw Pal trotting back and forth in front of the half-open gate to the barnyard. "Oh, my soul and body," she gasped. "Dad, Boris is out!"

Boris was their registered Holstein bull, and any other time he discovered the gate unhooked he would have been out. Not this time, however. Pal had seen the open gate, too, and it was a standoff. Boris stood in the opening, and then headed toward Pal. The dog ran at him. Boris retreated. This happened several times. Finally, Boris lumbered off to a shady spot behind the barn to get away from Pal's flashing teeth and incessant barking.

Pal barked so loud and long on Saturday night that Gramps swore he'd get rid of him the next day. Their neighbor Helen Johnson came over the next morning, however, with the news that something, a weasel probably, had gotten into her chicken coop and killed three of her Rhode Island Reds.

"My stars, that's what all the barking was about then," Gram said.

By the end of the first month, Gramps realized he had himself a dog. Pal was devoted to his new master and never strayed far from his side. He appreciated Gram as the source of his food supply, and he enjoyed tearing around the yard with any children who came to visit, but his life, his very existence, centered on Gramps and the work of the farm. Occasionally, he'd go with Gramps to help neighboring farmers when their stock got out or they needed help in loading or unloading an animal, but Pal knew where he lived and to whom he belonged.

It took a while, but Gramps actually seemed to take pride in his dog, grinning when he heard others talking of Pal's work with livestock.

The years passed. Then one hot summer day in the midst of haying season, Gramps fell ill. The doctor told him his working days were done. He and Gram sold the cows and other stock, keeping only a few laying hens. There was no longer much work for Pal to do. He began going across the road to help the Johnsons, and soon they were thinking of him as their dog. Every day, he brought their cows up to the barn. Every night, Helen put out a pan of food for him.

On warm, lazy autumn afternoons, he'd come over and snooze on the porch beside Gramps's rocking chair as long as Gramps stayed out. Then he'd leave and go back to round up the Johnsons' cows at milking time.

In October, Gramps's tired, old heart gave out. With funeral preparations and all the people coming to the house, none of us gave much thought to Pal.

Pal knew his master was gone, and his job was done. He moved across the road for good. After that, if he spied Gram out working in her flower garden or one of us kids in the yard, he'd lope over to sniff a greeting but never stayed long.

A working dog to the end, Pal never retired. One afternoon, about ten years after he came to my grandparents' farm, Darwin Johnson found his lifeless body stretched out beside the barn.

It was the first time since we'd known him that Pal missed bringing the cows up to the barn for milking at 5:00 p.m.

~Marie Latta

My Dog Sees Dead People

I have found that when you are deeply troubled,
there are things you get from the silent devoted
companionship of a dog that you can
get from no other source.
~Doris Gray

"Sallie, get out of those pajamas! Retirement doesn't mean lying around," my husband Paul said.

"I'm bored," I replied, yawning.

"That's it, come on. I'm going to fix this right now. We're going to go get that new dog that you've been talking about adopting."

"Today? I can't. I've got the California Women's Governor's Conference tomorrow, and I need to pick my break-out sessions," I replied, stalling.

"You can do that later. Let's go!"

Within the hour, we were at the Orange County Animal Shelter, wandering around the concrete rows of caged dogs. I brought a box of tissues because I knew I would cry when I couldn't save them all. There were so many sad faces in those cages, some hiding in corners, and others jumping around as if to say, "Pick me! Pick me!"

We took several out in the yard to get acquainted, but none of them seemed right. As we turned to leave, I passed a cage with a tiny, black nose peeking out.

"Paul, come see this one. She's adorable, and she's in cage 220, my birthday! It's meant to be."

She was a cute Beagle/Dachshund mix — and the tag said she was not available until the next day when her ten-day hold was up.

"Oh, Paul, I have to have her. She's perfect, but how can I do this? I have to be at the conference at 7:00 a.m. tomorrow and the shelter opens at 7:00!"

"Okay, I'll come get her for you, but let's let the office know we want her," he acquiesced.

The women in the office cautioned, "She's been very popular. You'd better be here early and take a number. First come, first served. We open the office at 7:00 a.m. but we don't start adoptions until 10:00."

"I'll be here," Paul said. I knew this was a big sacrifice for him. He had never been a pet lover and he had only tolerated all the strays we had adopted when the kids were young. That he would do this for me touched my heart.

I was so excited that I was up at dawn the next day and coaxing Paul up, too. I was afraid he'd miss his 7:00 a.m. appointment. I left for the conference with a spring in my step.

At the noon break, I called him. "Did you get her?" I asked anxiously.

"Well, barely. I got there early and took a number, but the lady next to me wanted her, too. I had to produce my #1 to prove I was first in line. She's yours now!"

"Oh, babe, thank you, thank you!"

So Mollie came to live with us, but a strange thing happened. Mollie must have belonged to a man before she was found wandering the streets of Santa Ana, California, because she only had eyes for Paul. It was like a boy and his dog. If Paul went out to the gazebo, Mollie followed. They went "gopher hunting" in our back yard together; Paul manning the hose while he yelled, "Get 'em, Mollie!" They napped together as Paul started becoming tired more easily. He was the only one she would play ball with. She was definitely Paul's girl.

Then Paul died suddenly. We all grieved heavily, even Mollie.

She moped around and wouldn't eat or play, so I started sending her to doggie daycare.

Meanwhile, I gave Paul's car to my granddaughter. She lived in San Diego, and the family would come up to visit frequently.

One day, soon after Paul died, Mollie became animated and ran to sit by the front door. I couldn't figure out her sudden exuberance. Up pulled my granddaughter in Paul's car. When the family came through the door, I could see Mollie's ears lower, and she was visibly disappointed. Then it dawned on me: She thought Paul was back. My heart broke for her.

Every time that car showed up, Mollie ran to sit by the door. And every time, she was disappointed.

The first two years rolled by, and we both grieved and held each other tight. One night, I called into a show on LA Talk Radio called "Dancing with Ghosts" where Rebecca Fearing is a well-known psychic medium. The next day was my birthday, 2/20, and I needed to hear from Paul.

"What's your name, and where are you calling from?" came the voice on the phone.

"Sallie from Los Alamitos," I replied.

"What can I do for you?" Rebecca asked.

"I wondered if you have any messages from the other side."

Rebecca told me how Paul had died, about our missed anniversary trip to Hawaii, and other things only Paul and I would know. Then she asked a question, "Who's the little black dog he's referring to?"

I thought she was speaking of dogs on the other side and started naming all the deceased black pets we had owned.

"No, he's insisting she's with you now." Mollie was lying beside me.

"Oh, that's Mollie. He adored her."

"Well, he said he loves her and talks to her every day." My heart did a flip-flop.

"Oh, that's so sweet," I mumbled, sobbing.

"Mollie can see him, Sallie, so when she's sitting and just staring at something, know he is with you both. She sees him, Sallie."

We ended our conversation, and I was glad that I had called. I know now that Paul is still looking out for Mollie and me, just like he did the day he fought to make her mine at the shelter.

~Sallie A. Rodman

Simba's Friend

*The deepest kind of peace and faith are represented by
the dove. It is thought to quiet our troubled thoughts
and renew our mind and spirit.*
~Author Unknown

Simba was our first "rescue" dog, and I do mean that in the truest sense of the word. He was about three months old, skin and bones, half wild, and as homely as they come. He resembled a mangy coyote. He was nervous, scared and would shy away if anyone came near his head to pet him. But my daughter saw him at the shelter and said, "He's the one."

He vomited all the way home and had diarrhea for days. However, with time and patience, Simba blossomed in our home, and he made us laugh and cry more times than I could count.

Simba's wild side remained with him throughout his life. I watched as he plucked a crow out of the air that was dive-bombing him. He came home with a wild turkey dangling from his mouth and made us cry each time he chased off coyotes that came near our property. We never knew if he would come back alive from those encounters.

When Simba was two years old, he was hit by a motorcycle and sustained a hip fracture. They removed the head of his femur (the ball of the hip). He healed quickly and never let it slow him down. Then he came home one night with a three-inch hole in his abdomen from an animal that had taken a big bite out of him. The wound had to heal from the inside out and took three months to do so, but it did.

Even with all those adventures, Simba survived and he was still with us at age fifteen, with a white face and paws. Then he developed Canine Vestibular Syndrome, and we thought we would lose him. We had to puree his food and feed him by hand. We carried him outside when he had to eliminate. He was unable to walk alone for two weeks. His recovery was slow, but the only residual effect was his head remained slightly tilted to the side. Simba was back to running wild and loving life.

In Simba's final months of life, he developed hyperthyroidism. His appetite was ravenous, but he was unable to keep any weight on and was slowly growing weaker. We had to stand beside him and support him to prevent him from falling. My husband and I had the "how long do we watch him decline before we do something" conversation every other day. Because Simba was still eating, drinking, and wagging his tail, we felt he still had quality of life.

Eventually, Simba spent his days just lying on his rug in the back yard, watching the birds in the feeder. We were wintering in Arizona at the time so the days were warm and sunny.

One morning while I was painting the house with Simba lying nearby, a white dove landed on the wall next to the house. The dove walked back and forth along the wall and watched us for hours. By the end of the day, he was eating out of my hand. He stayed until sunset, flew away and returned every morning thereafter.

That dove was intrigued by Simba and spent most of the day prancing around his bed, chasing the other birds away from the feeder, and sitting in the bushes above Simba's head singing his dove warbles. This sound greeted us outside the window every morning and remained until sunset. The bird became very friendly with the family and would often land on our backs or heads and crawl over Simba while he rested on his bed. He ate birdseed while Simba ate his dog food. He drank water out of Simba's dish. The dog and the dove were mesmerized with each other.

We never gave the dove a name and just assumed it was a "he." We called him "Simba's friend." We would hear him outside the window in the morning and tell Simba, "Your friend is here." The day would begin again with the two of them watching each other until the sun set. The dove returned daily for four months.

After seventeen blessed years with Simba, the day came when he died peacefully. It was one of the saddest days of our lives. Two days later, Simba's friend flew off at sunset and never returned. I always thought that he came for the food and stayed for the friendship that he developed with Simba, but I think he really came to bring peace to Simba in his final months of life.

~Dawn Hendricks

The Cycle of Life

No animal I know of can consistently be more
of a friend and companion than a dog.
~Stanley Leinwoll

Spring came late to my home this year. It usually begins in mid-March, but this year it did not come until May fourth. But then, I have a different way of measuring its arrival.

Years ago while driving through New Mexico, my wife and I were taken by the local tradition of cow skulls as decoration. They are a ubiquitous artifact of the Southwest. We returned home with one of our own.

We hung it over the door to the garage as a simple decoration, but within a week, two ambitious sparrows had moved in and began to build a nest. The large eye sockets made a perfect picture window for them with a view of our entire back yard, and the roof overhang protected them from cats and squirrels. That was in early March, fifteen years ago, and ever since then we have measured the arrival of spring by when a new family of sparrows moves into the skull.

They are industrious little critters that build a new nest in a couple of days. The male collects materials, and the female expertly weaves them into a comfortable home. With a two-week gestation and another couple of weeks for birth and flight lessons, the family will be gone five or six weeks after starting construction.

Sparrows build a new nest every year and will not re-use an old one, so every year I carefully remove the old materials. Right from the first year, I noticed that the nest was composed mostly of dog hair from our Labrador, Layla. Labradors shed like a snowstorm, and their hair is soft and pliable, an ideal material for a bird's nest. For fifteen years, our baby birds came into the world on a bed of our dog's hair.

Layla would always station herself on the patio as the monitor and guardian of the sparrow families. At the slightest activity, she would charge into the house to alert us. The best times were watching the chicks being pushed out of the nest to fly for the first time. They would plummet like a rock, frantically flapping their little wings, and then at the last second pull up out of the crash dive to fly back home. That usually brought a dog dance of joy.

Only once do I recall a little fellow not pulling up in time and crashing hard. Layla slowly walked over to the tiny bird and sniffed it. When it did not move, she prodded it with her nose and turned to me as if to say, "Do something!" I have rarely felt so helpless, but at the same time, I felt immensely proud of my dog's empathy for another living creature.

The birds became an important part of Layla's life, and some inner clock always alerted her to their annual return. When they were in residence, she watched them day and night. And when they left each year, the removal of the old nest became a ritual for both of us. She would bury her nose in it, making sure everyone was gone while taking in their scent, sensing that a part of her had kept them safe and warm. Over the years, I estimate that Layla mothered and guarded at least 100 sparrows and thought of each of them as her own pups.

We lost Layla a few months back, and maybe that is why spring did not come in March. But we have a new puppy now who is trying to fill some very large paws. On May fourth, she rushed into the house to alert us that something was happening. Outside, she had taken up her station on the same spot where Layla had kept her vigil for so many years, and the three of us watched two sparrows build a new nest in the skull.

Witnessing new life being born in the remnants of an old one is a profoundly thought-provoking experience, especially when I realize that for fifteen years I have been gifted by the cycle of life playing out in my own back yard.

And since the new dog automatically took up the station of the last, I choose to believe it is not a coincidence. Since all dogs go to heaven, I am sure Layla sent this puppy to keep watch over her birds.

~James Michael Dorsey

Tough Love

I can train any dog in five minutes. It's
training the owner that takes longer.
~Barbara Woodhouse

We're returning Henry to Dachshund rescue!" I declared to my husband, Ed, when he returned home from work. "I'm fed up with his barking and snapping every time someone comes to the house. I'm beside myself with what to do with him."

"No! He's not going back. We adopted him, so we're responsible for making it work," Ed replied firmly.

I felt stunned. In sixteen years of marriage, Ed had never said "no" to me. Tears welled in my eyes from a mixture of frustration and guilt.

We'd formed a strong bond with Henry in just five months, so it would be heart-wrenching to send him back. Nevertheless, I was at my wit's end with him terrorizing our visitors.

Ed defended him. "He's a loving dog and smart as a whip. We just have some kinks to work out. As we've discussed, it's hard telling how many foster homes he's already endured in his young life."

"I know you're right. He's a sweet boy, but he's only sweet to us!" I responded. "Are we going to gate him in your office every time we have company?"

"If that's what it takes, then that's what we'll do. I don't like the feel of returning him like a piece of damaged merchandise," Ed said.

I had an idea. "What would you say about finding a good trainer for him?"

Ed smiled. "I think that's a great idea."

Within two weeks, our seventeen-pound dynamo was receiving in-home doggie training. Natalie, Henry's trainer, came highly recommended. She explained, "I'm not here to train Henry; I'm here to train *you* so *you're* able to train Henry. Your sausage dog will be going through what I call Canine Boot Camp. Are you still ready to sign up for this training?"

We agreed.

"To begin," Natalie said, "Henry needs to learn that Ed and Cindy are the top dogs in this house, not him." She said we'd work with him to create a dedicated time-out area called "place" to use when we needed to manage his behavior. Henry came to us with a healthy ego, so busted to third in line was going to be a jolt of reality for him.

Natalie continued, "For three weeks, he's not allowed on the furniture, and he is to learn, without hesitation, to go to his 'place' when told to do so. He must work for his treats by using interactive toys. That means no tidbits pass his lips for simply being his adorable self! He only gets treats when he obeys your commands and properly uses his toys."

"So there's no cuddling on the couch while we're watching TV?" Ed asked.

"Not during the three weeks of boot camp. And after that, he's only allowed on the furniture when he's invited," she explained.

"Cuddling seems so essential in the bonding process. Withdrawing affection seems stern," I said.

Natalie explained that we were to take him on at least three walks every day, which would replace the bonding time. "Walking a dog is the best way to bond," she said. "If you walk him, he won't think affection is being withheld. In fact, in his view, he'll be getting more love and affection."

"What about getting him to accept visitors? He's totally okay with us, but he goes completely out of control, barking and nipping at everyone who comes to the house. We can't trust him, and we're afraid he's going to bite someone," I said.

"We'll cross that bridge later. The problem might resolve itself once his behavior is managed," Natalie said. Her rules sounded harsh to Ed and me, but we knew a good dose of tough love was necessary.

With that in mind, and a bag of healthy training treats in hand, Ed and I put Henry on a schedule and then followed it to the letter. It was a grueling routine, which took dedication on Ed's part and mine.

Henry embraced his training with gusto, and, fortunately for us, he responded well to the new structure. He was clearly a quick study and appeared eager to please us. Learning his "place" seemed simple enough for him, and he marched like a trooper during our walks. He was all business and on a mission to take direction.

Henry received high marks on his progress, and with each visit, Natalie praised all three of us on his improvement. On Henry's graduation day, I told Natalie that we couldn't be happier with her training techniques, and we felt his progress was largely due to her expertise. "His behavior is probably 90 percent better now than it was six weeks ago," I said to Natalie.

"He's done remarkably well, but why only 90 percent improvement?" Natalie asked.

"He has to be in a gated area whenever we have visitors. We're still fearful he'll bite someone, not to mention scaring the heck out of people when he charges them without warning," I replied.

"It sounds like it's going to take a long time for him to trust others. My guess is that in his previous family, someone loved him and treated him gently, while someone else in the family taunted and teased him. It's going to take him a long time to get past that kind of mistreatment. I think, too, excessive teasing might contribute to his nervousness because Dachshunds aren't usually this high-strung," she added.

"Keep using some of the techniques I showed you throughout training. Try to remember that he strikes out because he's frightened. It's a fight-or-flight situation, and he chooses to fight. Sadly, you might have to gate him until he adapts, if that ever happens. Remember, too, that there are usually some kinks with rescue animals that can stay with them indefinitely," Natalie said.

Some semblance of order has crept back into our home in the two years since Henry's training. Although the boot camp rules have softened, he remembers them quickly when they're enforced, and then he showers us with loads of kisses once he's released from his "place." We figure he's now approximately three years old; there are signs of him calming down and evidence of some maturing.

He's a charming, happy boy with healthy self-esteem who still spends his time in a gated area when we have guests. We sometimes allow him to mingle with visitors, but only when he's already met them a few times. He's learned the meaning of a water-filled spray bottle, which helps keep him under control around others. He seems to feel safe when he's in a room separated from strangers. Getting him accustomed to others is a slow, on-going process, just as Natalie predicted.

I'm so thankful Ed put down his foot and refused to return Henry, because now it's clear that his good qualities far outweigh his bad. He's a funny and lively little guy who brings joy to our lives.

~Cynthia Briggs

Mandy's Story

> *Until one has loved an animal, a part of*
> *one's soul remains unawakened.*
> *~Anatole France*

A number of years ago, while working as a preschool consultant for a local hospital, I had a client named Debbie who was visually impaired. She was a single parent, and on one visit she informed me that her guide dog, a beautiful ten-year-old yellow Lab named Mandy, was "retiring." My client had a new guide dog, and was looking for someone to take home for Mandy.

My husband and I had been thinking about getting a dog, but we couldn't agree on when. I said I would take Mandy, but I told my husband and our eight-year-old daughter that I was just caring for her for a few weeks until Debbie could find her a new home.

Mandy settled in very well, although she continued to guide for us — getting up every time we did and following us around the house, and stopping at each curb when we took walks. She wouldn't let us cross if any cars or obstacles were approaching.

We made her part of our life, and she joined us for trips to our cottage, long walks, and cross-country skiing. After a number of weeks, my husband and daughter voiced their sadness that she would some day leave our home to live with someone else, so I confessed that Mandy could live with us permanently. I was greeted with whoops of joy, and Mandy was given many loving hugs.

It took Mandy over a year to stop guiding all of us, and to fully retire and just become a well-loved family pet. We kept in contact with Debbie and even went once to visit her at her apartment. As soon as we got to the front of the building, Mandy knew where to find the elevator, which way to get off the elevator, and which door was Debbie's. They had a wonderful reunion.

As Mandy approached her twelfth year, she started to really slow down, often just lying outside my husband's home office, or by the fireplace or the back door. Mandy was not eating very much, so we had the feeling that her end of life was near. I called Debbie to ask her what she wanted me to do. She said that Mandy was our dog now, but she really would like her ashes to be spread outside in nature.

One morning, Mandy could not get up. I called our veterinarian, and she advised us to bring her in. She felt it was time for Mandy to go. My husband was away on a business trip, and my daughter was at school. I was so upset and didn't know how I could handle this alone.

So, I called Debbie, explained the situation, and asked if she would like to say some final words to Mandy. She did. I held the phone to Mandy's ear, and Debbie started talking. I did not hear everything that she said to that beautiful dog, but Mandy was wagging her tail back and forth across the floor as she heard her beloved Debbie talk to her. Oh, how I cried as these two beings who loved each other for so many years said goodbye to each other. After Debbie stopped talking, I told her that all her love had reached Mandy, and I would cover her with more love when I brought her to the vet.

Mandy died peacefully with my arms around her as I whispered all the names of the people who loved her. Because we live in the country with a very peaceful tree-lined back yard, we buried Mandy's ashes under a pine tree outside our kitchen window.

We've had a few other dogs enter our life over the past fifteen years, but that beautiful yellow Lab, who gave so much of herself to others, still holds the most precious place in all of our hearts. Gone, but never forgotten.

~Carol Bromby

The Three-Legged Wonder

You think dogs will not be in heaven? I tell you,
they will be there long before any of us.
~Robert Louis Stevenson

When we announced that we were moving to another state, our three boys were not happy. But we were smart and played the trump card. "We will get you guys a dog," my husband announced proudly. And as though a magical fairy had appeared, sprinkling happy dust all over the room, the mood lifted and the boys cheered. "A dog!" they shouted. "Yay!"

Two months later, before we had even unpacked the pots and pans, there were not-so-subtle reminders about the promise. "When is the dog coming?" they asked anxiously. And we always responded, "Soon. Very soon."

As luck would have it, one of my husband's co-workers was trying to find a home for a foster dog, a black Lab named Man. I eyed my husband skeptically when he came home, whispering the details so that the boys wouldn't hear. I had visions of a cute, fluffy lap dog, one that would be easy to contain. A sixty-pound, jet-black Labrador Retriever wasn't what I had planned to add to our already crazy household. But then came the vivid reminder: I was always outnumbered when the males voted in solidarity for anything.

Man arrived two days later like a bull in a china closet, knocking over lamps with a wag of his tail and jumping into our laps with wild abandon as he showered us with kisses. The boys were smitten. They immediately took off on adventures, exploring the new neighborhood with their buddy in tow, even sneaking him into the neighborhood pool for a swim. And if I ever needed to locate them, I simply had to look for Man, who would park himself outside of the homes of their playmates, sitting like a proud sentinel as he guarded his charges.

We soon learned that Man had a bit of wanderlust himself. He would stand at the door, whining pitifully to be released, where he would romp in the back yard, chasing squirrels and then jumping the fence as soon as we turned our backs. I think he enjoyed those moments of hide-and-seek, a game he played with regularity, much to our frustration.

One morning he jumped the fence as we all rushed around to get ready for school and work. Like most tragic accidents, it happened in a second. As we heard the screech of tires and the yelps that followed, we knew with alarming certainty that he had been hurt.

As the boys stood in the driveway crying, my husband sprang into action to get Man to the vet. Within hours, we received the news. His leg had been badly injured; it would need to be amputated.

Over the next few days, we feared for his future and the quality of his life. We tried not to joke about the fact that his fence-jumping days were over. But any concerns went by the wayside when we went to pick him up following his surgery. During his stay at the animal hospital, he had managed to charm the doctor and the rest of the staff, who were sad to see him go. And as he limped into the waiting room, his torso bandaged, his tail was frantically wagging a greeting for us, his family. We breathed a collective sigh of relief as we carefully put him into the car and headed home.

Man healed quickly, adapting to things like climbing stairs and jumping on the sofa. He learned to lean against the tree when he needed to raise his leg to pee. And we watched his spirits soar, ears flapping, as he half limped, half ran, keeping up with his beloved boys.

The years with our tripod redefined for us what it meant to be handicapped, as he inspired us with his strength, determination, and boundless love. During that time, we taught him how to retrieve the newspaper in the morning and delighted when he happily brought it to us as we rewarded him with a treat. And after we canceled our subscription we laughed as he made his way through the neighborhood, collecting papers from the neighbors and depositing them on our front porch. He showed us that he needed a job that provided him with a purpose.

Man was always resourceful. When the boys were too occupied to feed him, he would make his way into the pantry and pull a can of food off the shelf, following one of us around until we noticed. But his true culinary weakness was dog biscuits. We had taught him to sit and say "please" in his own unique doggie way, as he sat proudly waiting for one, drooling in anticipation. But between those rewards, we could often hear him sneaking into the box, crunching two or three at a time, much like a child steals cookies on the sly.

Because of his affinity for them, we were excited when the makers of Milk-Bone sponsored an open casting call for pets, along with ideas for a commercial. The boys brainstormed their pitch, finally deciding that Man should sit, stately and proud in front of a big box of biscuits. The caption would read, "I'd give my right arm for a Milk-Bone." He didn't win.

We were fortunate to have had Man for sixteen years, sadly watching him grow old, arthritic, and incontinent. The boys, who had grown into men, sat with us as we made the painful decision to help him cross over the Rainbow Bridge. And as we stood as a family in the vet's office, tearfully whispering our goodbyes, he thumped his tail one last time in response. He was our once-in-a-lifetime pet. Mighty Man, the three-legged wonder.

~Paula W. Millet

Disappearing Dave

None are as fiercely loyal as dog people. In return,
no doubt, for the never-ending loyalty of dogs.
~Linda Shrieves

He was named "David Letterman" by the teenage son of the first family that owned him. And like David Letterman, he was a rogue through-and-through, a rogue in a tuxedo — all black with a white beard and a white ruff at his neck. When he ate spaghetti, his beard would turn orange. I was told there were ten puppies in his litter, and they all looked alike, except Dave.

We lived down the street from his original family. The children were away at college and returned only sporadically, so the mother had given her blessing for Dave to come and live with us. My brother and I were in elementary school, and we couldn't wait to get home every day to play with Dave. But Dave always knew when his first family's son was home on a break from school, and he would run away from our house and drop by for a weekend visit with them. We speculated on how he knew the son was home. Could he distinguish among the sounds of different car engines?

Dave was well known for other small disappearances, as well. He would go from house to house, gathering up any other dogs who could get loose, and together they would go marauding — knocking over trashcans and gobbling up chicken bones and other food.

There were woods behind our house, and Dave often chased after a deer, raccoon, or opossum. Sometimes, he came home skunked, and we would give him a bath with tomato juice. On the other side of the woods, there was an ice cream stand that also sold pizza and sandwiches. Dave often emerged triumphantly from the woods with a stale bun locked in his jaws. How he got the buns out of the tall Dumpster, I can't imagine, since he was a medium-sized dog, fifty-five pounds at most.

His other trick at the ice cream stand was to walk up to the front, just as a regular customer would, and place his order. He would stand up with his paws on the countertop and howl until someone bought him a cone, or the owner, fed up with the noise, thrust one through the little window.

Once, when I went to look for him, a blond girl with chocolate ice cream on her face said to me, "That's the dog that ate my brother's ham sandwich!" I could picture it — the boy standing there dumbfounded while Dave happily scarfed down the goods. "Come on, Dave," I said, grabbing him by the collar and beating a hasty retreat.

When our friends and neighbors saw Dave loitering at the ice cream stand, they would stop and pick him up. He would happily get into anyone's car, sitting in the back seat with his ears perked up, confident they would chauffeur him home. Once in a while, someone we didn't know would pick him up and call the number on his tag, and we'd work out arrangements to have him dropped off or picked up.

And then he disappeared for good. After several months, we had to accept that he was not coming home. He never was very smart about crossing the road. He could have tangled with another opossum or one of the big beavers back in the pond.

An entire year went by, and nothing.

And then, on New Year's Eve, we heard a scratching at the screened door. It was Dave, with his tail wagging and his tongue hanging out. He was well fed, brushed, and had a red collar we had never seen before. It was a miracle.

We began making up stories about where Dave had been during his gap year. He sailed to Italy, the birthplace of spaghetti. He enjoyed the pizza, too, with pepperoni, sausage, and extra cheese. Then he hopped the train to Paris and took up sidewalk painting. He wore a beret and had a palette slung around his neck. He wintered in the Swiss Alps, catching snowballs thrown by blond ski bums, munching marshmallows and sleeping in a heap by the fire.

Although we never found out the truth, it was probably something like this: A little old lady picked him up at the ice cream stand and brought him to her house, kept him confined to a neatly fenced back yard, loved him, and fed him biscuits. He could not escape until New Year's Eve, when she had company who were careless about keeping the door closed.

After that, I always looked over my shoulder, afraid another family would come running up and say, "That's Blackie! That's our dog!" But I shouldn't have worried. After all of his adventures, Dave had come home to stay.

In his later years, Dave would sit under the maple tree as if he were on an invisible chain. We joked that he was retired. His hearing and eyesight went. When you threw him a ball, he would come back with a stick, or not come back at all, hiding around the corner of the house to take a break.

My brother and I grew up, too. When I came home after my first semester in college, Dave couldn't see or hear me. I knelt down and put my arms around him, and he shoved his snout into my sweater. When he smelled me, he began to shake all over with excitement. I realized then that he had had no idea where I had been for all those months, or if I was ever coming home again. That was his own little holiday miracle.

~Gwen Hart

Detective Carlos

You enter into a certain amount of madness
when you marry a person with pets.
~Nora Ephron

L aw enforcement canine handlers and their four-legged partners have an extraordinary relationship. They work together
in the "trenches" daily, performing a wide variety of specialized
and dangerous tasks. From narcotics and explosives detection
to search and rescue; from locating missing people to hunting down
"bad guys," canine teams are phenomenal in their commitment to
the job and to one another. All canine partners live with their human
counterparts and at home they are considered both a family pet and
a working member of the household.

A twenty-eight year, award-winning veteran of his police department, my husband Mike was himself a canine handler for fourteen of
his twenty-eight years on duty. His first canine partner was "Konny," a
German Shepherd who was tragically beaten to death with a lead pipe
during an off-lead search, by a robbery suspect who was hiding in an
abandoned warehouse. After receiving wide media coverage, enough
money was donated to the police department to be able to replace
Konny with "Vasko," another German Shepherd who could only be
described as one big squishy cuddle-lump.

Vasko loved strangers and friends alike and greeted everyone with
an enthusiastic and sloppy kiss. Unfortunately, big squishy cuddle-
lumps do not always make for efficiency in the field and Vasko was

eventually "retired" to a loving family. Mike was thereafter partnered with "Carlos," a Belgian Malinois he called his best buddy and his "career dog." Together, Carlos and Mike were responsible for setting national records in the seizure of drugs and drug money, and Carlos became known throughout law enforcement agencies in several states as the "Wonder Dog."

While maintaining an incredibly demanding work schedule, Mike additionally trained canine teams who came from all over the Southwest to work with him. A major component of training canines for fieldwork in narcotics obviously involves learning how to detect different varieties of narcotics. Actual drugs, evidence from past busts, are used during this training. Mike carried his training evidence to and from the training facility and once home, always kept it in a lockbox.

One Friday evening, Mike and I were expected at a wedding. We had both arrived home late from our respective workdays and were in a rush to change clothes and get out of the house. As I was putting the finishing touches on my uncooperative hairdo, Mike hurriedly put Carlos in the back yard and gathered wedding presents, car keys and venue directions. In our hurry to leave, Mike inadvertently left his lockbox filled with training evidence on the dining room table… and the back access door unlocked.

After a lovely evening of dining, dancing and celebrating, we returned home. We were looking forward to a nightcap and sleeping late the following morning—a rarity in our household. I'd headed into the bedroom to change into my standard lazy-time uniform of sweatpants and oversized T-shirt when I heard loud swearing coming from the dining room. I ran down the hall and around the corner, to find Mike in the doorway of the dining room.

There stood a very proud-looking Carlos, who had gotten into the house while we were out. He was sitting bolt upright in the middle of the dining room, next to overturned dining room chairs and a now-empty lockbox, surrounded by destroyed training evidence. Torn plastic bags lay strewn amongst all manner and incarnation of narcotics and drug paraphernalia—and in the midst of the mess sat Carlos, "smiling" widely with an "I'm such a good boy" look on his face. He was eagerly awaiting a reward for having "located" so much evidence.

I collapsed in hysterical laughter. Mike did not share in the levity.

After taking photographs of the room to accompany the dreaded but inevitable explanation that he would have to make to his superiors, Mike loaded Carlos into his police van and set off in the wee hours of the night for an emergency veterinarian visit. Although canines do not intentionally ingest drugs, Carlos still needed to be checked. I was left behind to clean up the remnants of Carlos's "job well done."

As I surveyed the wreckage, broom in hand and vacuum at the ready, I harkened back to television commercials of the 1960s and early 1970s, wherein a frustrated housewife would wipe her sweaty brow and stare at the floor in frustration, while a male voiceover boomed, "Have YOU ever tried to get that pesky pet hair/food/spill out of YOUR carpet?"

In powder form, cocaine is much like baby powder and in evidence form, spilled marijuana looks as though a box of dried oregano has been scattered all over the place.

Have YOU ever tried to get that pesky cocaine and marijuana out of YOUR midnight blue, thick-pile carpeting?

After two hours of sweeping, vacuuming, scrubbing and more vacuuming, the carpet was finally clean, the upended dining room chairs were righted, and Mike and Carlos returned home with a clean bill of health from the vet.

Peace was again restored.

Or so I thought.

Mike always taught that a dog's scent detection ability is about one thousand times more acute than a human's. He explained that if he came home and I was making spaghetti sauce, he would think, "Carole is making spaghetti sauce." On the other hand, if a dog smelled it and could talk, the dog would be able to describe what was in the spaghetti sauce. Further, canines are generally trained to "alert" on narcotics one of two different ways. One is by sitting down silently upon detection of the scent and the other is to bark and scratch and jump and carry on as though the house was on fire.

Carlos naturally alerted in the latter fashion.

In other words, all of the sweeping, vacuuming and scrubbing was not enough to completely eradicate the scent of "Carlos's Most Excellent Adventure" ... and when he would come into the house, the lingering aroma of narcotics to Wonder Dog's wonder-nose sent him into overdrive — an eighty-five-pound dog barking and racing around close quarters in hyper-vigilant alert mode (lending itself to frenetic chases and loudly stern and occasionally four-letter admonishments). It was not until we had the carpeting professionally cleaned — *twice* — that Carlos finally ceased to "alert" when he came into the house, although he did continue to take extreme interest in the dining room carpet.

Several years after this hilarious incident and after many more professional successes, Carlos retired from active duty, capping an illustrious, record-setting career. Shortly after his twelfth birthday, Carlos crossed the Rainbow Bridge... and just over two years after Carlos passed, Mike too passed away.

To this day, I love to visualize Mike and Carlos the Wonder Dog reunited, with Carlos once again running and barking and driving Mike to eye-rolling, laugh-out-loud distraction... and along with the "pesky cocaine caper," that vision will always bring a smile to my face and peace to my heart.

~Carole Brody Fleet

The Dog Really Did That?

Chapter 2

Dog-Gone Silly

I Saved a Dog

Mix a little foolishness with your serious plans.
It is lovely to be silly at the right moment.
~Horace

I save dogs quite frequently. It's a deep-seated instinct in me. A forlorn, lost, four-legged hairball running down the street is all it takes to set me off. I go into a frenzy. *MUST. SAVE. DOG.* My senses tingle; my synapses fire. My heart pounds and my breathing becomes raspy. Everything blurs and I become intensely and profoundly focused.

He must be scared. She must be hungry. He needs me. She might get hurt.

I become a determined woman on a mission… a mission to save the dog.

And, usually, I am quite successful. Most of the time, I save the dog and the day. Two weeks ago, I saved Cookie. I was driving down the street when I noticed a brown blur in my peripheral vision. My heightened instincts kicked in. I assessed the situation: *Yes, it's a lost dog and — gasp — it's barreling for the major intersection ahead!*

Immediately, I switched into Superhero Doggy Saver mode and started weaving in and out of traffic. The dog was slipping from sight, so I had to take fast action. I screeched my car to a stop, halted traffic, and ran at lightning speed toward the runaway dog.

I pushed a skateboarding kid out of the way. "Hey, old lady!" he shouted at me. But it was okay because he didn't know I was a superhero at work. I flew farther down the street. Just before the dog met with certain death from an oncoming car, I scooped him up.

I am sure I heard cheers and hurrahs. Horns were honking. My girls said, "Oh, my gosh, Mom! You almost killed us!" To which I responded with Super Hero Honesty, "I'm so sorry! I forgot you were in the car."

Cookie had a tag, and we called the number. We returned Cookie to her grateful owner and counted it as another successful mission. Just another day in Superhero Doggy Saver land.

But my family thinks I might be a tad obsessed. They've wondered if there is a therapy group for people like me. DRA… Doggy Rescue Anonymous. But I can't help it. When I think of a lost dog's fear and helplessness and innocence, it affects me in a way I can't describe. It's an emotional trigger. Even watching rescue videos on Facebook evokes it. When my girls walk in and see me at my computer with the tissue box, they sigh and say, "Mom's watching dog-rescue videos again."

But even if I do go a little overboard, there's no denying that I have saved a lot of dogs. Owners thank me, and at the end of the day, tears turn to joy. It's a wonderful, glorious, worthwhile thing that I do.

Last week I sprang into action once again. I looked out our front window and saw a beautiful German Shepherd sniffing around in our front yard. Wow. Now, lost dogs were even coming right to me. My savior reputation was getting around. I put on my imaginary cape and went outside to save the day.

The dog had no tag. I had never seen it before. *How would I ever find its owner? How long had it gone without food and water?* I was overcome with worry and concern for the poor dog. I switched into rescue mode.

I grabbed a leash and took the lost dog around to our back yard. I cordoned off our four dogs despite their protests. I got bedding and supplies. I enlisted my daughters to put their best art skills to work. We made lots of flyers and posters.

FOUND FEMALE GERMAN SHEPHERD

We diligently drove all around town, plastering up the dog's picture.

A couple of days later, we received a call. It was the dog's owner! The dog's name was Lilly. The owner sounded so frantic, so worried. He said he had just moved to a new neighborhood, and Lilly had wandered out the front door. He had only looked away for a minute, and he couldn't understand how she could have disappeared so quickly.

He had just bathed her, so her collar with her identification had been removed. He had been looking for her non-stop, without sleep, ever since. Needless to say, he was ecstatic we had found Lilly. He was overflowing with gratitude.

He said he was ready to get in his car and come get her. "Where do you live?" he asked.

"We live on Oak Street!" I said, eager to hear how far the dog had traveled.

The voice on the other end hesitated a beat. "Oak Street?" he echoed.

"Why, yes! Where do you live?" I asked enthusiastically.

"Oak Street," he said, flatly. "I'm your new neighbor. I live right next door..."

MUST. SAVE. DOG.

~Julie Theel

12

Rosy and the Wildebeest

*Give toys that are powered by their
imagination, not by batteries.*
~H. Jackson Brown, Jr.

I caught up to the family of three as I speed-walked around the campground in Summerdale, Alabama. Frank and Georgia were chatting while their chocolate Lab tugged on the leash, hoping the slowpokes would speed up a bit.

Being a sucker for dogs, I slowed, smiled, and said, "Hi." I joined in the conversation after Frank introduced his wife and himself.

"Beautiful dog," I said as I bent down to pet her.

"Rosy is such a clever girl," Frank said proudly. "She was trained by the monks of the New Skete Monasteries. You don't have to ask her to do anything," he said as he tossed his hat like a Frisbee onto the grass beside the walking path. "Now where did I leave my hat?" he asked, looking around while Rosy's head bobbed from side to side. It took her seconds to spot the baseball cap. She hopped to it, swooped in, grabbed it by the brim, and delivered it to Frank. With her tail wagging, she was obviously pleased with herself.

"Thank you, Rosy," he said with a flare and settled the cap back on his head.

From that moment on, I never passed her without giving her a pat, a scratch on the muzzle, and a mini-massage — my reason for being a favorite of most dogs.

A day or two later, I was sitting outside my camper, reading and enjoying my morning coffee, when Frank approached. "Could I ask you to watch Rosy for about ten minutes while we deliver a package to our neighbor?" he asked. "We won't be gone long. I just don't want to lock her up in the camper on such a beautiful day."

I gathered up my stuff, moved two doors down, and parked myself on one of their chairs. I petted Rosy, her head resting on my lap. I had seen her with a number of her squeaky toys, and since the door to the motorhome was left open, I asked her where her mouse was. She stared at me, her forehead creasing, looking somewhat confused.

"Where's your mouse?" I asked again, and got the same anxious stare as her head cocked to one side and then to the other side. I let the matter drop, and she seemed perfectly content to sit by me while I massaged and talked to her softly.

"Everything okay?" Georgia asked upon their return.

"Your dog doesn't understand me," I said. "I asked her to get her mouse, and she just stared at me."

"Shhhhhh," whispered Frank. "She doesn't know it's a mouse."

"What do you mean she doesn't know it's a mouse? What does she think it is?"

"She thinks it's a wildebeest," he responded.

"A wildebeest," I said, and off she ran, returning in seconds with the mouse squeaking with every bite.

~Joei Carlton Hossack

13

Bubbalicious

*A well-balanced person is one who finds
both sides of an issue laughable.*
~Herbert Procknow

"Really, you want me to give Prozac to my Golden Retriever?" I put my hand to my chest and reached back to feel for the chair so I could sit down to steady myself.

My vet smiled. She fondled the tips of my dog's ears before she started to chuckle. "I know it sounds silly. But, yes, we have found that the drug can be very helpful to dogs with Obsessive Compulsive Disorder."

I felt my own laughter start to creep up from my belly. "Isn't that a people disorder? I mean, he just chases shadows. True, he chases them all the time, but really… Prozac?" I leaned back into my chair. Bubba put his chin in my lap.

Just about the time my words slipped from my lips, Bubba's chin came up, and he lurched toward the wall. His one-hundred-pound-plus body hit the wall with a force that shook the pictures hanging on it. For a minute, I thought he might have broken his nose.

"Bubba!" I grabbed for his leash with my left hand while I tried to hold on to my purse that had turned upside down and was on its way to the floor. I had no more secured his leash when Bubba turned sharply to my right and dove under the exam table. I realized that my vet's watch tilted on her wrist as she spoke, and that the light caught its reflection and threw a shadow on the walls and floor.

It wasn't funny, but as I lay sprawled on the floor with my arms thrown around Bubba's neck, I couldn't help but laugh so hard that I began to hiccup. My vet was almost beside herself as she tried to keep her own laughter under control.

I pulled my sweet Golden Retriever close to my feet while I managed to put myself back onto the chair. My vet leaned an elbow on the exam table, peered at me over the top of her glasses, and said. "Let's just try it for about a month, shall we?" Then she lay her head on the table. Her giggles came in gulps.

I took Bubba home before I made my way to the nearest Walgreens for the Prozac. Every time I thought about the scene in the vet's office, my lips curled into a smile.

The clerk at the pharmacy raised her head and looked at me. "How can I help you?"

"I need a prescription filled, please."

She took the slip of paper from me. "Is Bubbalicious a male or female?" she asked.

A little taken aback, I said, "Male."

"How old is Bubbalicious?"

A giggle rose in my throat. "Two."

The clerk's eyebrows formed little peaks on her forehead. "Two? Did you say two? Do you realize this drug is for anxiety?"

Suddenly, it dawned on me that the clerk thought we were talking about a human. I just couldn't help myself before I started to laugh. The clerk had a look on her face of pure disgust. She backed away from the counter, opened her mouth slightly, and then closed it quickly.

I knew I had to explain. The four people behind me shuffled their feet. I heard some throat clearing, too.

"Oh, I am so sorry. This is for my dog. He chases shadows." I heard laughter from behind me. The clerk's face collapsed, and she also began to laugh. She drew a hand across her forehead and laughed harder. Then she looked up at me and said, "Do you want Bubbalicious to have a rewards card?"

Now the people behind me stomped their feet and laughed louder.

The pharmacist came to the window to see what all the commotion was about. The clerk gave an explanation to him in choked spurts, and in minutes his deep belly laugh chimed in with the rest of us.

The cash register made a whirring sound, I paid for the prescription, and the still-smiling clerk handed me Bubbalicious's rewards card.

I still laugh every time I tell the story. We tried the drug for a month, but it didn't seem to have any effect on poor Bubba. Being kind of a naturalist, I decided to stop the drug and distract the poor dog whenever he chased a shadow of a bird passing overhead—or any other shadow, for that matter.

A positive note to the end of my story is that, to this day, I am able to use Bubba's rewards card whenever I shop at Walgreens!

~Alice Klies

14

A Lick and a Promise

One of the things that binds us as a
family is a shared sense of humor.
~Ralph Fiennes

"**O**ne week to go!" Chris said, referring to our upcoming wedding. I squeezed his hand. There was so much to do before we said our vows.

"Remember to breathe," he said. I took a deep breath, and the salty sea air filled my lungs.

Shadow trotted behind us on the beach, a piece of kelp in her mouth. We were visiting my future husband's family in Kommetjie, a little coastal village near Cape Town, right at the tip of Africa. Shadow bounded after a seagull, barking excitedly. It took off, and she ran back to us for a quick pat before wading into the icy Atlantic Ocean for a swim.

It was hard to believe that, not too long before, this gorgeous, athletic dog had been sitting in an animal shelter, unwanted and lonely. Thanks to Chris's sister and parents, she was now part of a loving family.

They needed to be loving, because Shadow was pretty naughty. She barked at every person and vehicle that passed by, and no fence could keep her in. She roamed the beach and the neighborhood, and soon everyone in Kommetjie knew the sleek, black dog with the big, pointy ears. Shadow showed her appreciation for being adopted by licking everyone she met. She licked hands, faces, feet — anywhere she could find a patch of bare skin.

***

I had done most of the wedding planning myself. We would marry in a small, stone chapel with gorgeous, stained-glass windows, and have photos taken among the spring flowers on the sand dunes in front of Chris's parents' house. The reception was going to be at a quaint local hotel. The décor, menu, and music were all agreed upon, but I was still stressed. The small details made all the difference.

Our parents had never met and were to do so just before the big event, when my parents would fly down from Durban. I was nervous about this as it had the potential to be very traumatic (for me, anyway) if things didn't go according to script. My dad was quiet, but he had a propensity for dry humor and for saying unusual things.

I phoned my mom a few days before they were due to arrive. After the mandatory "hello" and "how are you?" I got straight to the point.

"Now," I said (I tend to be a little bossy), "just a few things to note, Mom. And please tell Dad, too."

I gave her a whole list of suggestions about what to say and what not to say, what to wear and what not to wear.

"Anything else to add to our list of instructions?" my mom asked. She knew me so well, and I could hear she was smiling. She was also a control freak, so she understood my need for order.

"Oh, yes, they have a slobbery dog called Shadow who likes to lick everyone, so just be prepared for her. And finally... this is the last thing," I said. "They have a problem with a rat in the wall panels, and Chris's mom is very embarrassed about it. So if you hear it scratching around, please don't say anything."

I put down the phone and placed a shaky tick next to the item on my list that said, "Brief Mom and Dad."

***

The big night before the big day finally came, and my parents arrived at Chris's parents' house for a pre-wedding dinner. I was sure I'd covered everything and felt quite calm after taking some Rescue Remedy stress relief medicine. Chris's sister had laid out a delicious spread, including fresh, succulent crayfish caught the day before by Chris's dad. We were all set for a wonderful evening.

My dad, feeling very awkward and nervous after the intensive briefing from my mom in the car, walked straight into the living room. Before anyone even had a chance to sit down, he blurted out: "So, where's the liquor?"

My mom looked mortified. My dad, on the other hand, looked bemused. I was speechless.

My mother-in-law-to-be, ever the gracious host, jumped in quickly and said: "What would you like? We've got beer, wine, whiskey…"

"No… no…," my father stammered, "the *licker*."

Just then, Shadow the rescue dog rushed in, slobbering profusely, and saved him with a welcoming lick on his hand. The perfect, un-choreographed ice breaker.

~Michelle Preen

15

A Dog's Prayer

Animals are such agreeable friends — they ask
no questions, they pass no criticisms.
~George Eliot

December 2003 was a very hard time for my family. My teenage daughter had missed a week of school due to a hospitalization and was saddled with a lot of makeup work. At the same time, my husband had the first of two surgeries. This particular surgery was a total hip replacement, and it was to be followed by a total knee replacement a few months later.

My parents drove up from South Carolina to Kentucky to spend a few days with us to help me out during this difficult time. They came to help around the house and watch my younger child, allowing me to spend time at the hospital with my husband and help my daughter get caught up in her studies.

My mother is no animal lover, but my husband is. We had three dogs at the time, and my husband might have wanted more if I hadn't insisted that three was my limit. My poor mother spent those few days trying to keep the house clean, stay up to date on the laundry, and cook meals for all of us.

She also fed the dogs and let them outside when they needed to go out. One particular day, it had rained the night before, so the back yard was quite saturated. All of our dogs tracked in mud that day, causing my mom extra work on the floors and carpet. One of my dogs, who loved to chew on wet grass, then proceeded to throw up this partially chewed, wet grass all over the family room carpet. My mother patiently cleaned that up, too.

That was the day my husband came home from the hospital, so by late afternoon we were all home. At dinnertime, he felt up to joining us at the table. As we sat around the dining room table preparing to eat the delicious meal my mother had lovingly prepared, we all bowed our heads to ask for the Lord's blessing on our food. It has always been my parents' custom to hold hands when they pray before a meal, so we all did that.

That night, my father said, "Let us pray." Then he bowed his head, closed his eyes, and extended his hands out to the person on his right and on his left. We all bowed our heads, closed our eyes, and reached our hands out for the hand of the person next to us, too.

When the prayer was over, my mother, with her hand still stretched out, lifted up her head, looked at my six-year-old son and asked, "Ty, why is your hand wet?"

"My hand's not wet," he replied. Then, lifting both of his hands out from under the table so that we could all see them, he added, "Grandma, you are not holding my hand."

My mother bent her head back down and looked at her right hand, which was still outstretched beneath the table. She let out a startled scream and jumped up from her seat.

When she finally regained her composure, she told us she had apparently been holding the nose of our dog — the very same dog that had been so much trouble to her all day!

Ty burst into laughter! He said he had watched it all happen and wondered why his grandmother had chosen to hold the dog's nose instead of his hand. It seems that when my mother reached out to hold his hand, this funny dog of ours stuck his nose in my mother's open palm. Ty said he reached his hand out to grab his grandmother's hand, but then saw her wrap her hand over the dog's nose instead, so he just put his hand in his pocket.

My mother's perspective was quite different. She reached her hand out after she had already closed her eyes and then felt what she thought was Ty's wet hand. She just assumed he probably had a good reason for it being wet. He was just a six-year-old, after all. So, she closed her hand around what she thought was the little, wet hand of her sweet grandchild.

I think maybe the dog was trying to make up to her for all the trouble he had caused her that day by patiently letting her hold his nose, for reasons he probably figured only she knew.

~Harriet E. Michael

16

Murray and the Three Dachshunds

Hospitality: making your guests feel like they're
at home, even if you wish they were.
~Justine Vogt

Once upon a time, there was a little street pup named Murray Dog. He had a lot of energy and decided one day to run through the suburbs of Eugene, chasing the autumn leaves as they fell from the trees. Soon, he came upon a beautiful turquoise house with a purple arbor and a creek in the back yard. He thought this looked like a great place to rest, so he shoved his snout against the front door. Magically, it opened.

The house belonged to three Dachshunds: Justin, who was in charge of rearranging the furniture; Penny, whose main job was making sure the floors were well-licked; and Watson, the archeologist of the family, who dug holes in the back yard to search for intelligent life beneath the dirt.

It so happens that on the day Murray Dog decided to trespass, Justin, Penny, and Watson were frolicking in the park.

Murray Dog scampered toward the kitchen because all that running and chasing had made him hungry. He saw three bowls lined up against the wall and walked over to check the first one out. It was the biggest bowl… and it was empty.

Well, this is disappointing, and not at all like the fairy tales I've read!

he thought as he moved on to the middle-sized bowl a few feet over. It, too, was filled with nothing but air. He licked it anyway.

Mmm, I bet that was some good food, he thought as he moved on to the smallest bowl, still optimistic that maybe a crumb had been left behind. It had not. One thing Murray did not know is that even on a glorious fall day with the leaves falling and the park calling, Dachshunds will never leave a morsel behind.

Still hungry, but not seeing anything to eat, Murray Dog decided to check for toys. He was in luck as there was a basket full of them nearby. He removed them one at a time, sniffing each one, then tossing it in the air to check the aerodynamics and mouth feel. He selected six toys and decided to take a quick nap.

He walked into the living room where he saw three chairs. He sat in the first, but the color clashed with his beautiful red hair.

This chair is NOT in my color chart!

He thought about sitting in the second chair, but it had too many blankets and pillows on it.

There might be a monster hiding under them!

He let out a tiny bark and moved on to the last chair. It was just right. So he grabbed each of the six toys he had chosen, circled twenty-seven times (Murray Dog was an overachiever) and lay down for a nap.

As he was sleeping, the Dachshunds came home. They rushed right over to their dog dishes, ever hopeful that they might again be filled with food.

Someone's been sniffing my bowl, growled Justin.

Well, someone's been licking my bowl, and he has puppy breath, thought Watson.

Penny said nothing because, while her brothers were complaining, she'd found a piece of carrot near the refrigerator and was happily chomping on it.

Then, Watson noticed that the basket of toys had been ransacked.

Someone's been playing with my toys! His big dog heart was pounding. Watson loved his toys, and the idea of sharing them with anyone really got his dander up.

Suddenly, they heard little snores coming from Penny's chair.

Someone's napping in my chair, Penny observed as she waddled over to see who it might be.

Watson and Justin joined her. When Watson noticed that half a dozen of his toys were being snuggled with, he lost it and started barking so loudly the neighbors probably thought a squirrel had decided to run through the house wearing a mail-carrier uniform.

Hey, those are my toys! No one plays with my toys! Justin and Penny nodded as fast as their long necks would let them.

Just then, Murray Dog woke up and saw the Dachshunds. Unafraid, he put his nose out to sniff each of them.

Hi, I'm Murray Dog. I was wondering if you had anything to eat, he seemed to be saying.

Penny, ever the hospitable hostess, showed him the extra pieces of kibble she had stored under the pillows in the haunted chair that none of them would sleep in.

Thank you for your kindness, Murray Dog indicated while he chewed.

I need you to know that if you're going to stay here, you have to leave the toys alone. They're all mine! Watson chimed in with a bark, even though he had already made his point.

I can stay? Murray Dog almost piddled himself in excitement. He'd been living on the streets, and this was such good news.

Sure, but you'll have to sleep over there. Justin pointed with his snout to a king-sized bed in the bedroom.

And they all lived happily (and noisily) ever after.

~Leigh Anne Jasheway

17

The Critic

For the best seat in the house,
you'll have to move the dog.
~Author Unknown

Dinner was over and we sank into the sofa with our steaming cups of tea to watch *2001: A Space Odyssey*. Cody had just completed his nightly ritual of stealing tissue from the trash. Looking innocent, he strolled across the living room, nonchalantly dangling a tissue from the corner of his mouth. He circled his spot on the red oriental carpet until it was just right and plopped down to join us.

Apart from an occasional scratch or flick of an ear, he just lay there, totally disinterested in this iconic film about evolution and the history of mankind. That was, until a large ape-man family came on screen. As soon as he noticed, Cody jumped up, got right in front of the TV, body tensed and alert with interest, and began to bark — a lot.

We looked at each other in disbelief. Cody had never shown any interest in the TV before. What was this big, brown Poodle doing, and why? "Dogs don't watch TV, do they? Can he really see what's on the screen?" But before we could discuss it any further, the commercials began. Cody trotted into the kitchen for some water, and then returned to his spot.

"Well, that was interesting," we said to each other, thinking this would be an aberration. But once the movie came on again, the same thing happened. Cody jumped up, went to the TV, and began barking at the ape-men until the commercials resumed. This time, he stayed alert. And as soon as the movie apes were back on, he was at the TV screen barking.

This behavior didn't stop until the apes had fully evolved into humans. At this point, Cody lost interest, yawned, and began napping. Entertained — more by our dog than by the movie — we wondered if this was a one-off or something more. We'd soon find out.

One night, when Cody was carousing in the back of the house, looking for trouble, he suddenly galloped from the kitchen, through the dining room, to the living room, and up to the TV screen, barking furiously. He had spied an oncoming TV horse that looked so tiny that I could hardly see it up close. That was impressive.

Wanting to share this phenomenon with friends and family, I decided to videotape him interacting with the TV. I put the recorded cassette in the VCR and turned it on. As soon as Cody saw himself on the screen, he was beside himself, barking, jumping, and moving his head from one side of the screen to the other.

As time went on, we noticed that Cody developed certain prefer- ences. Although he liked any animal on screen, he had favorites. Dogs were, of course, of great interest to him. Those he liked got licked, and those he disliked got growls. Cats always riled him up.

He also formed relationships with some ongoing TV characters. One of his favorites was the Pillsbury Doughboy. When the doughboy's belly was tickled and he uttered the famous "Ha-ha," Cody got a huge dog smile and licked and licked the doughboy's face.

Cody regularly tried to figure out who or what this strange rect- angular being was. He circled the TV slowly many times, giving special care to the back, where all the wires came out. Sniffing, licking, looking, and listening, he continued to be stumped. No animals or doughboys ever popped out of the back of the set, nor were they living under it or in a nearby corner. Poor puppy.

Then one evening, he gave the rectangular box one final try, again to no avail. At this point, he stopped and stood for a few moments.

And then, just like that, Cody let it go. He was done figuring out the TV. Instead, he had made peace with it by accepting our television set as a friend.

From then on, when we went to bed each night, Cody gave each of us a goodnight kiss. And when he was done, he walked over to the TV and gave the screen a giant lick. The TV had now become a cherished member of Cody's pack.

~Linda Zallen

18

Making a Splash

Whatever you do, wherever you go,
don't be afraid to make a splash.
~Anil Sinha

've shared my life with three Yorkshire Terriers over the years, but the quirkiest one to ever grace my world has been Sissy, my latest. She has a host of peculiar behaviors, not the least of which is her love of fish. Tuna, cod, and salmon make her prance and go crazy. But it is her agoraphobic tendencies that are the most striking. She's happy to stay home all day and she is always going in to hiding. Sometimes, I feel as though I'm living with a covert CIA operative!

Over the years, Sissy's hiding has become a game and sometimes a battle of wills. I work from home, and there are days when Sissy and I get up and have breakfast together, and I don't see her again until dinner. I've gone on plenty of search missions only to find her hidden under my bed or beneath the skirt of my upholstered sofa. And after ten years of living with Sissy, nothing really surprises me anymore. But one day, when she was still a brand-new pup in my life, she completely floored me.

Sissy and I had battened down the hatches as a raging nor'easter was pummeling our little corner of northern New Jersey. The rains had come and stayed for forty-eight hours, complete with *kabooms* of thunder and zigzags of lightning that tore through dark skies. Sissy didn't like it — not one bit. She was shaking and shivering with anxiety, and I cuddled her five-pound body close… and she let me. The covert operative had turned into Velcro!

When it seemed as though the storm had finally passed, Sissy detached from me long enough so I could finally take a shower. I gathered some clean clothes and towels. Before I flipped on the water in the tub, I decided to keep the bathroom door ajar just in case Sissy wanted to be near me again. I figured she could curl up and wait for me on the throw rug.

I soon regretted that decision as the open door created a draft, something of a wind tunnel. The vinyl shower curtain kept billowing into the tub, sticking to my wet, soapy body. With the handheld showerhead, I doused the curtain, trying to weigh it down so it would adhere to the painted steel of the tub. But the curtain kept ballooning back toward me, which made soaping up and rinsing off quite a challenge.

At one point, Sissy's nose suddenly popped around the curtain. She stood there, quivering and wide-eyed, her beige front paws on the side of the tub.

"Privacy, please. I'll be done in a minute," I told her, yanking the curtain closed.

By the time I was through and finally flipped off the water, a loud rumble of thunder and a bright flash of lightning pierced through the mini-blinds shrouding the bathroom window. I squeezed the water from my hair as a few droplets of hard rain pelted the roof. Then there was a thunderous boom. In the silence that followed, I heard a tiny splash.

What was that? Did I drop something… maybe the bar of soap? I looked, but all was clear.

As I ripped open the curtain and stepped out of the tub, something caught my eye — a splotch of beige and brown rising up from inside the toilet bowl. I did a double take, reaching for my towel and drying my eyes to get a better look. Two triangular shapes, like dorsal fins from baby sharks, rose from inside the toilet.

The pointy ears and wet face of Sissy emerged — a drowned rat with doleful eyes.

I gasped. *Yikes — what a place to hide!*

The dog was shivering. Her pitiable look seemed to telegraph,

Help! Get me outta here!

Quickly, I reached into the bowl. Drenched, trembling Sissy jumped into my hands as if my fingers were magnets, and she were made of iron.

She licked my wrist and looked up at me with a warm, grateful gaze as I wrapped her in a dry towel and drew her close, feeling as though the storm had bonded us.

When the sun broke through the clouds a little while later, Sissy, her hair blow-dryer soft and smelling squeaky clean from her very first bath, went back to normal — *her* idea of "normal." She scampered away from me and went into seclusion. I didn't see her again for hours.

~Kathleen Gerard

19

He Wouldn't Hurt a Fly

He was a gentle giant, a big guy with a big heart.
~Ann Murphy

When my wife and I first married, I was working sixty hours a week. I was concerned about leaving her alone at home so much, in terms of both company and security, so we decided to go to the local shelter and rescue a German Shepherd. They showed us a litter of eight that someone found in a box at a local park a few weeks earlier. They had been there overnight. They were newborns when they were found, far too young to have been separated from their mother.

When the litter was shown to us, they all stole our hearts, of course, but one stood out to me because he was very awkward and shy. When I held him up and talked to him, he couldn't even make eye contact with me. Human beings may *admire* a creature or fellow human with beauty and strength, but they *love* one with imperfections. We're more likely to shower affection on a mutt with a lame leg than a perfect show dog. So we took him home, determined to undo whatever damage his rough start had done to his mind. On the way home, my wife joked, "Oops! We were supposed to get a confident guard dog." We both laughed and said we would make him confident somehow.

We named him Charlie. Over the years, his gentle nature became apparent — in how he reacted to people and other animals, of course — but also in some humorous ways. For instance, he was an "only dog" so we worried he was lonely when we went out for the day and left him in the back yard. We came home one day and were watching him through the window without his knowledge. He appeared to be entertaining himself by trying to catch flies.

I said to my wife, "Look! The killer instinct is finally coming out! He's hunting!" Yes, they were only flies, but it was a start. However, as we continued to observe him, we realized he wasn't trying to hurt the flies. Quite the opposite — he was licking them, trying to make them his friends! He literally "wouldn't hurt a fly." The flies, however, didn't enjoy the company as much as he did. In fact, they all died in a sea of spittle. Licked to death. When the drowned flies stopped moving, Charlie would nudge them with his paw, wondering what happened and why they didn't want to play anymore. It would have been sad if it weren't so cute.

When Charlie was all grown up and our first daughter was born, we were never worried that he would intentionally hurt her, but instead that his size and the puppy-like clumsiness he never outgrew might cause him to injure her accidentally. Instead, Charlie slowed down around her, and to our immense surprise, his protective instincts finally began to emerge. When someone came to the door, his barking had a ferocity we had never heard before she was born. When our second daughter arrived three years later, he grew even more protective.

Our two girls took up most of our time, time that used to be devoted to Charlie, so we again worried that he was lonely when we were out. He was still kissing flies to death, but the grief of losing them, and perhaps the knowledge that he was somehow responsible for their deaths, had to be depressing for him. So we rescued a second dog, a Maltese-Yorkie mix, or Morkie for short. We named her Pixie. They were a sight together. The long and short of it. David and Goliath revisited.

Pixie was very docile at first, intimidated by their vast size difference. But it didn't take long for her to figure out Charlie was the nicest dog on earth, or for her to take full advantage of it. She tormented him incessantly, jumping at his face, trying to nip his nose. Charlie would open his mouth wide and growl but he never bit her. I once saw him sleeping, or trying to, while Pixie chewed one of his ears. Again, it seemed that he had no temper whatsoever. He could have ended this torture with one chomp, but he didn't.

Pixie is now the mob boss and Charlie is her dopey bodyguard. But it's company, and they're both happy.

Charlie persists in his attempts to establish friendships with insects, and not just flies but crickets, June bugs, grasshoppers, and anything else he can catch. They all meet the same grisly fate — drowning in a sea of saliva. But now, Charlie has Pixie to help him mourn the loss of his bug friends.

We wanted a fearless guard dog, but we got a lover, not a fighter. I thought I would teach him to be ferocious, but he taught me about kindness and tolerance instead. And we all love him just the way he is. We didn't get what we thought we wanted, we got what we needed. And Charlie did, too.

~Mark Rickerby

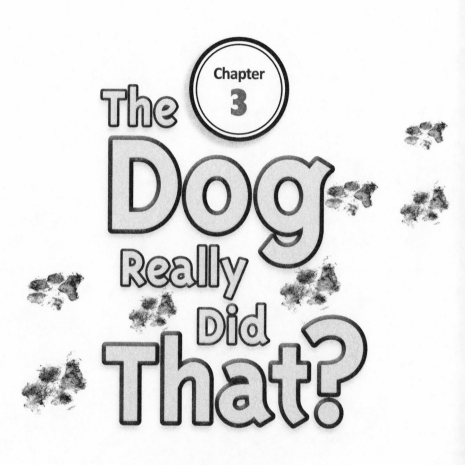

Chapter 3

The Dog Really Did That?

So Smart!

20

What a Buddy

Things are never quite as scary
when you have a best friend.
~Bill Watterson

had been coaching kids in gymnastics classes all day, and I decided it would be fun to stay for an adult gymnastics class. And it was fun — all the way up until my last vault. I landed on a spring on the mini trampoline and felt an odd movement in my foot. It moved oddly again when I tried to stand up and walk on it.

My husband had to pick me up, and after an ER visit and a subsequent appointment with an orthopedic doctor, I got the bad news.

"You have a dislocation in your foot, and this will require surgery. You should have had surgery last week. I cannot believe they missed this in the ER," my orthopedic surgeon informed me. "You'll be on crutches for around three months."

All of our fall plans for travel, for camping and hiking, were gone just like that.

After the surgery, I was sent home to recuperate. I got situated in bed, and my husband cuddled with me and our dogs while we watched movies for the day.

When the nerve block wore off, I could start moving around a bit. I got up the next morning to go to the bathroom, and our Terrier, Buddy, followed me. I noticed he wasn't using his right rear leg. He was only walking on three legs.

"Hey, babe, did you notice if Buddy fell or anything recently? He's not using his back leg at all," I inquired of my husband.

"No, he was running around like normal when I put him out last night. This is new this morning."

We poked around and felt up and down his leg. He didn't seem to have any pain. But he continued to use only three legs. We figured we would see if it got better after a couple of days, and if not we would take him to the vet.

He became the most helpful dog, and we saw a side of him we had never seen before. He had always been one of the smartest dogs I had ever met, but it amazed us how observant he was. One morning, one of my crutches slipped on the dog blankets. It wasn't major, but the next morning when I got up, Buddy had dragged the dog blankets to the corner of the room and out of my way. He did this every morning while I was on crutches.

Our hound dog, Lucy, was quite the opposite of Buddy. While she was the sweetest dog, she could be a bit clumsy. She would dart straight down or up the stairs as fast as she could, despite what was in her path. Buddy would block her until I got fully up or down the stairs on my crutches, and then he would move out of the way and let her follow me. It really was the most amazing behavior.

But Buddy's leg never seemed to improve. After about a week of him on three legs, we finally got him to the vet. The vet checked his leg and X-rayed it, but they couldn't find anything wrong. Buddy didn't show any signs of pain, and he was happy and playful. The vet saw he was attached to my side at the appointment (as he was every day), and suggested he might be "empathizing" with me, not using one of his legs because I couldn't use one of mine.

We were astounded. We had never heard of such behavior, but it was all the vet could come up with. He sent us home with some anti-inflammatory drugs for Buddy, and we were told to keep an eye on him and follow up. But since there was nothing in the X-ray, and he wasn't showing signs of pain, the next step would be an MRI if it didn't improve. We figured as long as he wasn't showing any pain and was happy, we would let him be and see what happened.

Finally, toward the end of three months, I was moved into a walking boot. Initially, I began with partial weight-bearing on the crutches until I could fully ambulate in the boot, and then something quite remarkable happened. The first day I was without crutches, Buddy began using all four of his legs again.

"Babe, look! Buddy is walking normally again!" I exclaimed when I saw this.

"Well, would you look at that? Incredible! Do you think he really was 'empathizing' with you?"

"I have absolutely no clue," I responded, just as perplexed as he was.

To this day, we don't know if he had an injury that happened to correspond with mine. We and the vet believe he may very well have been sympathizing with my injury. I'll never forget the complete love and companionship that dog gave me. Buddy truly lived up to his name.

~Gwen Cooper

21

The Sting

A dog that runs after two bones catches neither.
~English Proverb

W e had built a new home in the country, and it was time for a dog. I surprised my husband with a Beagle for his birthday — Belle, an adorable, little, sable-colored female with a perky black nose, pretty brown eyes, and the cutest little bark I had ever heard. When they saw each other, it was love at first sight.

To say that Belle was energetic would be misleading. Let's just say that whenever she was in the house or garage, as soon as the door cracked open, I looked around to see who had fired this dog out of a cannon! She ran laps around the yard as hard as her little Beagle legs would allow, with her ears laid back and her tongue hanging out. It was truly comical.

We decided there was only one thing to do about Belle's boundless energy. She needed a pal. Enter Beagle number two.

Bo, a male Warfield Red Beagle, was a hilarious addition to the family, and laughingly referred to as "Belle's dog." Bo was a pretty smart dog, but his intellect paled in comparison to Belle's.

I never knew a dog could use psychology on another dog until I witnessed Belle in action one fall afternoon. We had purchased rawhide sticks for the dogs to chew on, and they had been carried off to various locations known only to the dogs. Bo had retrieved one of them, and was happily chewing on it on the cool garage floor.

Belle spotted him and began to scheme. I could see it in her eyes. She wanted that rawhide stick.

At first, Belle walked over to Bo and tried to take the rawhide away from him. But he managed to hold onto his prize.

Next, Belle plopped down on the garage floor a few feet away and watched Bo with envy as he contentedly gnawed on his rawhide. After a few moments, she got up, went out into the yard, and found a twig. She brought it into the garage and began playing with it. She shook it, threw it in the air and caught it, and then plunked down and started chewing on the twig.

She seemed to be having such a good time.

Bo took notice and stopped chewing his rawhide stick. The more fun Belle seemed to have with that twig, the more intrigued he was. When it became too much for him to endure, he dropped the rawhide stick and went over to Belle to try to take her treasure away from her.

She brilliantly put up enough of a fight to be convincing. How could she possibly give up her wonderful twig? But, slowly and reluctantly, she allowed him to steal the twig away from her.

With a satisfied look, Bo plopped down and started gnawing on the twig.

Belle moseyed over to the rawhide stick, picked it up, and started chewing on it. I'm not sure if Bo ever figured out he'd been had.

~Anna Scates

22

Locked Out

From there to here, from here to there,
funny things are everywhere.
~Dr. Seuss

Duke and Daisy came to us as foster dogs from the local shelter when they were five weeks old. Weighing just over four pounds, they were small enough to be held in one hand. They may have been tiny, but they stole our hearts in a huge way, and as soon as they were available, we officially adopted them.

Because they were Boxers, these pups were high energy and always getting in trouble.

Daisy was the smarter of the two. You could almost see the wheels in her brain turning as she considered each new situation. She reminded us of the Velociraptor in the original *Jurassic Park* movie… especially in the scene when it learned how to open a door.

The doors in our home were fitted with handles instead of door-knobs. To open, we had to pull down the handle and push the door forward. Daisy watched and learned… and she learned fast.

On the other hand, we were slow students.

"Honey, I thought you put the dogs in the bedroom."

"I did."

"No, you didn't. They're here in the living room."

"Yes, I did. You must have let them out without realizing it."

We repeated this conversation a few more times until we actually saw Daisy jump up, pull down the handle, and push open the bedroom door. She was less than three months old.

At first, we joked about it. We bragged to our friends about how smart she was. Privately, we were thankful that Duke wasn't quite as smart or bold as his sister. They were already double trouble without him upping the level of mischief.

A few months later, I visited a family member in another state. The second night I was away, I called home to see how things were going. When my husband answered the phone, I chattered on about the beautiful afternoon my cousin and I spent together, giving him all the details of our day. I spoke for a few minutes before he interrupted me.

"That's nice. Would you like to hear about *my* day?"

Hmmm. That didn't sound at all good. "Uh, okay. How was your day?"

To say he had a bad day would be an understatement.

That afternoon, he had taken both puppies out to the front yard to do their business. Then he brought them in the house and went back out to clean up their mess. Since it was a hot, summer day in south Florida, and he didn't expect to be outside for long, he was only wearing a pair of gym shorts.

At first, all was quiet. He picked up their messes and then pulled a few weeds. That's when he heard noises coming from the front door. It sounded as if someone was jiggling the door handle. Of course, he thought, Daisy was trying to get out.

He stood and waited for her to come bounding out, her brother following on her heels. It didn't happen. When the noises stopped, he went back to pulling a few more weeds, pleased that she had been foiled in her attempt to open the door.

A half-hour later, hot and sweaty, he finished his work, eager for some water and a shower. He tried the door. It wouldn't open. He tried again. No luck. Was it stuck? No. It was *locked*. She must have hit the deadbolt with her paw in her attempts to push down the door handle.

Daisy had locked him out of the house!

The poor man lost it. He pounded on our front door, yelling, "Daisy, let me in! You open this door right *now*!"

Of course, that didn't work. She's a smart dog, but she hadn't yet learned how to unlock the door, and it's doubtful she understood his yelling. So my dirty, sweaty, and shirtless husband had to knock on neighbors' doors until he found someone home who could call a locksmith. Two hours later, after paying the weekend emergency rate of $120, he finally re-entered our home.

To add insult to injury, Daisy and Duke had reveled in their unsupervised liberty. Chaos reigned, and several couch cushions lay shredded on the floor.

I confess, as I listened to his account from a thousand miles away, I tried to stifle the giggles. But the picture of him pounding on the door, demanding that the dog let him into his own home, was more than I could process without doubling over in laughter.

Good sport that he is, he let me laugh for a bit. But his next statement cut short my mirth.

"Glad you find it funny," he said. "But I hope you realize that now our neighbors will be looking at you with pity… and not because you're married to someone who was locked out of the house by his dog."

I thought about it for a moment, and then he explained. "Everyone in the neighborhood will be wondering why, while you were away, someone named Daisy was in your house and locked out your half naked husband."

Hmmm… he had a point. When I returned home, the first call I made was to a dog trainer.

~Ava Pennington

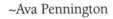

23

An Unexpected Angel

If your dog doesn't like someone,
you probably shouldn't either.
~Author Unknown

When I was twenty-two years old, I found myself living every California surfer girl's dream — going to college in Hawaii and living with my high-school sweetheart (who then was working in law enforcement on Oahu). Life was awesome, although between going to school full-time and working two jobs, it was also incredibly busy. So when my sweetie called to tell me we were adopting a dog from the local shelter, I was not thrilled. It was not because I am not a dog lover; I am. It was just that, as much as I loved this man, I knew our new furry family member would become my responsibility — something I just didn't have the time for.

Well, any frustration or doubt quickly dissolved as soon as I looked into those sweet, golden-brown eyes. Sammy (as we named her) had the sweetest temperament. She was always incredibly affectionate and calm. She would even snuggle with our rescue kitty, Benny. So it came as a huge shock and embarrassment when she tried to attack a member of our neighborhood ground-maintenance crew.

I was home studying for a mid-term that warm afternoon. I had the front door and all the windows open to let in the tropical breezes. When one of the workers came up to my door asking for a glass of water, Sammy immediately lunged at him and stood on her hind legs, coming face-to-face with the now clearly scared worker. She was growling viciously and showing all her teeth. If our screen door hadn't been metal, I believe she would have gone right through and attacked the man.

Needless to say, I was embarrassed by her behavior and my inability to calm her down. This poor guy just wanted a glass of water on a hot day, and my dog was ready to rip him apart. So I did the only thing I could do: I apologized and shut the front door. That ended our little domestic drama, and I went back to studying.

Two weeks later, my sweetie came home after what appeared to be a particularly tough day on the job. He began to tell me about an assault call he had responded to earlier that day that took place only a few blocks from our house. A man working with ground maintenance had gone up to one of the homes and asked for a glass of water. When the lady of the home went inside, he followed her in and savagely assaulted her. Every hair on my body stood up as he finished telling me about this poor woman's violent attack. Recalling my previous encounter, I began to feel incredibly guilty. There I was feeling embarrassed, while Sammy was busy protecting me.

In the thirteen years that I had the pleasure of sharing with this amazing dog, that was the one and only time she ever growled or showed any type of aggression.

We thought we were simply giving a shelter dog a new life. As it turns out, she was preserving mine.

~Maria Atlan

24

Ding Dong

Some of our greatest historical and artistic treasures
we place with curators in museums;
others we take for walks.
~Roger A. Caras

My son was a senior in high school and I was looking ahead to my empty nester years. I had grown up with dogs, although my mother had always been the one to care for them. Now, with my son leaving, I felt I had the time to take on this responsibility.

On a chilly December day, I selected an adorable puppy at the local shelter. The first two nights, I cuddled up with her as if she were my newborn baby. I imagined the trauma she went through living at the shelter for three months, and I wanted her to feel human love and security, perhaps for the first time. I was also anxious about how she would react to being taken from her sibling, but she quickly adapted. In no time, Cocoa was displaying her exuberant personality and sweet disposition.

As Cocoa grew, I experienced Raising a Puppy 101. She learned the essentials: The yard is the bathroom, food offered is food eaten, and a leash means we walk.

I learned much more. For example, I learned the hard way that even the most lovable and well behaved puppies have an innate need to chew, and this phase can last a couple of years. Cocoa went through dog toys as if she were speed dating—some lasted less than three minutes. She also discovered the couch, the screen door, shoes, and the basement staircase. She cut her new teeth on them all.

But for all her episodes of destructive behavior, her puppy days were filled with sweetness. Cocoa adored me unconditionally. Invited or not, she would often jump into my lap, lick me as if I were a melting Popsicle, and delight me with her unbridled excitement when I returned home from work.

After my son left for college, Cocoa and I became best friends. I talked with her about bad television, and she listened with an understanding frown. I complained to her about politics, and she hung her head in disgust. She cried when thunderstorms frightened her, and I comforted her. And when she longed to go for a walk and nudged at the leash that was hanging at the door, she was so adorable that I could not refuse.

One day, when Cocoa and I were just hanging at home, she astonished me with a completely new behavior. She was outside in the yard, and the doorbell kept ringing. Every time I peered through a window at the front porch there was no one there. I was puzzled, but imagined that a neighborhood child playing a prank was ringing the bell.

Finally, after it happened a few times, I opened the door and looked outside. The only "person" anywhere near the door was Cocoa, who was wagging her whole back end and grinning dog-ear to dog-ear. By standing on her hind legs and using her front paws like fingers, Cocoa had been ringing the bell. I reinforced this behavior by opening the door for her, and now she rings the bell every time she's ready to come indoors. I haven't stopped marveling at this trick, and I love to see the surprise on my guests' faces when they witness Cocoa's doorbell trick for the first time.

Cocoa and I have been housemates for nine incredibly enjoyable years. She has provided me a companionship that I could never have imagined and offered hours of entertainment. She has comforted me, shared my joy, and stuck by my side when I've been lonely. She's also driven me crazy with her anxiety and angered me with destructive behavior. But this much I know without a doubt: One day, she'll be gone, and the doggie doorbell ringing will cease. I will miss her profoundly.

Until then, ringing the doorbell is Cocoa's signature move, and I will continue to be the proud parent, bragging about my talented dog.

~Debbie Robertson

Willy, the Ecumenical Dog

God will prepare everything for our perfect happiness
in heaven, and if it takes my dog being there,
I believe he'll be there.
~Billy Graham

Willy, my Wire Haired Fox Terrier, was never trained to sit, stay, speak, roll over and play dead, but he did something amazing and much more meaningful without any training. How he knew when it was Sunday, I am not quite sure. Maybe it was because we slept later. Whatever it was, he knew when it was Sunday.

His first stop on Sunday morning was at the Munson residence. He waited on their front porch for Mrs. Munson to come out, and then he walked with her to the Norwegian Lutheran church. After being sure Mrs. Munson was safely inside the church, he left. Then he went to the Nuffer residence where he waited outside the front door for Mrs. Nuffer. He accompanied her to the Catholic church. From there, he came home.

My parents never walked to church, but Willy dutifully went home to watch my parents drive out of the garage on the way to the Presbyterian church. Willy ran after the car. He often made it to the church before they did. After they were safely inside, he came home to be sure that I walked safely to Sunday school at the same church.

In my hometown of Luverne, Minnesota, stores would stay open until 10:00 p.m. on Saturday nights because that was when farmers went to town to do their trading. My parents kept their car dealership open until after 10:00 so as not to miss any business. This meant that they were often tired on Sunday morning, sometimes sleeping in and missing church. That did not keep Willy from accompanying me to the church for Sunday School.

One Sunday when my folks decided to sleep in, Willy walked me to Sunday School. Willy came home from church with a note for my parents tied to his collar. It read, "Your dog came to church. Why didn't you?"

~Doris Schoon

26

Staying True to the Red, White, and Blue

*There is only one smartest dog in the
world, and every boy has it.*
~Author Unknown

t was Friday evening, and my husband and I had just finished eating a lovely dinner at my parents' house. We were ready to head home for some relaxation with our pups and some movies.

As we were putting on our jackets and getting ready to head out to the car, my brother's dog Gwen started getting excited and whining. She was a sweet German Shepherd who was staying with my parents while my brother was deployed in Afghanistan.

Gwen had her nose pushed to the door. She was rigid with determination, making it clear she wanted to go home with us.

"What do you say, pretty girl? You want to come join us for a sleepover?" my husband asked her, as he lovingly scratched her large, expressive ears. She whined even more, and knocked once on the door with her paw, then jumped at our feet with her two front paws, herding us out of the house.

"I think that was a most definite 'yes,'" I said, as I laughed along with everyone else and went to grab her leash. "We'll bring her back tomorrow," I told my parents as I hugged them goodbye.

This was the first time Gwen had been to our house since my

brother left. Before my brother had joined the Army, he would come over to our house every other week or so to hang out. He would bring Gwen along, and they would usually crash on the futon downstairs for the evening.

That dog was shaking with excitement throughout the entire car ride home. When we got home, she bolted immediately for the front door. We heard whining from behind the door — our Hound baying with happy excitement and our Terrier bouncing with joy for us to be home. They knew we had brought a guest for a puppy sleepover, just for them, of course.

What happened next, though, melted our hearts. Gwen kindly greeted our dogs, but then she bolted down the stairwell, and we heard her push open the door to our living room. We followed her down and found her nudging and rifling through the blankets on top of the futon.

"She's trying to find her dad," my husband whispered to me as he put his arms around my shoulders. My eyes welled up with tears as understanding hit me at the same moment.

While she did not find my brother there that evening, she did sleep in the blankets all night, as they held his scent. She dragged the blankets with her when we took her home to my parents' house the next day, and she slept on them every night her dad was away. We told my brother about what had happened, and it touched his heart so much he decided to give Gwen a surprise when he returned home safely from Afghanistan.

Six months later, early on Christmas morning, we brought her home with us again for a special field trip. It was the same emotional process. She could hardly stand it, and she shook and whined the entire ride over to our house. She bolted downstairs, found the original blanket, which we had snuck back onto the futon, and started searching it. But this time she found her daddy inside, ready to snuggle and love his puppy.

"I sure missed you, girl," my brother said as he hugged Gwen while she inundated him with puppy kisses. We were all laughing and crying along with the dog. Sometimes, we forget that we humans are not the only ones to miss our American heroes; our furry friends, too, have to help hold down the fort and stay brave while our loved ones are overseas fighting for our freedoms.

~Gwen Cooper

27

Good Things Come to Those Who Wait

She had no particular breed in mind, no unusual
requirements. Except the special sense of mutual
recognition that tells dog and human they
have both come to the right place.
~Lloyd Alexander

"P lease, please, please, let us get a dog!" our four children sang in unison. My husband and I looked at
each other sheepishly. We didn't know how much
longer we could withstand the begging for a dog.

It had all started a year before when my daughter Heather became
infatuated with her best friend's dog. Her constant chatter about the
pup and all her antics got her younger siblings on the bandwagon for
wanting a dog as well.

That evening, Harold and I discussed once again the pros and cons
of having a dog join our family. We feared the children, ages three to
twelve, would only see a dog as a playmate. We told them they would
all need to help with feeding, walking, and bathing their dog.

I had grown up in an apartment complex in Brooklyn, New York,
where no dogs or cats were allowed. My only pets as a child were fish
and birds. I didn't know the first thing about dogs, their care or breeds.
All I knew was they were adorable. I was afraid of the responsibility.

Harold had dogs growing up. Eventually, he convinced me it

would be the best decision we ever made to get a family dog. I had one condition: The dog had to be adopted through an animal shelter. Harold agreed. Our children were ecstatic when we told them the news. I wish I could say I joined in on their excitement. I was a bit hesitant about our new adventure because I didn't know what to expect.

The following week, Harold took the three girls to look at a dog that was in a foster home. I stayed home while my youngest child, Alex, napped. About an hour later, the girls came running through the door, all talking at once, full of excitement. "Whoa, slow down! One at a time!" I insisted. Heather went on to tell me all about Duke, a Golden Lab/German Shepherd mix. The other kids chimed in with bits and pieces of how amazing Duke was. "I started the adoption process. If all goes well, Duke will be ours in a few days," Harold said loudly above the kids' chatter.

I trusted Harold in choosing a dog for our family since he had a few dogs growing up. "He really is a sweet dog and was great with the girls," he continued. The foster family told Harold that Duke was approximately eleven months old. He was found several months prior, walking alongside a road. He was thin, and it looked as though he had been abused. My heart sank.

After all the paperwork, the adoption was finalized. The day had arrived for us to get Duke and bring him home. Once again, Harold went with the three girls while I stayed back home with our youngest. In less than an hour, our new family member came trotting through the door. "Mom! Meet Duke," Kimberly, my youngest daughter, yelled with glee. I looked down to see the most beautiful dog! Duke had sandy-colored fur, blond eyelashes, and amber-colored eyes. And he was *big*! At first, he was timid about all the commotion and excitement. But once everyone settled down, Duke felt at home immediately and claimed the couch for himself.

It only took a few days for me to get used to having a dog in the house. As the months rolled by, the kids kept their promise and helped with feeding, walking and bathing Duke. We soon found out Duke was quite the charmer and singer. All we had to do was sing, and Duke would join in with us, half howling and half barking. His role in our family chorus was soprano! During the first year with Duke, he especially loved birthday celebrations. When we sang, Duke would sit on a chair at the table, wearing a birthday hat, and sing his version of "Happy Birthday."

Duke proved to be a loving and loyal dog to our family. When I became pregnant with our fifth child, Duke was very protective of me. "Duke, you don't have to worry," I soothed him. When I had a bad cold in my ninth month of pregnancy, Duke sprawled on the couch with me, his head across my belly. He was a great comfort. After I had fallen asleep, I was awakened by Duke's whimpering. "What's the matter, boy?" I asked. Duke seemed unusually antsy, so different from his usual calm personality. He started to pace back and forth in front of me. I stood up to see why he was so on edge. As I got up, I felt a sharp pain in my lower abdomen. Somehow, Duke knew before I did that I was at the beginning of labor!

When I got home from the hospital with my brand-new baby boy, Spencer, Duke was the first to greet us at the front door. He was so excited to meet the new bundle in my arms. He followed me over to the couch where I set Spencer down. Duke rested his head across my newborn's belly, just as he did to me a few days before. He stayed there gazing at Spencer until they both fell into a sweet slumber. As I looked down at my sleeping babies, I felt so blessed. I was thankful that my children had the opportunity to grow up with such a sweet, funny, and protective dog.

Our Duke lived a long, beautiful life. He enriched our lives more than I could ever have dreamed of. Duke went over the Rainbow Bridge at the age of sixteen. Although I never had a dog until I was an adult, I smile as I think, "Good things come to those who wait."

~Dorann Weber

Frisby Loves Bacon

And hey, bacon made everything better.
~Jennifer Estep, Spartan Frost

I was driving home in my 1949 red Chevrolet coupe with the windows down, the ocean breeze flowing through the car, and the Beach Boys on the radio singing "California Girl." I was enjoying the Manhattan Beach scenery—the vastness of the ocean horizon, the curling waves, the seagulls, and the smell of the salty sea. Everything was great until I tried to turn onto my street and found my way blocked by a police car. When I looked past it, I saw smoke billowing out the front door of my own apartment!

Parked in front were two large, red fire trucks, with their lights flashing and sirens blaring. A fire hose stretched across the lawn, up the stairway and in my front door. There were police cars too, and an audience of beachgoers.

My demeanor changed in a flash. I smelled smoke. And then I panicked. My dog was in there. Where was Frisby?

I parked my car and ran to a police officer. I was in hysterics. "That's my apartment. My dog's inside. I need to rescue him."

With a harried voice, he said, "You'll have to wait for a few minutes."

My heart pounded. Almost in tears, I pronounced my words slowly and with clarity, "My dog is inside my home. Don't you understand what I'm saying?"

Frisby was a Wire Fox Terrier who was a rascal. After he had destroyed our living room couch, we switched to keeping him in the kitchen while we were gone. That morning, I left him in the kitchen while I ran an errand. But I hadn't realized that the bacon grease that I saved, which was sitting on top of one of the stove's metal burner covers, would be so tantalizing to him.

Apparently, he had been jumping up and down in front of that stove trying to get that bacon grease, and in doing so his paw had turned on one of the burners. The bacon grease had started to melt, then boil and smoke.

Eventually, the kitchen filled with the strong odor of burning bacon grease and volumes of smoke. The fumes seeped out the open kitchen window, under the closed kitchen door into the living room, and under the front door to outside. The haze rose over the roofline. A neighbor noticed the smoke and called 9-1-1.

The firefighters got into my apartment in time. There was no fire, and once the bacon grease container was removed from the stove, it didn't take long for the smoke-filled apartment to clear.

And where was Frisby? They found him standing on the kitchen table with his head out the open window. One firefighter said, "That is no dumb dog. He knows where to find the fresh air!"

~Gayle Fraser

29

All in a Day's Work

A dog will teach you unconditional love. If you can
have that in your life, things won't be too bad.
~Robert Wagner

The pain in my shoulder was excruciating as I lay in a crumpled pile on the floor. It had only been a few days since I had a double mastectomy due to breast cancer. I had just made a foolish decision to lean over to pick up a piece of paper when I suddenly slipped off my chair and landed on the floor.

The floor was not a bad place, but there was nothing nearby that I could use to pull myself back up to the chair. I yelled for my husband Dave to help me. However, he was in the garage working with his power tools and could not hear me call. So I lay there, waiting.

Just when I needed it most, I felt the soft, wet tongue of our dog, Sandy, licking my face. She was trying to bring me comfort as only she could. I began thinking back thankfully to the day when she became a member of our family.

"Oh, come on, Mom. I really need a dog!"

"Travis, don't you mean you *want* a dog?"

"Well, I want one, and I *need* one. Tim has his own dog. If I had my own dog, then it would be even. Don't you see, Mom? You could teach me to have a sense of responsibility if I had my own dog. I would do everything for him — feed him, walk him, and wash him. You wouldn't have to do a thing — no extra work for you!"

"We will see what Dad says when he gets home. I don't see why you boys can't share the dog."

After this conversation, I felt my resolve beginning to weaken. I knew Travis had a birthday coming up soon. Perhaps a dog would serve as a birthday gift.

There is a bond that exists between a boy and his dog that transcends all other relationships. A boy can share his deepest, darkest secrets with his dog and never fear exposure. The dog always understands when his boy is having a bad day and still loves him unconditionally.

Travis went to school while I went to my job managing a local tax-preparation office. Coincidentally, there was a sign in the window of the dry-cleaning shop next door. It was a homemade flier with a picture of a litter of puppies and the caption: *Free Puppies!*

The puppies were adorable, part Golden Retriever and part Yellow Lab. Dave and I decided to honor Travis's wish. We agreed to pay all veterinary expenses, and Travis would be responsible for the dog's care. Travis picked out a male with very light blond fur and large, dark eyes. Travis's first comment was that her fur was as light as the sand on the beach. "Let's call her Sandy!" proclaimed Travis.

Eventually, Travis finished high school and got a job that involved a lot of traveling. Sandy was very lonely while he was gone, so Travis began leaving Sandy with the "grandparents" while he was on trips. Sandy became known as the mascot of the tax store.

This sweet, little puppy now tipped the scales at an imposing eighty-four pounds! Sandy's demeanor was very calm and gentle. She was the official "greeter" of the tax office. People who tended to be very brusque and curt would look for her. Their mood would immediately change as she lovingly licked their hands.

Now I was so glad to have this sweet dog licking my face as I lay on the floor. She couldn't help me, but at least she could comfort me while I waited for Dave to come back inside and find me.

Sandy had other ideas, though. She lumbered over to where the kitchen chairs were pushed under the table. Slowly, she pulled a heavy wooden chair out from under the table with her teeth. I was shocked as I saw a very determined dog push the wooden chair with her nose and front paws across the kitchen to the spot where I was lying on the floor. I was able to pull myself back up as a result.

I thought she was a hero, but what did Sandy do? She lay back down on the rug and took a nap.

~Alice M. McGhee

30

Wonder Dog

Properly trained, a man can be dog's best friend.
~Corey Ford

When my siblings and I were young, our uncle had a brown-and-white, droopy-eared mutt named Palooka. He was a friendly, affectionate dog who looked like a combination of Beagle, Basset Hound, and Dachshund. Our uncle called Palooka a "wonder dog" because he said every time he looked at Palooka, he just had to wonder.

So, when our uncle's job relocated him out-of-state and into an apartment, he offered Palooka to us. My siblings and I were thrilled. Our parents, not so much.

"I'll take care of Palooka," I promised my parents, as every other ten-year-old in the world has ever pledged. "I'll feed him, walk him, and teach him tricks and stuff."

"I'll help, too," said my brother.

"So will I," promised my sister.

My parents agreed reluctantly to adopt Palooka with the stipulation, "You kids are the ones who'll clean up the dog doo-doo in the back yard!"

So… our family got a dog.

Palooka ate anything we offered him. He especially liked hot dogs, pizza crust, apple pie, and buttered toast. Palooka slept on my sister's bed, and he napped under the kitchen table while we did our homework. He chased us around the back yard while we tossed a Frisbee. We loved Palooka, except for one thing…

"Time for doo-doo duty in the back yard," Mom would announce every afternoon when we got home from school.

And then it would start:

"It's your turn to clean up!"

"No, it isn't! You do it!"

"No fair! I did it last time."

"You did not! I did it last time!"

"You do it!"

"No way! You do it!"

Eventually, Mom would get frustrated, storm out the back door, grab the shovel and clean the mess herself—all the while grumbling about those kids and that dog they just had to have.

The doo-doo duty conflict became a blistering catalyst for tension in our house. Palooka's mess was a constant source of irritation.

Then, one afternoon when we got home from school, calamity had struck. Palooka was missing: his leash twisted limply across the back yard, his doghouse empty.

"Palooka's gone," I told Mom. "We don't know where he is."

"He probably slipped out of his leash and wandered off," she replied. "Check around the neighborhood."

So, we hopped on our bikes and pedaled down the street, calling for Palooka. We checked the neighbors' yards, the corner playground, and around the Dumpster behind the grocery store. Palooka wasn't anywhere.

That night, at the dinner table, Dad cleared his throat and broke the silence. "You know, I'm not surprised Palooka ran away. The way you three are arguing about doo-doo duty lately, I'm half tempted to run away myself."

"That's true," agreed Mom.

"You think Palooka ran away because of our arguing?" I asked.

"Who knows?" Mom shrugged. "Palooka is pretty smart."

My siblings and I sat silently for a while, and then we all took turns apologizing.

"Sorry I yelled at you," I said.

"Sorry I didn't take turns with doo-doo duty," mumbled my brother.

"I'm sorry, too," added my sister.

"Well, it's good to hear children being civil to one another," said Mom. "Now, everyone try to eat something."

After dinner, the three of us went out and cleaned up Palooka's mess. Working together, doo-doo duty only took a few minutes.

We all apologized to each other again before bed.

The next morning, when we shuffled half-asleep into the kitchen for breakfast, Mom clapped her hands and announced: "Look who is back!"

She opened the back door, and Palooka danced in, jumping up on us and barking loudly. We all took turns hugging and petting him.

"Thank goodness, he came back!" my brother said.

"Must be that he heard household peace was restored," said Dad, pouring his coffee. "And decided to return."

"I wonder where Palooka went," said my sister.

"I guess we'll never know," replied Mom.

I can't say that the three of us never argued again, but we stayed true to our promise to share doo-doo duty, and Palooka never ran away again.

Years later, when I was away at college, Palooka, at the ripe of old age of fourteen, had to be put down after a short illness. I came home for a weekend shortly afterward and, over a pot of coffee at the kitchen table, I asked my parents what had happened with Palooka when he had mysteriously disappeared all those years ago.

"Oh, your father boarded Palooka somewhere overnight," said Mom, nudging Dad with her elbow. "Didn't you, honey?"

Dad shrugged. "How should I know? You're the one who boarded him. You never told me about it."

"What?" Mom shook her head. "I didn't board Palooka. You did that."

"Nope," replied Dad. "When I got up that next morning, the kids were asleep, you were out jogging, and Palooka was in the back yard. I always assumed you brought the dog home early."

"So, neither of you boarded him?" I asked.

Mom was thoughtful for a moment. "Apparently not, but I always thought…"

"So, Palooka really did run away," I said. "Then came back on his own the next morning after we all made up."

"I guess so," said Mom, shaking her head again.

"Huh," grunted Dad.

Obviously, what my uncle had said was true: Palooka really was a "wonder dog."

~David Hull

31

The Fire Marshal

*People who do not like dogs do not know dogs. It is
very difficult to dislike a being who worships
you and would gladly die for you.*
~Roger Ebert

The ad read: "Free to Good Country Home."

"Check this out," my husband said, handing me the flyer. "He might just be the dog for us. We'd have plenty of room for him to run."

This wasn't a decision I took lightly. It would be our kids' first dog. Ours, too. *Would he be gentle?* I'd always envisioned a fluffy, Golden Retriever puppy, but we'd recently bought a house, and purebreds were expensive.

So why was this purebred free?

"We didn't know what else to do," the owner explained, wringing her hands as we walked that afternoon. "Buster's a good dog. But then he got loose and found the school."

I nearly walked back to my car right then.

"Oh, but he loves kids," she assured me, "only we don't have any. That's him, there."

She pointed down the hill to where a well-built Golden Retriever raced back and forth on a run made from a long lead rope snapped onto a clothesline wire. His paws had worn a smooth rut into the bare yard.

"I don't like it much either," the woman murmured, noticing me frown at the arrangement.

After our introduction, I checked out the dog, running my hands across his back and over his hips. His owner checked me out, too, appearing satisfied when I felt beneath his collar for sores. He felt good.

"We have to keep him tied now. He heads for the school — every time. At the playground, the dogcatcher only needs to open his car door, and Buster jumps in. I love him, but I've paid $250 in bail. I can't anymore. It's this or the rescue league. Your acreage is how big?"

"Three acres. Six miles from any school."

With not a fence in sight, I thought, praying silently. *Lord, is this guy for us? My clothesline barely holds our clothes.*

I knew God's answer the moment Buster sat in front of me. Extending his huge paw toward mine, we shook politely. I knelt to look into his brown eyes. Then he moved his head closer, resting his jaw softly against mine.

"Come on, boy," I said, opening my car door. The big dog obeyed, riding home like the gentleman he would be for the woman who'd rescued him from his life on a clothesline.

At home, he stepped out of the car as if he owned our place. And in a way he did. Walking up boldly, he sniffed the tomcat that came with the house. My husband introduced himself, rubbing his hands through Buster's ruff. Then he set the dog free.

"What if he runs off?" I argued when we left to buy dog food.

"Susan, we're not tying him. It's best we know now if he'll stay or not."

When we returned, Buster lay beneath the tree looking very pleased. The nine lazy farm cats perched high in the tree's branches looked not so pleased. Beside the garage, Ol' Tommy smoothed his fur into place. Apparently, he'd come to an understanding with the new dog. Within the week, the farm cats took sanctuary in the barn.

Buster soon developed a routine of morning rounds. Crossing the dewy front yard, he'd walk down along the edge of the gravel road disappearing behind the pines. I followed one morning, watching as he stopped at each of our four corner posts to bless them. After claiming his property, he'd finish his patrol by signing off on the mailbox post and then settling down on the front porch to wait for the kids.

Despite open fields, Buster stayed home. With children of his own, he'd found all he needed. Wherever they played, he was nearby fanning his tail, sometimes knocking a toddler over in his enthusiasm to race them to the swing set.

We had protection now, too. The winter before, coyotes frequently traveled the nearby valley. They'd line up in formation atop the high bank of the ditch across from our house. Then, in a hair-raising wail, they'd begin their midnight serenade.

Not long after Buster's arrival, they returned one evening. First one lone cry, followed by a choir. Then Buster's bold, deep bark gave way to a racket of scattering yips and whines. That was followed by a blessed silence.

Every evening afterward, our big, golden sergeant posted himself at the driveway's edge. Through the window glass, carried on the frozen night air, came distant chatter like that of schoolchildren laughing. Then came a deep, heavy growl. Then one bark, for Buster was a dog of few words, and those yippy coyotes withdrew.

Several winters later, while stoking the basement wood burner for the night, I picked up a pile of veneer scraps I'd peeled from an antique table. Without thinking, I tossed three armfuls of brittle wood onto the gleaming coals. The old varnish quickly ignited, filling the stove box with a scorching blaze before I could slam the stove door. Flames leaked out from behind the door even after I kicked the latch shut. Then I waited in the dimly lit room for the fire to die down before adding the nighttime logs. Funny how I'd never noticed the flue stack glowing before.

Breathless from my narrow escape, it took me a while to notice barking outside. Buster never barked much, but that night his frantic, high-pitched calls would soon wake the kids. I set aside the remaining veneer scraps and went upstairs. That dog was hysterical when I stepped outside, running circles around me. Yet everything outdoors appeared serene.

Then Buster jumped on me.

"Get down!"

As I shoved away the dog, a glowing ember floated between us.

Buster leaped into the air after a trail of fireworks now drifting from on high. Two stories up, sparks and flames shot from our chimney. Glowing cinders were sweeping across the dry shingles like the panic sweeping across my heart.

My girls were upstairs asleep. Our garden hoses were stored for winter, and that dog wouldn't stop barking. Suddenly, I remembered the extinguisher stick. Gathering dust in the basement, it waited for a chimney fire.

Ripping it from its box, I grabbed some gloves before touching the stove's handle. Fanned by the fresh air, flames burst from the opening door. The stick went in. The door slammed shut. The chemical's reaction suffocated the burning creosote lining the long, chimney pipe. Several times, I ran from basement to outdoors before falling into a heap on the steps. There were no more sparks.

Standing in the doorway, Buster looked in uncertainly. I called him over, throwing my arms around his big, yellow neck.

"You saved us, Buster. Thank you for saving us."

~Susan A. Hoffert

Chapter
4

The Dog Really Did That?

Crazy Canines

32

The Battle for the Sheep Pillow

*Siblings are the people we practice on, the people
who teach us about fairness and cooperation and
kindness and caring, quite often the hard way.*
~Pamela Dugdale

Sometimes, my two dogs do things that remind me of the two sisters, Sue and Diane, I used to hang around with when I was a kid. At least once a week, the sisters would fight over something one of them had... and the other one wanted.

For example, one Easter Sunday, Sue came over to show my family her new Easter outfit. As we were admiring it, Diane stormed into the house, ran over to Sue, reached up underneath her dress and yanked her slip — a frilly half-petticoat — down to her ankles.

"Give me back my slip!" Diane shouted.

"No!" Sue shot back. "I need it for this dress!"

A tug-of-war, accompanied by ripping sounds, then ensued.

Well, last Christmas, my Rottweilers, Raven and Willow, made me believe that after fifty years, Sue and Diane had actually returned in canine form.

It all began one day when I was Christmas shopping and happened to see a fluffy dog pillow in the shape of a sheep. It was on sale, so I thought I'd buy it for Raven. My other dog, Willow, already had a stuffed bunny she carried around all the time, so I figured Raven deserved the sheep.

Well, my gift to Raven was a big hit... with both dogs. Willow decided she wanted that sheep pillow, and she was going to stop at nothing to get it.

Thus began endless days of sheep tug-of-war, Rottweiler style, which included growling in a variety of octaves and decibels. Because Raven sounded like a cross between Godzilla and a rabid wolf when she growled, she usually won the battle. Then she would take the sheep to a far corner of the room and plunk down on top of it to conceal it.

But Willow would wait, lurking behind the recliner or under the kitchen table, until an opportunity arose, such as when Raven would leave the room to get a drink of water. Then Willow would swoop in like a vulture that had been eyeing a fresh carcass and snatch the sheep. When Raven returned to her spot and saw the sheep missing, she'd run and jump on Willow, and the fighting would begin again.

I began to feel as if I had a front-row seat at a World Wrestling Federation match.

There was only one solution to the problem. I had to buy another sheep pillow and give it to Willow. But as luck would have it, when I returned to the store, all of the sheep pillows were gone.

So I did the only other thing I could think of to resolve the problem and restore peace in the house: I took the sheep pillow away from Raven and hid it in the basement.

Although I felt certain I'd been sneaky about hiding the sheep, Raven seemed to instinctively know I was guilty of sheep-napping. She developed a creepy habit of standing and staring at me — a really evil-looking, "I want to drain your jugular vein" kind of stare. When I was watching TV, there she'd be, standing next to it and staring at me. When I was trying to read, she'd be peering out from behind the end table, her eyes boring into me. She didn't blink, she didn't move, she just stared, sometimes for more than twenty minutes at a time. It was like the Vulcan mind meld, where she was attempting to merge her thoughts with mine. And those thoughts were saying, "Give me back my sheep pillow... or else!"

About a week ago, I was in a department store and happened to spot a colorful display of pillows in the shapes of animals. I searched through them, hoping to find a sheep to give to Willow, so both dogs would have one, and I would be able to live in a calm, quiet house once again. There was no sheep, so I bought a hippopotamus, thinking Willow wouldn't know the difference.

The first thing Willow did when I gave her the hippo was rip out its eyes and spit them onto the rug.

Her message was clear: She wasn't all that fond of the hippo pillow.

Meanwhile, Raven continued to stare at me. When I woke up one morning and opened my eyes to see two dark Rottweiler eyes glaring into mine, that did it. I decided I'd rather put up with the dogs fighting than risk waking up without my jugular vein. I went down to the basement and brought the sheep pillow back upstairs.

Almost instantly, the dogs transformed into Hulk Hogan and The Rock, using their best headlocks and scissor holds on each other as they battled for the prize. They crashed into the end table near the sofa. I'd just set down a cup of tea, and it splashed everywhere. And Raven's growling got worse, kind of like a buzz saw on turbo speed.

Yesterday, just as I was on the verge of taking the sheep pillow for a long walk in the woods and "accidentally" dropping it into the brook, Raven suddenly decided she didn't want it anymore. When Willow grabbed it away from her, she didn't make any attempt to resist. Even Willow seemed stunned by the abrupt change of attitude. She brought the pillow over to Raven to taunt her with it, which, in the past, always had incited a battle. Raven only yawned and looked away.

As it turned out, the reason why Raven lost interest in the sheep pillow was because she decided she'd rather have the hippo. She picked it up and carried it to the corner, then fell asleep on it. I figured maybe she felt sorry for it because it had no eyeballs.

And the moment Raven woke up, Willow pounced on her because she wanted her hippo back.

Here we go again.

~Sally A. Breslin

33

Stupid Dog Love

Good judgment comes from experience, and
experience comes from bad judgment.
~Rita Mae Brown, Alma Mater

My partner Hellen and I were driving to my brother's family home in eastern Ontario's cottage country to share Christmas dinner with my siblings and parents. Meandering carefully along the winding, snow-covered road, I was jolted by the erratic dodging of a large, black Labrador Retriever. I slammed on the brakes, skidding and missing him by inches. When I glided to a stop, his big, dumb, happy face was looking in my driver-door window. I opened it and told him firmly to go home.

For some dogs, the suggestion is all they're looking for. It has been my experience that many will simply wander off and do as they're told, but not this guy. We played a game where I would move forward, and he would run in front of the car. I would stop, and he would visit the window. This went on for a bit. Finally, I got out of the car and aggressively shooed him off the road. For a few moments, I had a clear path to proceed without possibly killing the dog and wrecking my Christmas.

Having arrived and settled happily at my brother's house, I was told by two subsequent carloads of guests that each had nearly hit a big, black dog on the way in. I looked at my partner and said, "That dog is going to die today."

In my mind, I saw the dog's fate more precisely — that the speeds people travelled would more than likely result in a collision that, rather than killing him instantly, would gravely injure the dog. He would hobble into the woods and die slowly and painfully in below freezing weather.

I had to go and rescue this dog, despite the protests of my family members who don't have dogs: "Don't bother. Don't worry. He'll make his way home."

I was having none of it. If he were lost and/or abandoned, he was at risk of freezing overnight even if he managed to avoid being hit. It should be noted that this dog seemed convinced that moving vehicles came along at random intervals to play fetch or tag with him.

This dog was not going to die if I could help it. After several kilometres of retracing my route, out he jumped, narrowly missing my front bumper. Again, the big, dumb, happy face at my window and the scrabbling paws on my door. This is the part where non-dog-loving people start paying attention, but I was much less concerned with a few scratches on my already dented RAV4 than I was with getting this kamikaze Labrador to safety.

I opened my back door, and in he jumped like he belonged there. We visited half a dozen homes clustered sporadically in the woods. There were mixed responses as to where this silly dog could have come from. Some had never seen him. Others pointed in the general direction of a house where he might live. The compass spun on me as I tried to piece together all the evidence. I followed the general path toward a house on the main road. I left him in the car and went up to find a child-friendly home with a backyard rink and many days of his footprints and waste near the front and back doors. Lights were on, but no one came to the door, so I assumed they, like me, were out for Christmas dinner. The lit foyer featured the tell-tale stay-out-of-the-living-room doggy gate, and I imagined the convolution of events — one kid's job is to let him out before departure, another's job is to let him in — he said, she said — et voilà, doggy day-pass.

With crazy dog in tow, I looked around the back for a rope to tie to his bright green collar, but there was none. At this point, I tried the garage door and, finding it unlocked, thought that I would just leave him in there, but it was colder in there than it was in the bright sunshine. I spied the door from the garage to the house, tried the handle, and opened it. The dog ran in, lay down sideways, and banged his tail against the floor. Mission accomplished. I thought of the kid who forgot to do his or her duty, and I said happily, "You're welcome."

Christmas dinner at my brother's house was a joyful, stressful, routine affair. We all drove home not having to worry about hitting the Lab and knowing that he was comfortably safe in his family's foyer. My brother called me on Boxing Day to tell me that he had taken his sled by the house, but there was no sign of the family's return. This was *not* good. The two possibilities posed increasingly menacing significance. The first possibility was that the person tasked with seeing to this dog's care had fallen down on the job. The second possibility was that this dog had told me an elaborate lie, and I'd put him in a house where he did not actually live. Either way, we were anxious to go see to the dog's welfare and get him to the SPCA so his real owner could find him.

As my brother had assured me, there wasn't a track in the overnight snow other than muted ones my car had created the previous day. I opened the garage, went to the door and opened it. The dog darted out happily to meet Hellen and be restrained from any more road drama. The blood drained from my face, and then returned with a vengeance as panic rose within me. This was indeed *not* this dog's house. He had spent the last sixteen hours destroying everything he could get at. Baseboard and trim were ripped and snarled from drywall. The doggy gate was askew. Garbage, torn pillows and couch cushions were in tatters as far as the eye could see into the living space.

I stood in the doorway to the foyer trying not to vomit. I composed myself enough to walk, closed the door and the garage door, and strode zombie-like toward Hellen. The Lab was playing — jumping straight up in the air and diving nose-first into the snow — coming up with a face full of snow crystals and licking his snout like a bonehead. Hellen's smile melted away as she saw me walk down the driveway toward her.

I said, "Not only is this *not* his house, but he trashed it!"

Hellen's expletive said it all. We stood gawking at this crazy dog as he dove and jumped and tried to "retrieve" us so we would play in the snow with him. I felt a deep affection for him in that moment — partly because he was completely worthy of it and potentially a Freudian defence to prevent me from running him over with my car. Fortunately, my love of animals is as deeply rooted in my psyche as any stress-induced revenge tendencies, so the big, dumb, happy dog grounded me for the emotional onslaught.

The tears flowed freely down my cold cheeks as I was bombarded with images of this family coming home to undeserved chaos. My mind played a slideshow of every moment of my life when I was bad and wrong and stupid and in trouble. It isn't always the MO of our partnership to rise beyond the stress to support one another. Sometimes, it's an echolalic storm of expletives — both of us reacting gracelessly in fear and angst.

Not today. Hellen suppressed images of evaporating dollar signs and me in handcuffs. She denied in that moment the fear that my actions might constitute a revision of the Criminal Code for what we are now calling "stupid dog love." She embraced me with her whole heart and assured me that she was with me one hundred percent in my good-faith judgment of the situation and that, ultimately, everything would be fine.

She called the SPCA to come and get my partner in crime, and I called 9-1-1 to make the dumbest report ever. I spoke to a string of constables, each with his or her own unique sticking points for understanding why I would put a dog I don't know in an empty house I don't own. Once I made my case that I believed in all good faith that he belonged there, that significant evidence existed to propel my decision, and that my actions were humanely motivated, each of them was downright kind to me. These facts and a quick investigation into my background of upstanding citizenship allowed them to ascertain that no criminal charges would be laid.

The police notified the owners, who were out of town and had a large Springer Spaniel (with them). After the police investigation wrapped up, insurance adjusters and lawyers took over, and many thousands of dollars of damage were rectified. The impact on my liability premiums is yet to be determined. Through a lawyer, I was able to express my deep regret to the family for this situation, and they acknowledged that they understood it as an innocent mistake. As for the dog… A harried owner, who had been searching since Christmas Eve and lived several miles away, located his big, dumb, happy dog at the SPCA and was charged $300 to get him back.

Truthfully, I have a long history of stopping on the roadside to rescue wayward mutts who play in traffic. No, this wasn't my first dog rescue. It wasn't even my first black Lab rescue. There have been many. It's been months since that fateful Christmas day. The angst of waiting for financial and legal details in the wake of this debacle had almost obscured an important fact. I saved that dog from a potentially miserable fate and, if called upon again, I would do the same thing… except for the wrong house part. I will never again trust a Labrador Retriever to tell me where he lives.

~Barbara Clarke

34

A New Leash on Life

Dogs bring out the best in us.
~Author Unknown

"Mom! Get your dog off me!" I yelled, two seconds after walking through her door. It was Christmas Eve, one of the few days a year when I dress up. My thirteen-year-old daughter Desirée and I had arrived to pick my mom up for church, and before I even closed the door behind me, my mom's Shih Tzu, Verdell, had gotten her light-gray hair all over my nice black pants.

Instead of pulling Verdell away with both hands and messing up her own clothes, my mom grabbed the dog's collar with her index finger. Verdell was so excited to see us that she spun around in circles trying to free herself. But instead of freeing herself, she twisted the collar around my mother's finger, tightening it more. My mother's finger was stuck and Verdell couldn't breathe.

My mom screamed and got down on her knees. I thought she was screaming in pain but it was more than that. She was trying to unfasten the collar but it wouldn't budge and neither would the dog. Verdell was motionless.

I could see the fear in my mom's eyes as she realized her closest companion couldn't breathe. She tried pulling her finger out but couldn't. There was no time to spin the dog back around to free her. My mom frantically found scissors but I grabbed them away from her, fearing she would nick the dog trying to cut the collar with one hand. I wasn't comfortable cutting it off with both hands but I knew it was our only hope.

My hands shook rapidly as I pushed the blade under Verdell's collar, freeing her and my mom. Verdell's head fell to the floor. I had never seen her still before. I put my ear to her chest to check for a heartbeat. There was nothing. I looked up at my mom, shook my head, and said, "She's gone."

"Noooo! Nooo! Nooo," my mom wailed. My daughter, who grew up with Verdell, ran to the bathroom and locked herself in. I stared at the dog in shock. I couldn't believe Verdell was gone just like that. Only a couple of minutes earlier, she was greeting us at the door. It didn't seem real. The lively little dog, who was never short of energy, lay there lifeless.

My mother's sobs penetrated my heart. I had never heard her cry like that. I thought her grief would kill her. I was never close to Verdell. I'm allergic to dogs, a bit of a germophobe in general and, as if she knew that, Verdell always went after me, of all people. Aside from the shedding, she'd drool on me and even manage to slip her tongue into my mouth — a doggie French kiss.

I don't know what happened, but something clicked inside me. I grabbed Verdell's slobbery mouth, took a deep breath, and proceeded to do CPR. I didn't even know if CPR worked on pets or if I would remember all the steps, but it all came back to me. I tilted Verdell's head back, put my mouth over hers, and breathed. Then… I pumped her chest.

"One-one thousand, two-one thousand, three-one thousand," I recited, and then breathed. "One-one thousand, two-one thousand, three-one thousand."

I checked for her breath and heart beat. There was nothing.

"One-one thousand, two-one thousand, three-one thousand," I said, and prayed to myself. *Please Lord. Bring her back for my mom. She can't take this. Verdell's all she has.*

My mom looked on quietly with hope and expectation, as if I knew what I was doing. I listened for Verdell's heartbeat again. It wasn't there.

"One-one thousand, two-one thousand, three-one thousand," I lamented.

I checked Verdell's vitals again. Nothing.

"One-one thousand, two-one thousand, three-one thousand." Now I could barely get the words out.

With tears rolling down my face, I checked Verdell one more time, looked up at my mom, and finally said, "That's it."

My mom burst into tears again, and I along with her. In the background, I could hear my daughter's muffled cry coming from the bathroom. My mom and I looked down at Verdell. I zoned out looking into her eyes. For a second, I thought I saw one of them blink. I shook my head to snap myself out of it.

"Did you see that," my mom asked. "She blinked. There it is again!"

I wondered if we were both wishful seeing.

This can't be, I thought. Then Verdell's tail wagged.

"Look, look, loo loo look... her her tail. Her tail!" my mom jumped up screaming.

"She's alive!" we cheered. "She's alive! She's alive!"

I embraced my mom, not something we normally do in my undemonstrative family, as we watched Verdell slowly come back to life. Her blinking and tail wagging got faster and faster. Then Verdell lifted herself up by her front legs and joined our celebration as she joyfully ran around the house dragging her back legs behind her.

Little by little, Verdell's hind legs regained strength as well and she jumped all over us. I held her in my arms and she attacked my face with kisses. I didn't resist. Verdell ran back and forth between me and my mom like a puppy pleading to play. Then suddenly she stopped dead in her tracks and made a beeline for the bathroom where my daughter remained barricaded. Verdell scratched on the wooden door, but Desirée didn't answer. She couldn't hear anything over her sobs.

"Desirée! Open up," I yelled through the door.

"Nooo!" she yelled back.

"Open the door," I said. "Someone wants to see you."

"No!" she shouted. "I don't want to see anyone right now."

"It's Verdell," I said. "She's alive!"

Desirée opened the door just a crack to peak out but enough for Verdell to push her way in. Desirée looked down at Verdell in shock. And then excitement.

"Verdell, Verdell, Verdell," she screamed, through her strained voice.

Desirée came out with Verdell in her arms. The dog squirmed, wanting to get down and run around some more. We called an emergency veterinarian. He wasn't surprised by our Christmas miracle and said CPR is often used on animals. The vet asked a few questions about Verdell, congratulated me, and said we didn't need to bring her in. I thought it was all too good to be true but he assured us that she was fine.

We never made it to church that evening but Jesus definitely made His way to us. Verdell and I had a special bond after that night, a special connection that only we shared.

~Adrienne A. Aguirre

Canines and Car Washes

*You don't get anything clean without
getting something else dirty.*
~Katherine Whitehorn

t seemed like such a good idea at the time… sunny day, dirty car, no line at the carwash. I didn't think about my two dogs in the car.

I plunked down my money for the deluxe car wash — the one with all the bells and whistles and the longest cycle: seven minutes, which proved to be the longest 420 seconds of my life!

At the first downpour of pounding water and pummeling brushes, my Westies went ballistic — howling, growling, snapping, and yapping. The flashing green and red lights didn't help. At the same time that my car was shimmying and shaking, my dogs were leaping from the back seat to the front seat, into the dashboard, my lap, and into each other. They were desperately trying to escape or attack the water and brushes. (Anything that moves is fair game for a Westie.) I understood what it must feel like to be inside a washing machine.

I gripped the wheel in panic as I realized I was stuck in this car with two flying, freaked-out dogs! Plus, I was trying to keep my eyes on an immovable object in the distance so I wouldn't get carsick and throw up.

I watched the cycles light up on the bar above the car. We were only on cycle three, one of countless rinses. We weren't even halfway done!

I was astounded at the insanity of my dogs and their stamina… that they could keep up this level of hyperactive madness for seven minutes.

By the time the car wash spit us out, I was a sweating, hyperventilating wreck. The outside of the car sparkled; but the inside looked like the aftermath of a tornado. White tufts of fur stuck to the ceiling and dashboard, scratch marks scarred the leather seats, my sunglasses lay broken on the floor, and the contents of my purse littered the front seat. And, to top it off, my macho-male MacTwo had peed everywhere and my dainty lady Mulligan had pooped in terror in the back seat.

Will I ever take my dogs to a car wash again? NO WAY!

~Sherri Goodall

36

Down by the Bayou

It's not the size of the dog in the fight;
it's the size of the fight in the dog.
~Mark Twain

George Mutt loved adventure, and we, his "parents," loved canoeing. George also loved being on the water. He had a Labrador Retriever's soul in a Yorkie body. So it was easy to put George in a life jacket and take him along on our canoe adventures.

With not much time that day, we decided on a day trip to Armand Bayou. On an earlier trip, Roy had seen an exceptionally beautiful, large buck near an oil-company tank farm on the bayou across from the nature preserve that it ran through. We thought we'd go out, locate the buck again and take photos. So, with Roy paddling stern and me paddling bow, George contentedly scanned the banks of the bayou from my lap as we embarked on our adventure.

It had been a wet, cool spring, and George's dives into—and returns from—the bayou left both George and me wet and muddy, but we were having fun. We paddled some distance, and just before we reached the tank farm where Roy had seen the buck, the bayou necked down.

"Okay, now let's start sneaking the right-hand bank so we don't scare the buck," Roy suggested. We didn't want to startle him into running off before we had a chance to get his picture. We were also half-afraid that if George saw the deer, he would jump out of the boat, and the chase would be on. We figured if we "sneaked" the opposite bank, maybe the deer would remain out in the open, and George would stay in the canoe — or we could at least catch him in the water before he hit the opposite bank. That was the plan, anyway.

We paddled past the last bend in the bayou before the tank farm and were edging along the right bank just inches away from land. There was no deer in sight on the left bank, and we were totally absorbed in trying to locate it. I halfway noticed a gray clay hill on the right bank as we approached it. George was blissfully sleeping in my lap, tired out from his swimming sessions. My paddle touched the bank and… the earth moved. In a split second, the gray "hill" turned into a ten-foot alligator that locals had nicknamed "Fat Albert." His massive, tooth-filled head swung around, staring at us up close and hissing his annoyance.

George, feeling me recoil in fright, sprang into action to protect me. We'd been paddling this bayou for a couple of years, and Roy had told me about this legendary gator. But since I had never seen him, even when we went looking for him, I thought he was just that — a legend. Today, George protected his family and leapt from my lap toward the gator's open mouth. I screamed "No!" and snatched George by the nape of his neck mid-leap.

How our actions did not turn the boat over, I'll never know. I guess we knew subconsciously that if we turned over, we were done for. George was in a huff — not being able to attack our foe — but valiantly barked at the hissing alligator. "Fat Albert," on the other hand, was annoyed at being awakened from his nap. Tired of having his sensibilities disturbed by a yapping snack, he took one last piercing look at us, rolled down to the bottom of the bank and plunged into the bayou — swimming away directly under our canoe.

When I asked Roy what we should do, he said, "Nothing. Don't do a thing — and don't paddle." No problem. Both of us were prepared to brace the canoe if the gator tried to turn us over, but we watched in nervous silence as the bubble stream of the gator bisected our canoe's position and traveled upstream.

It took a couple of minutes, but when we recovered from our scare, we took note of what George was doing. He was sitting proudly on the bow of the boat, no doubt patting himself on the back for chasing off the marauder.

~Janice R. Edwards

37

Maddie and the Invisible Raccoons

A person can learn a lot from a dog,
even a loopy one like ours.
~John Grogan, Marley and Me

Our first dog was a copper-haired Cocker Spaniel named Maddie. She was a delightful, happy, little dog who shared her unbridled enthusiasm for life with our family for more than ten years. Maddie loved every human she met, had an amicable relationship with one cat and two rats, and liked most dogs. But she *hated* raccoons with a burning intensity.

Our back yard is terraced; the bottom strip is long and narrow, and flanked by several towering blue spruce trees that lean over the fence toward our property. A cornucopia of creatures has lived in those trees over the years, including crows, robins, starlings, squirrels, rats, and *always* raccoons.

That being said, we never actually saw those raccoons. We heard them chattering and rustling through the branches at night, and occasionally glimpsed a tip of a tail heading over the fence, but we never saw the creatures themselves.

Maddie, though, had a very personal relationship with those raccoons. She chased them back and forth across the bottom terrace every single day. Or, she *thought* she chased them back and forth. There was never any sign of a raccoon during this process, only Maddie racing along the back fence, nose to the ground, frantically sniffing and barking.

One can only assume the scent was so powerful that, in her little doggie mind, it was as if those raccoons were really there.

This practice continued for years, and we, supportive family that we were, enjoyed making fun of her. We would call to her as she freaked out, "Go get 'em, Maddie. Chase those nasty, invisible raccoons."

And so she did, over and over and over, until the entire neighborhood knew about her propensity to chase invisible raccoons.

Then, early one cold October morning, when my older daughter was the only one up, preparing to leave on a school trip, everything changed.

Maddie asked to go out; Sarah complied and returned to her packing. A few minutes later, urgent barking drew her attention. Concerned, she opened the front door to let the dog back in. From around the corner of the house came the sound of running feet, and Maddie's extremely distressed yelping. The little dog flew toward the open door, followed far too closely by an enormous and apparently angry raccoon.

Horrified, Sarah tried to close the door before the raccoon made it in.

She missed.

A whirling dervish of raccoon and dog entered our foyer. Screams erupted, from Maddie and Sarah, and perhaps even the raccoon.

Upstairs, sleeping snugly, I was jerked awake by a terrified voice screaming, "Daddy!" This was followed by the sound of Maddie's high-pitched squeals of pain.

I leapt out of bed. *Oh, my God. Maddie's been hit by a car,* I thought to myself. I flew down the stairs prepared to find the worst. Halfway down, I stopped, frozen into immobility by shock. A battle was taking place at the foot of the stairs: mud, fur and even a few drops of blood exploded from the animals, splattering the floor and walls.

Sarah stood a few feet away from the pair, throwing shoes, coats — anything she could find. Winging the objects at the writhing ball of fur and tails, she tried in vain to dislodge the raccoon.

I screamed, "My poor baby!"

In my mind, a scene played out. I would reach in, grab the raccoon by the tail, and twirl it over my head before tossing it through the open door. As my hand moved in slow motion toward the angry creature, I recalled another possible scenario.

A friend, when faced with a similar situation — but not, I must say, inside his house — had poked at a raccoon with a broom handle. And the raccoon immediately crawled up the handle and attacked him.

With my hand in mid-air, reaching toward the raccoon, I considered the inadvisability of my plan. My husband came pounding down the stairs behind me. One look was all he needed to determine my intentions. He swatted away my hand. "Good Lord, Leslie. Don't you dare!" Then he picked up Sarah's duffle bag and threw it at the pair still spinning in a violent circle of fur.

The raccoon remained unfazed; the dog, however, did not. Her screams sent me into a panicked frenzy. "Tim, do something."

He slammed the door against the dog/raccoon, hoping to force the creature to let go. I worried this would injure Maddie, but then decided a bashing with a metal door was the least of her worries.

Finally, with one massive heave, Tim managed to hit the raccoon on the shoulder hard enough to force it to release the dog. Turning to face us with claws bared, it hissed. Not only did I not know raccoons hissed, but I had no idea how long their claws were! Then it turned and waddled out the door. The nasty thing seemed not only uninjured, but unconcerned by the whole debacle.

Once we all calmed down, Tim took Sarah to catch her bus, and I sat on the stairs comforting my poor Maddie. Physically, she suffered only minor scratches and bites. Thanks to her shaggy mass of hair, her body had been protected from both teeth and claws.

Psychologically, she didn't fare as well. Her small, furry body shook as she sat on my lap, staring blindly into space. She muttered an odd "Arr, arr, arr" every few seconds. It took over three hours for her to calm down enough to function.

From that day onward, she always stopped at the top of the stairs to our back yard before heading down, obviously trying to decide if it was safe. A few weeks later, on a walk with some friends, we encountered a garage door covered with large photographic images of a family of raccoons. Maddie was terrified and refused to approach the images. I'm certain she had nightmares for weeks afterward.

She didn't chase her "invisible raccoons" for over a month, but eventually time soothed her traumatic memories, and she returned to her favorite pastime.

Now convinced of the reality of her invisible raccoons, we did not return to our teasing.

~Leslie A. Wibberley

38

Say Goodnight, Gracie

An animal's eyes have the power
to speak a great language.
~Martin Buber

She broke the hearts of everyone in our neighborhood, this little Dachshund. She was half-starved, beaten up, and left outside her gate in the cold Colorado winter. All of us tried to help her. "Come here, Gracie. Here's a treat, Gracie. Let us help you, Gracie."

But she was street-hard and mean. Her owners were incapable of keeping her safe. They left her out in the cold and the heat, locked her in the basement when they were gone for the weekend, forgot to feed her, and then beat her when she barked.

She had learned to survive on her own, running up and down the alleys of our neighborhood. Animal Control picked her up and, astonishingly, kept returning her to her owners. Within a few days, she would be running wild again, barking frantically, and nipping at all of us who tried to rescue her.

Enter Karen, the Dog Whisperer. She has a lot of other talents — this warm, smart, hilarious friend who lives with us — but speaking the secret language of dogs is one of her specialties.

She started leaving little dog bones outside our gate. Sure enough, that little bloodhound smelled them all the way up the alley. The next step, which took about a month, was to move the treats inside the back fence. By the end of summer, Gracie had ventured all the way into the yard, over to the patio dinner table, and onto my lap.

"Way to go, Karen," I said, resignedly. "You have successfully groomed Gracie and me into thinking she lives here."

From there, all it took was a short walk and a plate of cookies to seal the deal. The neighbors, God bless them, recognized that Gracie was safer with us. We exchanged the cookies for her leash and vaccination records. And it was at just about that moment, after the handshakes and farewell hugs, that the real Gracie chose to reveal her hidden diva.

Victim? I don't think so. From the second it was clear that she was safe, that she had three adoring adults at her beck and call forever, this sad little dog with the big eyes morphed into the pampered celebrity canine she longed to be.

The first order of business was to apprise the neighbors that there was a new boss in town. There would be no casual stopping by the house in which she was now Dog-in-Chief. Never mind that these were the same kind folks who had tried to help her through the years. From now on, she would decide, through much embarrassing sniffing, patting down, and barking to wake the dead, whom she would condescend to let come into her yard. Dignitaries bearing gifts were obviously jumped to the head of the list.

Next up was to teach us all her preferred foods. Dog food was so passé. During her years on the street, she had developed a taste for Dumpster delicacies like restaurant leftovers and the goodies from neighborhood barbecues. True, she would humor us by eating her Purina. But she obtained most of her calories from obsessively shadowing me in the kitchen, like a linebacker, watching me until I slipped, spilled, or dropped whole chickens off the counter and into her gaping maw.

We had to learn the hard way, of course, that this dog with the sensational olfactory protrusion could not be tricked into thinking the kitchen was closed. One Christmas Eve, my husband Ben and I came home from Midnight Mass. Something seemed off. The lights still twinkled on the mantle. The presents sparkled under the tree. And the table was still beautifully decorated with the china for tomorrow's Christmas brunch.

Odd, though. The foot-long Polish Christmas bread, lovingly

baked by our friend for this feast, wasn't proudly sitting in the center of the table where we had left it two hours earlier.

Slowly, we turned. Step by step, we followed the torn pieces of foil but no crumbs, curiously to the piano, where they lay, like discarded Christmas paper, under the bench. And under that telltale cluster of foil was the triumphant Gracie, licking her paws and settling in for a long winter's nap. As she stretched out, paws languidly poised in the air, eyes glazed over, we could clearly see the oblong shape of the entire loaf of bread in her gut.

But, of course, that was our fault. We should never have been so careless as to leave a double-wrapped loaf of bread on the table, flanked by tall dining-room chairs that could be tugged and pulled into the perfect formation needed for Gracie to get high enough to pull the bread off the table.

Merry Christmas.

Her tour de force, though — the performance for which she is hailed throughout the 'hood — occurred one wintry day in 2012. My pharmacist-husband Ben was having a drugstore built in a retail neighborhood nearly a mile from our house. In the ten months before our Grand Opening, Gracie and I walked up there every day to say "hi" to the workers and inspect the grounds.

Eventually, Gracie had to adjust to having the house and yard to herself during the long days while we were at work. After a few weeks of this, she had permanently chased off the cat that had roamed freely through our yard for years, and convinced our mail carrier that we somehow had a mountain lion chained up in the back. Once those brief distractions wore off, enough was enough. Queen Gracie was bored.

"Gracie's out," Scott, our long-suffering neighbor, announced when he called Ben at the drugstore to tell him that our back gate was open.

"Oh, brother. I wonder how she did that. I'll be right home."

Ben raced off on his bike, ready to search for Gracie in all her favorite haunts. But no worries! There she was, happily padding up the street. She had walked eight blocks, changed direction from north to east, crossed a busy, four-lane boulevard, and was within a few feet of our store when Ben stopped her determined advance.

"Bad dog! Bad dog! Funny, sneaky, endlessly entertaining, bad dog! You kill me. And not in a good way."

Our genial mail carrier, Dawn, is a riot with Gracie, who saves up her most ear-piercing barking for her. One day, I overheard Dawn talking to Gracie as she howled her head off at the window. "I'm so sorry I'm late. I know you've been waiting for me all day. I got held up. Have you been terribly anxious?"

An astonished neighbor saw her the other day. "Is this Gracie? We used to give her treats when she wandered down this way. She's so nice now. She's gained weight, and her coat looks so shiny."

Lap it up, Gracie. You came back from the brink. You deserve all the love the world is lined up to give you.

Now stop whining and go get your leash. It's time for your victory lap around the neighborhood.

~Kathy McGovern

39

Hyper Ready

Everything I know, I learned from dogs.
~Nora Roberts

made the mistake of looking outside. It was an innocent mistake. I needed to let my husband, who was mowing the yard, know that dinner was almost already. As I peeked out the window, I saw a little white dog running around with the neighborhood children as they played football on the unseasonably warm October day.

A few minutes later, the chicken was ready and I opened the front door to summon my husband in for dinner. The little white dog I had seen minutes ago across the street was now running around in our yard.

"Does he have tags?" I asked my husband.

My husband narrowed his gaze. He knew exactly where I was going with this simple question. Slowly, he shook his head. I didn't give him an opportunity to protest. I opened the front door and called out to the puppy.

Without hesitation, the little white dog wandered willingly into my home when I called to him. Our black Lab Kody sniffed him and walked away uninterested. I offered the little dog some food. He gobbled it up.

We walked the neighborhood that night knocking on doors. No luck. I borrowed a pet crate and took him to the vet the next day. They estimated him to be a little less than a year old and informed us that he was a Wire Fox Terrier mix. He needed a name besides "little white dog." My friend suggested we call him Franklin after the street he was found on. It seemed to fit him, so the name stuck.

After we posted signs in the neighborhood and the vet's office, notified the local pound and police department, and posted on Facebook, no one came forward to claim him. By then, Franklin had become part of our family.

I wasn't looking for another dog. In fact, that was the furthest thing from my mind. I was actually waiting for the news that my husband, daughter, and I were cleared to travel overseas for our son's adoption.

This crazy Terrier turned our house upside-down. He wandered in and out of rooms, finding anything and everything he could get into. He tore up paper. He opened cupboards and managed to take the lids off Nutella jars. He jumped onto the table and snatched dinner from unsupervised plates. He ate batteries and tore into our daughter's best friend's brand-new sleeping bag. The remnants of white fluff filled her room.

One morning, minutes before leaving for work, I called for Franklin to come inside. Kody stood in the corner of the yard barking relentlessly. I glanced toward his direction to see that Franklin had somehow managed to wedge his little head in the tiniest of spaces between the house and the fence. He was stuck.

Like a crazy lady, I ran to a nearby neighbor's home begging for a saw. Two young men looked at me wide-eyed. I caught my breath and explained the situation. They nodded, and within a few minutes, rescued this pup of mine.

A couple of months later, our family headed overseas for the adoption of our son. We left our dogs in the care of a dear friend and returned a week later. When we brought our son home from the Philippines, Franklin was not sure about this new "critter." He nibbled our son's toes when my son was in my arms.

The addition of a five-year-old boy to our family brought a whole new dynamic to our home. He was active. He was energetic. He was ornery. Yet, I was somehow prepared. This crazy, active, energetic, and ornery white puppy had already prepared all of us to expect the unexpected.

Many years have passed now. Franklin still runs around our home. He still gets into trash. He still does crazy things like drink out of the toilet. Franklin is blind, now, though. He has developed diabetes. He fumbles his way around, often running into the wall and random items in his way.

The crazy, white dog. The crazy, five-year-old boy. Both have aged and matured. They are now the best of friends. And that crazy little terrier did us such a favor by preparing us to be flexible and spontaneous. He prepared us for the gift of our son.

~Tammy Allison

40

Do-It-Yourself Dog Wash

*Anybody who doesn't know what soap
tastes like never washed a dog.*
~Franklin P. Jones

With keen interest, I had been watching some curious activity just up the road from the strip mall in the rural town where I live. What had been a long-abandoned house — or, to be more accurate, an overgrown shed — was being transformed into some new commercial establishment. Every day as I drove by, I observed the progress: new roofing, replaced clapboards, a fresh coat of paint — pink! I speculated to myself what sort of enterprise it was going to be and finally decided it must be a gift shop. To me, this seemed an unwise business venture in our particular neck of the woods, since I had never heard any of my neighbors pine for scented candles, elegant soaps, and precious pottery figurines. But I was wrong. Soon, a large sign appeared over the doorway: "Dunkin' Doggy Coin-Operated Dog Wash." I hadn't heard of such a thing before.

My wife and I never washed Arthur, our three-year-old Lab. The vet had assured us that healthy dogs were generally self-cleaning and only needed human intervention if they happened to get into something bad. And that had not happened... until now. A few months after the shop opened, Arthur was in the dog park and found something on the ground that was, at least to him, irresistible. Before I could reach him, he had thoroughly rolled in it, smearing it all over his fur.

Taking him home was out of the question. I didn't even want him in the car, but I remembered the new dog-washing establishment, and it was only a few blocks away. Arthur and I headed there with deliberate speed.

There were no other customers when we arrived, nor was there an attendant. The entire place was set up like a laundromat, except that instead of washing machines and dryers, there were several enclosed booths. I peeked in one. It contained a large tub, a hose with a sprinkler end, plastic bottles of mild soap, and a secure ring with a short chain to attach the dog's collar (in case Fido decided he did not like the accommodations). Clear instructions were printed on large placards attached to the wall. There was also a coin box outside of each booth.

I went to the change machine and fed it several dollar bills. Armed with a pocketful of quarters and several towels from a pile in the lobby, I entered a booth. The process seemed clear enough. They even provided an oversized plastic apron to wear so I didn't have to share in the bath. I coaxed Arthur into the tub, snapped the chain to his collar, donned the apron, and then stepped out to feed the coin box eight quarters. I turned the lever.

Nothing. The water was supposed to start spraying out of the hose, but it did not. I turned the lever again, but that had no effect. I re-read the instructions on the wall to see if I'd missed something, but no, the water was definitely supposed to start as soon as the lever was turned. *Well, this one's broken,* I thought to myself. *I'm out two bucks. No big deal.* I disconnected Arthur, vacated the first booth, and headed to the second. Arthur safely attached once more, I slid eight more quarters into the second coin box and turned the lever. Again… nothing.

The dog still stinking to high heaven, and down four bucks now, I said a few choice words, which luckily Arthur could not understand. Then I resorted to the old-fashioned method of getting machines to work. I tapped the coin box gently. Nothing. I thumped it with the palm of my hand. Nothing. I pounded it with my fist — twice. Nothing. Though I am generally of a very peaceful nature, I must admit that an image of my worst enemy passed through my mind as I gave the coin box one final wallop, and — *voilà* — the water started pouring through the nozzle.

I stepped inside the booth, latched the door, and began soaping up Arthur. Things were going along swimmingly, so to speak, for a while. I don't know how long a dog bath is supposed to last, but evidently I was taking way too much time because I had only just lathered him up when the water cut off. No problem. I had plenty of quarters left. But when I tried to leave the booth, the latch wouldn't slide. It was stuck. Can you picture this? Arthur was standing in the tub soaking wet and covered in soapsuds. I was standing next to him wearing a ridiculous plastic apron with the picture of a pink Poodle on it. And we were locked in the booth, wondering when, if ever, another customer or the attendant would show up.

I grabbed one of the towels to dry my hands, and then used it to protect my fingers as I tried again with both hands to slide the stubborn latch. Thank heavens, it finally gave way. I determined to leave the door ajar from then on. Out of the booth once more, I figured the whole farce was finally over. I dug out eight more quarters and fed them to the machine. Nothing. *That's all right. Now at least I know how the contraption works. All I have to do is give it another death blow!* I drew back my fist and slammed the coin box once again. The sound echoed, the wall vibrated, and then the hoses in both booths started at once!

~Richard Matturro

41

A Bittersweet Victory

Accept the challenges so that you can
feel the exhilaration of victory.
~George S. Patton

I wasn't with Ron the day he spotted the Free Puppies sign. Later he claimed when he almost passed it, our car spontaneously swerved into the gravel driveway and lurched to a stop, flinging grit and tiny pebbles in all directions. That automobile reacted the same way whenever it neared Garage Sale and Yard Sale posters, too.

"You should've seen them, honey," he grinned as he recounted the story. "Those puppies kept climbing and tumbling out of their cardboard box. Each one scampering around the lawn was cuter than the next. Little fuzzy bundles of black and brown rolling around…"

"Oh, I would've loved to have seen that," I interrupted.

Ron nodded and continued. "When I crouched down and called to the pups, one in particular ran all the way across the yard, and practically jumped into my arms. That did it. I told the owner I'd be happy to take that little guy off his hands and give him a good home."

I was thrilled with his decision. The puppy was cute and cuddly. His soft fur was mostly black, with tiny patches of light brown above each eye and on all four legs. I forgot to ask what breed he was, until he grew bigger by the day. At six months old, his paws were almost as big as the palm of my hand. I later discovered he was part Gordon Setter and part "some kind of really big dog."

We agreed to let my then eleven-year-old son, Scott, name our new pup. He chose Rocky and it seemed to fit perfectly.

You know how intelligent adults sometimes do the stupidest things? We lived in a small, two-bedroom apartment on the second floor of an old complex. We both worked full-time and Scott was at school all day. Still, we thought leaving Rocky home alone all those hours during the day was a perfectly okay thing to do. Although he took to paper-training, he became bored as he grew older and searched for things to amuse himself.

The months went by and my daily phone call from Scott became the highlight of the afternoon for my co-workers. I knew every day at 3:15 my phone would ring, and Scott would recite Rocky's activities for the day. I didn't even say hello anymore.

"What did he do today?" I would sigh. The men and women in my office would stop what they were doing. A hush came over the room as they leaned my way and sat perfectly still. As I listened to Scott's account of what happened, my facial expressions would change from shock or surprise to disbelief or anger. On some days I just gasped and snorted.

"He did what?"

"Oh my gosh!"

"Are you kidding me?"

"Can you clean it up?"

"Did you tell him 'bad dog'?"

"Well, close the cabinets."

"Well, close your closet."

"Well, shut the drawers."

Rocky's days continued to be filled with mischief. He had a fondness for standard dog provisions: shoes, newspapers, magazines, tennis balls, pretty much anything else he could find. He even teethed on my lovely bentwood rocker. I wondered and worried how he could eat the things he did and not get sick. He chewed up, and evidently swallowed, chunks of our dilapidated couch, including foam stuffing, fabric, and wood. One day, he managed to dig out our wedding album and chomp on some of the photos, leaving visible bite marks.

In a way I was surprised our downstairs neighbors never complained of noise, but I assumed they worked during the day, too. Eventually, one morning I received the dreaded phone call. It was from my elderly apartment manager.

"Hello, Becky?" I immediately recognized her raspy, smoker's voice.

"Mildred! What's wrong?"

"I think you'd better come home. There's been a lot of racket going on in your apartment, and some people have complained." She coughed and hacked for a while before continuing. "I walked over that way and heard it before I got to your building. Your dog was barking like crazy and it sounded like things were falling and breaking."

"Oh my gosh. I'll get there as soon as I can."

I slammed the phone down, grabbed my purse, and dashed out of the office. "I gotta go. Rocky's in trouble."

I barely remember driving home or pulling into the parking lot. I was too preoccupied with the images floating around in my mind. What could possibly have happened? I jumped out of my car, ran into the building, and dashed up the flight of stairs. It was absolutely quiet, which I hadn't expected.

I hesitated, then silently slid my key into the lock and slowly turned it, afraid of what I might see. As I swung open the door I saw Rocky sprawled on the floor, apparently exhausted from the morning's events. Scattered all around him were pieces of my once beautiful, massive philodendron, missing so many leaves it resembled a vine. Most of the tiny nails that served as a trellis in the wall were also gone. Hopefully, they were mixed in with the many piles of potting soil and greenery.

I stepped inside the apartment and surveyed the damage. Tip-toeing between little mounds of dirt, stems and leaves, I knew my cherished plant would never be the same.

It was so terrible, it was funny, and I couldn't help laughing. That's when Rocky looked up at me with his tired, sad eyes, not even lifting his head. I'm sure he was humiliated, so I bent down to pet him and whispered soothing words.

"Poor baby, Rocky. What happened here today? Did that bad old plant attack you?"

I smiled and he began to wag his tail, slapping it against the hard floor. That's when he stood up and I noticed that not only was the floor covered with dirt, but so was he. It was in his fur. It was in his ears. It was in his nostrils. He began to shake from head to tail and dirt flew in every direction. As he walked over to his water bowl, I bent down to dig through the layers of soil and found some nails. I was fairly sure he hadn't actually swallowed any, but if he did I was sure he'd be okay. We always said he had the stomach of a goat. Nothing made that dog sick.

I should've expected something like this to happen. Often, when Rocky loped past that plant, the sheer movement caused the leaves to flutter and wave. He seemed a bit skittish and occasionally growled at it.

Dog versus defenseless plant. Although Rocky appeared to be the victor he certainly wasn't acting like it. I guess victory isn't that sweet when it's such a dirty fight!

~Becky Lewellen Povich

Chapter 5

The Dog Really Did That?

We Are Family

42

The Housewarming Gift

Once you have had a wonderful dog, a
life without one is a life diminished.
~Dean Koontz

Watson continued to lie by the front door, waiting for his buddy Frodo to come inside after our car ride to the vet's office six weeks earlier. He stood watch, day and night, anticipating that Frodo would walk through the door at any moment. But his brother wasn't coming back.

How could I help my beloved dog, so steeped in grief, let go? We watched helplessly as our Collie became more distant each day.

"Look," I said to my husband Michael, "Watson left a single kibble in his food bowl for Frodo." We were never sure why Watson offered the morsel after each meal. An acknowledgement that Frodo was the alpha dog? A sign of brotherly love? Or a bribe to keep his daytime antics a secret from us? All we knew was that Frodo stood nearby, eagerly awaiting the gift. And after Frodo's passing, the continuation of this loving gesture was sadder than Watson's refusal to play, go for a walk, or wag his tail.

"He needs a playmate," I said as Michael and I lay down to sleep one night.

"Who needs a playmate?"

"Watson."

Michael turned on the light. "What do you have in mind?"

I reached over to the nightstand and grabbed a picture that I'd printed from an earlier e-mail from Tri-State Collie Rescue. "I've completed an application, and the Collie rescue has this dog available. His name is Hunter."

"Don't you think it's a bit early to get another dog? It hasn't been that long since Frodo died." Michael handed back the photo. "But he's certainly nice looking."

I glanced again at the tri-colored dog with forlorn eyes and a scruffy coat. "Hunter needs a loving, forever home, and Watson needs a buddy to pull him out of his depression. They need each other."

Michael sighed and turned out the light, a signal that the discussion was over. Frodo was his dog, and he struggled with the thought of replacing him. After a few minutes, Michael rolled toward me. "How old did you say the dog was?"

"Three," I whispered across the dark expanse and smiled, knowing Hunter would soon be ours.

"So where is this dog?" Michael tossed over his shoulder the next morning as we ate breakfast.

"It's a bit of a drive."

"How far is 'a bit'?"

I fidgeted. "Uh... West Virginia."

"Are you kidding me? Do you realize how far that is from St. Louis?"

"I know, but I've already had three phone interviews with the Collie rescue. Hunter's perfect for..."

"We're not driving to West Virginia for a dog. There are hundreds of local dogs that need a home," Michael said, buttering his toast.

I recalled my conversation with Hunter's foster dad. How Hunter had been infested with fleas and ticks. How he suffered from ear infections, dermatitis, and malnutrition, but still showed such zeal for life. I knew Hunter was meant for us, meant for Watson.

"The foster dad is willing to drive him closer."

Michael's brow furrowed. "How much closer?"

"Columbus, Ohio. So it will only be a fourteen-hour round trip instead of twenty."

"Oh, is that all? Well, if you really think he's the dog, then go. I'd go, but I have to work."

Could I actually do it? To say that I was directionally challenged would be an understatement. Fortunately, our nineteen-year-old son Holden agreed to accompany me, but I was still nervous driving so far with a new dog.

Three days later, as Holden and I navigated across the Midwest to meet our new family member, I discovered an unforeseen bonus of sequestering my teenage son in the car. He had to talk to me.

We joked. We laughed. We bonded. We shared a mission, he and I, to save a rescued Collie who needed a loving home.

Four roadway stops and seven hours later, Hunter stood before us, and my eyes drifted to his protruding hipbones, his brittle coat, and his tail stowed safely between his hind legs. He needed mending of both body and spirit. Hunter's foster parents had loved and cared for him, and now it was time for them to let go, their job completed.

We gathered the dog's antibiotics and eardrops, and we placed Hunter in the travel crate to go home. It was a fresh start for a dog that had been so neglected prior to his rescue. He needed a new name for his new journey, and our family chose Thor — something strong and bold.

Halfway home, Holden asked, "What do you think Thor is thinking right now?"

I laughed. "That two strangers just kidnapped him and are driving him to an undisclosed location." I looked in the rearview mirror at the courageous dog that had not only survived his previous neglect, but also continued to trust humans. He was a lesson in bravery and forgiveness for us all.

At midnight, we pulled into our driveway, knowing we'd need to introduce Thor to Watson outside on neutral territory. With both dogs on leashes, they sniffed and investigated each other without incident... until we went inside. Almost immediately, snarling commenced, followed by growling. The encounter ended in a tussle, and Watson lost the bout, suffering a gash on his nose. Needless to say, I was shaken, along with the dogs. Second-guessing my decision to bring another male dog into our home, I retreated to my home office with Thor, and we spent the night on the floor. As he nuzzled next to me, placing his muzzle across my chest and giving a deep, contented sigh, I knew I'd made the right decision.

Unfortunately, the next day brought a skirmish more intense than the first. The tally—Thor: 1, Watson: 1. I knew that if Thor were to bond with Watson, I needed to call someone more knowledgeable about dog behavior. Luckily, my circle of dog friends runs deep, and I received a referral to a dog behaviorist who quickly made a home visit.

As she dangled hot-dog strips in front of the boys, she started the training that would eventually bond them together, as well as bond them to us. Within a couple of hours, the Collie boys sat side by side with ears touching, earning their rewards. Their defensive body language and jockeying for authority had diminished. Watson, who was already well-trained, waited patiently for Thor to catch on, even showing by example.

"Remember, we want Thor to think that when Watson's around, great things happen," the behaviorist said.

And they did. Over the next couple of weeks, the dogs eagerly partnered during their training with Michael and me. Soon, they began sleeping next to one another and playing with a tug toy without incident, a true test of companionship. A grieving dog and a broken dog had learned the value of friendship. Watson no longer lingered by the front door, wallowing in sadness, and Thor no longer tucked his tail in fear.

Recently, Michael smiled and pointed down at Watson's food bowl. There, a single piece of kibble lay untouched at the bottom. Watson stepped aside and let Thor claim his belated housewarming gift.

~Cathi LaMarche

43

Andy

*Dogs are great. Bad dogs, if you can really call them
that, are perhaps the greatest of them all.*
~John Grogan

He came from a no-kill shelter that was being shut down by the state — too many animals, not enough caregivers. Because of the large number of dogs needing to be placed, the older ones were to be destroyed. The others were distributed to refuges around the country. A volunteer at the shelter called me. She already knew me and was desperately trying to save the old dogs she had cared for over the years.

I had taken in abused and abandoned animals since I was a child in my parents' home in England. Now I lived in America and was limited by space and law, and we already had our quota of abused dogs. But this was an emergency. Andy and Cheyenne arrived the same day.

Cheyenne was a sweet dog who fit into the household perfectly. Andy was a different proposition altogether. He was eleven years old and spent his entire life in the no-kill refuge, having been abandoned as a puppy. He trusted no one. If he was told to do something he didn't want to do, he turned sullen, lifting his lips in an aggressive snarl. And having been an outdoor dog, he was totally unaware that he would be expected, after a reasonable amount of time, not to use the entire house as his own private bathroom. In spite of all my careful tutoring and frequent daily (and nocturnal) trips to the yard with him, he still preferred to use the carpets in the house.

After two weeks, I was becoming more and more frustrated with him. We had patiently tried everything in an attempt to make him feel at home, but he had rejected all our efforts. Kind words fell on deaf ears; any attempt to pet him was met with a stiff-legged grumbling retreat to another room. A show of teeth greeted anyone if they approached him directly. One day, I needed the space he was occupying and politely asked him to move. He rushed at me with bared teeth, and I knew he was not bluffing. I grabbed a chair and held it between us until he retreated into a corner.

As a family, we had always made allowances for his shortcomings. He had lived in a shelter with no chance of bonding to a special person, and it was obvious from his many scars that he had been in fights over the years. We were ready to love him in spite of his aggressive, ill-tempered behavior, but after about three weeks my patience was stretched to the limit.

On this particular day, he was sitting in a corner of the dining room, and I noticed he was staring at me with a challenging look on his face. A large, unwelcome souvenir lay beside the dining-room table, and Andy was already growling at me, hackles raised.

With all my other commitments, I was finding it harder and harder to cope with an aggressive dog that was upsetting the entire household. I picked up the phone and called the shelter, which was still dispatching animals to different refuges. Suffering pangs of guilt and feeling a complete failure, I told them I was bringing Andy back.

Two days later, I had a call from the shelter. Apparently, Andy was howling incessantly, biting the wooden slats of his kennel, and clawing the wire of the run in a frenzy.

"I've known Andy a long time," the caregiver said, "and I've never seen him like this. He's trying to get back to you. Isn't there any way you can take him? Otherwise, he's old so he'll be destroyed."

I was frankly astonished at the reception I received when I drove back to the shelter to pick up Andy and bring him home. He danced around me, licking my hands and uttering little whimpers of joy. He pulled me on the leash toward my pickup and scrambled in by himself as soon as the door was opened.

All went well for the first week. There were no more "accidents" in the house, and Andy was a model of decorum. Then it happened! I needed the dogs outside for some house cleaning, and they all ran obediently out into the yard on command — all except Andy. He took up his position in the living room, defiantly staring me in the face with no intention of moving. When his lips lifted in a threatening snarl, I made up my mind: Desperate situations call for desperate measures!

Making sure the door into the garden was wide open, I put my plan into operation. I selected two large, metal cooking pans from the kitchen and went to find Andy. He was lying complacently on the floor in the living room, no doubt congratulating himself on winning the first round of the battle. I advanced toward him with my weapons held high, one in each hand. Suddenly, I clashed the two pans inches above his head, shouting, "Bad dog, bad dog," as loudly as I could.

The noise was appalling. Andy jumped to his feet and made for the back door in terror, legs slipping and sliding in a frantic effort to escape. He shot out through the open door and fled to the bottom of the garden with me in hot pursuit, clashing the pans and yelling "bad dog" over and over. He remained there for the next few hours, and when he finally appeared at the back door, it was with head held low and tail between his legs.

From that moment on, life in our household vastly improved. I was now top dog, and I only had to pick up a pan for him to do my bidding. Andy never growled at me again, and soon even a pan was an unnecessary incentive for good behavior.

The transformation was not immediate. He remained independent and watchful, but obedience and attention to commands started to replace the snarls and hostile behavior. One day, I found him standing by my side, and when I bent to stroke him, he didn't move away. That was the first step toward integration into the family circle. Then, a few weeks later, as I spoke to him, he tentatively wagged his tail, perhaps for the first time in his life. Soon, he started to join the other dogs, following me around the house or sitting beside my chair when I was writing.

Our love for each other blossomed, and within a few more weeks we had truly bonded. The more he learned to trust, the more he craved attention. Within months, he was offering me a paw, crawling up onto my lap to be cuddled, and sleeping on my already overcrowded bed.

Andy lived the rest of his life with us. When he finally passed over into doggy heaven, at almost fifteen years of age, he was a loving, important member of the family, blissfully unaware that he owed his life to two large, metal cooking pans.

~Monica Agnew-Kinnaman

44

Jazmine's Journey

A kind gesture can reach a wound
that only compassion can heal.
~*Steve Maraboli*, Life, the Truth, and Being Free

The pony-sized, white dog pressed her head against my thigh. Standing on all fours, her fluffy crown hit my hip. As we slowly walked side-by-side around the highway rest area, the dog paused. Her head drooped slightly, leaning into my leg. I bent down and placed my hands on her face. I looked into her somber, amber eyes, which seemed to question what was happening in her life.

Her name was Jazmine. She was on a journey, and I was part of her adventure.

I had transported dogs for various rescues before, but this Great Pyrenees mix was the first one for an organization called Big Dogs Huge Paws, which rescues large breeds like Great Danes, Newfoundlands, and Saint Bernards. Based in Colorado, at times the group needs people to handle dog transport for part of the journey through Wyoming, the least-populated state in the nation. As often as I can, I travel up to four hours to help dogs in rescue either go into foster care or be united with their adoptive families. Jazmine was leaving rescue and going to her forever home in Canada.

When she arrived at my car, Jazmine had already traveled more than four hours from her foster home south of Casper. I was taking her another two-plus hours north, and someone else was transporting her an additional two hours into Montana. From there, she would go to Calgary, where her adoptive family awaited her.

I gazed at Jazmine's elegant, yet scarred face. The story shared by the rescue organization pulled at my heartstrings. Jazmine had been abandoned in the wilds of southern Wyoming's Red Desert. She and her tiny twelve puppies had been left in the searing heat during mid-summer. Fortunately, some hikers had discovered them and brought them to safety. All survived, and eventually the puppies were adopted. Jazmine was the last to be re-homed. I pondered the journey this persevering pup had already traveled: finding a way to survive, protecting her babies from predators such as coyotes, and receiving battle scars for her endeavors. Then, being helped by strangers: removed from the desert of almost certain death, going into rescue and foster care, and now in transit to her new home, meeting different people at each stop. I would have understood if she had acted aloof or wary, but this gentle giant was leaning her head against my leg, once again entrusting a stranger with her future.

I marveled at Jazmine's resiliency and the durability that I've seen displayed by most rescue and shelter dogs. It takes courage to go from one family to another, having to adjust not only to new humans, but to a different home, often with new rules and expectations. It takes tenacity to live through the periods of time at an animal shelter filled with strange voices, sounds, and smells. Then there's the waiting, whether in cages or in foster homes, for yet another family, and trying again to settle in and be accepted. And here was Jazmine, with me being the third person in a day she'd accompanied, and her journey had barely begun. She had almost a thousand miles still to go and she would encounter another four transporters at least before finally meeting the family who had adopted her.

I began a routine at that moment: I prayed for Jazmine. I prayed her journey would be safe as she continued, and I prayed her life would be happy. I prayed that her new family would be as faithful to her as she, and nearly all dogs are, and that she would be protected physically and emotionally, for she had already endured so much. I have prayed a prayer over every single transport I've taken since. I want these dogs to know that, no matter the upheaval in their lives, there are caring people wanting only the best for them. And though they may not understand what is happening as they go from transporter to transporter, someone awaits them at the end of the journey, to love and care for them.

My time with Jazmine opened my eyes to this truth: It takes a village to rescue animals. From the organization's staff and volunteers, to the donors who support it, from the transporters and foster families to the people who adopt — rescue is a collective endeavor. It takes a community of compassionate and passionate people to rescue animals, but it starts with individuals, people like me who respond to the need. It starts with one, and I am one, one who can make a difference, and I answer the call whenever I'm available to fill that transportation role.

Jazmine and I finished our walk around the rest area that afternoon. I petted her and talked to her. I hugged her and prayed for her, and then I finished the two-hour transport north. I handed her off to a couple from Montana along with her paperwork, food and water, dishes and toys, which included a stuffed animal. As I placed that cloth-covered lamb next to Jazmine in the back seat, I thought how often humans use teddy bears for comforting children. I hoped the plush toy would bring consolation to this large, lovely dog as she continued traveling, meeting strangers and seeing new places. I hoped her journey would end with a happily-ever-after.

And it did.

A few weeks later, I learned via e-mail that Jazmine had arrived safely in Canada, although a bit woozy from days of car travel. She and her adoptive humans were getting along wonderfully. The family had two young children, and Jazmine seemed smitten with them. A photo arrived as well, showing the people and their new furry friend in the back yard. Jazmine's big-dog smile was apparent, and the photo captured her giving a kiss to the man in the family. Her journey may have been long and fraught with uncertainty, but Jazmine's faith in humans and her courage had been rewarded.

~Gayle M. Irwin

45

The M&M Twins

There's no buddy like a brother.
~Author Unknown

"You just have to meet him; he looks like Monroe!" my friend exclaimed, showing me the intake photo of a scruffy, gray-and-white Terrier our local shelter had recently posted online. It really did look like my rescue dog, Monroe, who I had saved from the streets and rehabbed over the previous two years. But she was still very nervous around other dogs. I just knew in my heart that she wasn't ready.

On the other hand, I was haunted by how much alike the dog in the photo looked like Monroe. I decided to go to the shelter myself and see this little dog in action. I knew I wouldn't be able to take him home if he was another rehab case. Secretly, I was hoping he would be, so I could shake this nagging feeling in my gut to bring him home.

At the shelter, I walked through the doors of the adoption room, and there he was, curled up asleep behind those cold, steel bars amidst all the noise of the other dogs barking for attention. They had named him Clifford. As I approached the front of the kennel, he awoke. Immediately, he was full of pep and ready to play. A staffer helped me take him to a visitation room. Once he was securely inside, he whirled around, bouncing about. He was so gleeful because someone had come to see him. He wasn't a rehab case at all. Instead, he was pure joy. He was the most adorable, friendly, little guy, and nothing was going to get him down, not even the shelter.

I decided to go back the next day with Monroe. She would be my true test of whether we could bring another little soul into our family. If she responded poorly, then we wouldn't take that step.

When we arrived at the shelter the next day, Monroe surprised me by entering the building with hardly a flinch. The staff brought out the happy pup I'd seen the day before. He was still friendly, still joyous. But he was calmer. It seemed that somehow he knew he needed to go slow meeting Monroe, letting her adjust to him first.

And then magic happened. My tiny rehab dog, who had never reacted well to another canine, simply looked at him, sniffed, gave one small, low growl and then went about her business. We all joked that since their resemblance was uncanny, her lack of reaction was because she thought she was looking at her own reflection in the mirror. Whatever the reason, remarkably, she was fine.

I looked at my mother, who had tagged along for this meet and greet, and I simply said, "Monroe has given us our answer. Let's take him home."

Clifford was renamed Monty, and he and Monroe are now affectionately known as the M&M twins. Monroe still struggles with any other dogs, but Monty has been the perfect companion for her, helping her overcome some of her fears, and being the playmate she needed. This scruffy Terrier who is so full of joy has completed our family and brought much love to our days.

~Jennifer R. Land

46

Our Daisy

Every dog must have his day.
~Jonathan Swift

"What kind of a name is Daisy?" asked JJ, our twelve-year-old daughter, when I told her about the (mostly) Golden Retriever in foster care that needed a home. "That doesn't sound like a Golden Retriever name."

"Let's not judge a book by its cover," I said. "Besides, if we do adopt this dog, we can always consider changing her name."

It was a big step to even be contemplating another dog. Our family had been going through a rough time. JJ was diagnosed with epilepsy at age eight, and her seizures were becoming more frequent and violent as she approached puberty. We never knew, from one day to the next, when a seizure would strike.

There is no cure for her type of epilepsy. I was consumed with finding the right medication or treatment so that she would gain better seizure control. Life felt like a marathon. And it became unbearable when Rhapsody — our beloved, neurotic Blue Merle Sheltie and JJ's best friend from birth — passed away one week shy of his fifteenth birthday. We were heartbroken and devastated. JJ was inconsolable. A dark pall seemed to grip our house.

Fourteen months passed. In my entire adult life, I'd never been without a dog for such a long period of time. JJ healed enough to want another dog and started asking for a Golden Retriever puppy. Though

I fiercely missed the joys of having a dog, the thought of dealing with a non-housebroken puppy was just too much.

That's when a friend called to tell me about the already housebroken thirteen-month-old mostly Golden Retriever that needed a home. And that's when JJ voiced her opinion about the dog's name.

"I guess it won't hurt to meet this dog," JJ said, "but as I've told you and Dad a trillion times, I really want a Golden Retriever puppy. So, if we don't adopt this dog, I want to get a puppy immediately."

"One step at a time," I replied.

Joyce, the foster caregiver, invited us into her home. "Have a seat," she said graciously, pointing to her sofa. The dog was not present. Joyce started interviewing us, asking pointed but valid questions. "Have you had a dog before? Did the dog live in the house or did you keep it outside? Did you walk your dog? If so, how many times a day? Did your dog enjoy frequent exercise and play? How often did the dog go to the vet? Will your vet give you a good recommendation?"

JJ answered each question, and I added commentary. But JJ was getting restless. She was anxious to see the dog. Finally, Joyce ended our grilling session. "If you'll excuse me, I'll go get Daisy," she said. JJ looked at me and raised her left eyebrow, conveying, "It's about time."

Joyce returned with a beautiful, red-coated, very small (mostly) Golden Retriever, and JJ and I experienced an immediate endorphin rush. We weren't even next to the dog, but just seeing her brought back memories of dog joy. Joyce held onto Daisy's collar, and the dog obediently sat by her side. "She's very smart," Joyce said, "and she's also very loyal. But this dog is extremely skittish around new folks. It takes her a very long time to engage or respond to unfamiliar people."

"What happened to her?" JJ asked.

"Well, we don't know everything. Someone witnessed her being thrown from a truck. She was brought to the shelter, but wasn't doing well, so I was asked to care for her."

JJ longed to pet Daisy. I knew because I was aching to pet her, too. But Joyce kept talking, in no apparent hurry to let go of Daisy's collar. She told us about her two dogs and a cat, and that she'd had them for eight years, and how, even though she wanted to keep Daisy for herself, the law where she lived was clear: three pets maximum. She spoke about her experiences as a foster caregiver. Unknowingly, she let go of Daisy's collar, but her arm draped over the dog's back.

Daisy looked right at us as Joyce told me, once again, that Daisy had been spayed. The wait had become excruciating. Joyce, still droning on, was now in full-repeat mode. "She's very skittish around new people. She doesn't warm up to new people quickly. It takes time to establish a relationship with this dog." I started to wonder if Joyce was ever going to allow us to interact with Daisy.

JJ tuned out Joyce. She looked at Daisy and said softly, "Here, Daisy. Will you come here, girl?"

And then the most incredible, heartwarming, powerful, and unexpected "moment" happened. Daisy, the dog who was supposedly very wary and skittish of new people and who needed so much time to warm up to unknown folks, boldly and without hesitation walked over to JJ. The dog sat down right next to her with an ease that seemed to say, "I'd love it if you'd pet me, old friend." JJ stroked Daisy's head and chest with both hands. Joyce stopped talking mid-sentence.

I couldn't hold back any longer. I, too, began petting Daisy, quenching a thirst that had been ignored for too long. My eyes filled with tears. As I stroked Daisy's head, I imagined the pall hanging over our house dissipating.

There was no need to ask JJ if she wanted to adopt Daisy because it was abundantly clear. It was equally obvious that Daisy wanted to adopt us. "I... I... I've never seen her do that. Not ever. She's never done that!" Joyce stammered, finally able to talk again.

Soon, we were Driving Miss Daisy home. JJ sat in the back seat with her, still petting her with vigor. She looked so happy. We were both so, so happy.

I'll never know if it was divine... or canine... intervention that convinced Daisy to respond to JJ that day. Perhaps it was both. What I do know is that Daisy is a truly remarkable, intelligent dog with a great sense of humor and an unbelievable vocabulary. She's been a wonderful, loving addition to our family for the past ten years. We cannot imagine what life would have been like without her. She continues to make us laugh every day. Daisy is a dog that radiates joy.

We never did change her name. Despite Shakespeare's line that "a rose [or in our case, a Daisy] by any other name would smell as sweet," her name became synonymous with all the goodness, loyalty, love, and joy that is our Daisy.

~Debby K. Simon

47

Pierre, the Gentle Giant

My most treasured possessions are not things; they
are only things. My friends, family and
animals are what counts.
~Olivia Newton-John

One early summer afternoon, my little brother and I were about a quarter-mile from our home, deep in the woods by a river we liked to play near. It wasn't unusual for kids to wander around by themselves back then. We felt safe in these familiar woods, and we liked pretending to be explorers. We found interesting rocks, arrowheads and, once, something that might have been a fossil. We'd stay out so long that my brother usually kept snacks in his pockets so we wouldn't need to go home until suppertime.

My brother spotted Pierre drinking from the river. He wanted to go pet him, but I wasn't so sure it was a good idea.

Pierre was an extra-large German Shepherd. That didn't scare me. I loved big dogs. But on the day we found Pierre, his appearance was frightening. He had many blood-encrusted wounds, and he was so emaciated that we could see his individual ribs (and many of his bones). He had sparse, dull fur, and was completely filthy. But when I looked at his posture, I could see that he was petrified of us. As we got closer, I could tell he was shaking in fear. My heart went out to this poor, abused dog, but I wasn't sure how to help him.

Even at only five years old, my brother was more adventurous and brave than I was. While I was debating how best to help Pierre, he approached the scared dog and offered him some of our snacks. Pierre stopped shaking, and his eyes lit up with hope. We'd grown up around animals, so my brother knew to go slowly and carefully, and hold the food just right so it was easy for the dog to eat it out of his hand without biting him.

When Pierre carefully ate and then nudged his big head into my brother's little hand for petting, my fears melted away. He was clearly a good dog who had been in a bad situation. My desire to help him overrode my fear of his appearance.

My brother was eager to bring him up to the house right away, but Pierre looked like he'd been outside alone for a long time. So I thought we should clean him up a bit before bringing him home and asking if we could keep him. We gave him as good a bath in the river as two little kids can manage without any soap. Pierre patiently endured our efforts to make him look more presentable. He seemed to understand that we were trying to help him.

That quarter-mile trek home was up a very steep hill. Pierre limped from some of his injuries and seemed so weak that I wasn't sure he could make it. But I knew we weren't strong enough to carry him ourselves, and we just couldn't leave him alone in the woods. He'd suffered enough already. We stopped to rest a couple of times on the way up the hill, and Pierre somehow found the strength to make it all the way up. It had to have taken every bit of his energy reserves to do so, even with the snacks my brother provided.

The woods eventually opened to a clearing that was our back yard. It was a decent size, with a big shed, picnic table, and plenty of grass. We hadn't figured out how to approach our mom about Pierre yet, so we concealed him behind the shed. I asked my brother to give the dog food and water and to do his best to keep Pierre quiet.

I went inside, and Mom asked where my brother was. I told her he was playing happily in the back yard and asked if we could have a picnic supper there. I figured if Pierre could "happen" to come to the table while we were eating, she would see how skinny he was and want to feed and keep him. She said sure, since it was nice out, and then asked me to set the picnic table for dinner.

I hoped that Pierre would stay behind the shed at least for a few minutes, but before we all sat down to eat, Pierre timidly approached the table. I didn't know it at the time, but my mother was afraid of big dogs. Pierre's pathetic appearance must have calmed her nerves because while she looked anxious for a second, she took a deep breath, and then slowly and gently approached him.

It was probably best that we had already given him a bit of a bath. He did smell better. And his wounds didn't look quite as bad. Unfortunately, it turned out that Pierre was afraid of adults. When Mom got close to him, he hung his head, his tail dipped down between his legs, and from the sudden smell, I think he might have wet himself.

So even though my mother is one of the most animal-loving people I've ever known, it seemed best for her not to touch him just yet. My brother and I gave him more food and water, and did our best to comfort him. He took to my brother and me like he'd been with us forever, but he took a few days to warm up to Mom. Her gentle, loving nature did win him over eventually.

Pierre's body healed faster than his emotional wounds. Before summer was over, he had a luxurious coat and a strong, healthy body. His ribs were covered by powerful muscles. He looked like a whole new dog. He was great with us, but remained afraid of strange adults, especially men.

With lots of good food and loving attention, Pierre became the physically powerful dog he was created to be. Although he looked like a purebred German Shepherd, he must have been mixed with another larger breed because he was taller and bigger than other German Shepherds I've seen.

Pierre was so big that my brother would ride him like a horse. We played with him for hours every day, and he soaked it all up happily. He loved us unconditionally. Pierre, our gentle giant, was the best treasure we ever found in the woods.

~Phyllis Wheeler

48

Bob and Becky

Every once in a while a dog enters
your life and changes everything.
~Author Unknown

Our five-year-old Border Collie, Becky, is the weirdest dog we've known. But my husband, Bob, and I couldn't love her more.

Border Collies are known for herding sheep. Plus, they need much more activity than other dogs, and are considered one of the smartest and bravest breeds. But apparently Becky swam through the genetic pool without soaking up one drop of it.

If a gun-wielding gangster broke into our house, Becky would go after him with the courage of a SWAT team commander. But when a fly is anywhere in the house, she runs, trembling and whimpering, behind the toilet, where she stays until I've spent half the day finding the fly.

Bob had always wanted a Border Collie. We adopted Becky because we were told she was bred to need no more activity than any other dog, and that she didn't have the herding instinct that all Border Collies do.

That was a bunch of hooey. Becky is not only on the go 24/7, but she herds everything in her universe.

She herds:

1. The vacuum cleaner.
2. Our empty-headed cat, Murphy, who doesn't even notice.
3. Apples that fall out of the shopping bag.

4. Anything that drops on the floor, including tomatoes, but especially meatballs.

Becky spends time in our fenced-in back yard herding her flock. No, not sheep. It's her flock of clay plant pots that once contained pretty flowers. Using her nose to move them along, she herds the pots one by one from the left to the right side of the yard. Then, crouching down with that intense Border Collie stare used for the purpose of intimidation, she makes sure that none of the pots make a break for it and flee from the rest of the pack.

Then she herds all of the pots to the left side of the yard. Then back to the right; then left. This keeps her happy for hours.

Becky doesn't bark. She screams. When she does, she sounds like a woman.

She screams when she sees that a miniature painting has been moved three inches. She screams when she sees a truck in our driveway — our truck.

One day, Bob decided it would be fantastic for Becky to follow her genetic instincts and see sheep. We drove to a farm that had lots of sheep and chickens.

Bob's chest was bursting with pride and anticipation to see her in all of her historical splendor. He said to the farm owner, "Would it be okay if I kept my dog on a leash and took her over to your sheep?"

"Sure."

Gracie, our other dog, stayed with me in the truck and watched.

Bob walked Becky to the pen where there were a dozen sheep. He looked so proud, just like a shepherd with his Border Collie in the ancient hills of Scotland.

When they got to the pen, Becky peered at the sheep, and her body crouched for a full two minutes in that concentrated Border Collie stare. It truly was a beautiful sight to see her in her timeless glory.

Then she let out a scream so earsplitting that all the chickens jumped a foot off the ground.

Bob rushed Becky back to our truck while the farmer came running over, looking around frantically for what he must have thought was a severely injured woman.

Meanwhile, all twelve sheep kept doing what they had been doing all along—eating stuff from the ground, still ignoring the doofus Border Collie that was scared to death of them.

Becky also does something that she has never been trained to do. When she sees Bob, and he, as always, kneels down to greet her, she slowly stands on her hind legs, puts her front legs gently around his neck, rests her head against his and hugs him. She doesn't move, no matter how much time Bob spends hugging her and kissing her forehead.

Becky loves Bob the way Juliet loved Romeo. And he loves her the same. When Bob leaves the house, Becky stays by the door, no matter how many hours it takes for her beloved leader to return home. She will not move, eat, drink, or do anything other than stand at her post... waiting.

When he comes home, the first thing they do is hug. Bob keeps his eyes closed in ecstasy. To me, love is love, whether it's between adults, between parents and children, between dolphins, or between whales.

But especially between Bob and Becky.

~Saralee Perel

49

Megan's Mia

Petting, scratching, and cuddling a dog could be as
soothing to the mind and heart as deep meditation
and almost as good for the soul as prayer.
~Dean Koontz

'd had a rather stressful day at work. It didn't help that I'd also had another argument with my teenaged daughter that morning. By the time I arrived home, I eagerly anticipated getting the most out of my evening power walk. Having some time to myself would help clear my mind and give me perspective.

I was unaware of my surroundings during my walk, which was unusual for me. I've always enjoyed immersing myself in the outdoor sights, smells, and sounds of our scenic neighborhood. However, this evening I found myself still processing the challenges of the day. Despite my preoccupation, the beauty of my little corner of sunny Florida was getting through to me. My turmoil diminished, enabling me to focus on my location. Two miles down, another two to go.

It was getting cloudier and I could tell that rain was coming. No problem. I would be home long before the liquid sunshine fell.

The intense walk worked off much of my excess physical and emotional energy. I slowed my pace, but a quick glance down startled me. The cutest Jack Russell Terrier had appeared out of nowhere and was keeping pace beside me. I knelt to pet her, delighted to discover that her ears were as soft as velvet between my fingers. She reminded me of my childhood dog. She had the same coloring as Lucky — white with a large black spot on her back and side, brown face, and white snout.

"Where did you come from, little one?" She was not wearing a collar or identification tags. I remembered seeing a Terrier when I drove into the neighborhood a few hours earlier. It had darted into the street in front of my car, but I had assumed she lived in the area. She must be the same dog.

I continued my walk, thinking she would find her way home on her own. The little stray continued to keep pace, walking next to me as if we were age-old companions. When I picked up my pace, so did she. When I slowed, she slowed. She never left my side.

When I looked around, I was not surprised that, other than the dog, I was alone on this dreary night. The sky had already darkened. I was worried. If I left her out there she might be hit by a car. I wondered if I should just take her home.

The timing was ironic. My sixteen-year-old daughter, Megan, wanted another pet. Our family dog, Daisy, had slowed considerably in her old age, and Megan hoped we would adopt a younger, livelier dog, one that would be a suitable friend for a teen. We had resisted her requests, since she would be leaving for college in a couple of years.

It didn't make sense to add another pet to our family. My husband, John, and I were looking forward to a little more freedom. The last thing I wanted was the additional responsibility of caring for another animal. Besides, I had a more immediate reason for not wanting to bring home a new dog. Megan and I had not exactly seen eye-to-eye earlier that day. I didn't want it to seem as if I was rewarding her after yet another argument.

The heavens opened, and rain pelted hard. I made my decision. Of all possible breeds, I would never have chosen a Jack Russell. Their energy level is usually off the charts. At that moment, though, it didn't matter. I could not leave this adorable animal out in the rain — even though I knew in my heart that once she walked through our front door, she would never leave. It looked like Megan would get her dog, and we would have a new addition to our family.

I broke into a jog, but the little stray never left my side. As we turned the corner, a neighbor called out and asked if I had adopted a new dog. I smiled and told her it certainly looked that way, but in actuality, the dog seemed to have adopted me. She mentioned this Terrier had been seen running around the neighborhood for the past several days. Some speculated that her owners had moved and abandoned her.

The neighbor offered to give me a spare leash, and I accepted gratefully. We still had to cross a busy street to get home. The dog sat calmly as I looped the leash into a makeshift collar and placed it around her neck. I wondered if she understood what it meant. Together, we jogged the final half-mile home in the rain.

I paused at our front door. Did I really want to do this? My heart overrode my brain, and I knew the answer was a resounding, "Yes!" When I opened the door, the Terrier rushed in and ran straight to Megan in the family room. She and her dad rapidly fired questions regarding the little dog. Who? What? Where? None of my answers mattered once this bundle of energy jumped into Megan's lap and claimed her for her own. I wiped away a tear as I watched my precious daughter hug her kindred spirit.

Our little visitor made herself at home immediately, even as I cautioned that we should not become too attached to her. We still did not know if her owners were looking for her. The staff at Animal Control confirmed she did not have an identification chip. They offered us the option of leaving her at the shelter or keeping her at home for the two-week waiting period before we could officially adopt her. John spoke for all of us when he said we would keep her at home and take our chances.

Two weeks later, Mia became an official member of our household. Megan was a standout soccer player in high school, and she named our new addition after her role model, the famous soccer player Mia Hamm.

My heart was full as I watched Megan and Mia playing together. I knew then that we would not only survive these turbulent teenage years, but that we would thrive... and we did.

~Sharon Dunn

50

By My Side

*Our prayers may be awkward. Our attempts may be
feeble. But since the power of prayer is in the one
who hears it and not in the one who says it,
our prayers do make a difference.*
~Max Lucado

My husband Jake and I dropped off our four-year-old daughter Patty at her favorite play place — my parents' house. Then we made the short drive east to the breeder whose ad had read, "Wolf-hybrid pups for sale. Home-raised dam and sire. Great dispositions."

We found a huge disparity between the ad and reality. An overpowering stench of dirty diaper and puppy poo assaulted us as we entered the house.

"We put them pups in the kitchen so you could see 'em," the grubby owner said, jerking his thumb toward the animals.

A mucus-crusted baby crawled across the gritty floor toward the wolf-dog puppies. The child's mother lounged against the grimy wall picking her nails.

Jake and I exchanged glances. No way would we buy an animal from this pigsty house.

The alpha male swaggered up to my husband. While Jake petted the large, frisky pup, the runt of the litter locked his canine laser gaze on mine. Target acquired.

The small, tan pup wobbled forward, his head the same height as my ankle. I petted the tiny fur ball while steeling my heart. I refused to bring "doggie cooties" home from this filth hole.

"Will they be weaned soon?" I asked.

"Oh, they can go now," the man said.

Jake shot the man an incredulous look. "They're too young to be separated from their mother."

"They'll be fine," the breeder's wife said. "Besides, other folks are buying them this afternoon."

I moved to block their runny-nosed tot from exploring the electric outlet. The pup squeezed himself against my right foot as if glued there.

Jake gave the playful alpha pup a final pat and told the owners, "We'll let you know."

We headed toward the front door. The runt stayed glued to my side.

I ruffled his fur and scooted him back toward the others. A second later, his baby claws clicked against the linoleum as he scrambled after me.

"Jake, he's following me. Isn't that adorable?"

"The alpha would be better, but we're not getting anything from here," Jake whispered.

The runt placed his teeny front paw on my shoe and leaned against my ankle. I carried him back to the other pups and walked away.

His frantic whimpers erupted, and he hurried back to my side. Jake shook his head as I scooped the pup into my arms and crooned, "You're a sweet baby."

The breeder sensed my weakening resolve. "He's 78 percent tundra wolf," he offered.

Jake watched me cuddle the smelly pup, sighed, and pulled out his wallet. I threw one arm around my husband and snuggled the pup closer with the other. "Let's name him Tundra," I said.

Tundra and I bonded over weeks of round-the-clock bottle feedings. My husband's visions of an intimidating guard wolf dissolved when Patty dressed Tundra in Barbie ball gowns and Cabbage Patch clothing.

Tundra outgrew those indignities and graduated to "royal robes" of fuzzy baby blankets thrown over his back. Patty led him around the house with her pink jump rope while proclaiming, "All hail, Prince

Tundra."

After playtime ended, Tundra always scampered back to my side.

He bypassed the normal puppy pitfalls of chewed shoes and carpet baptisms, so it shocked me the day I found him engaged in a clothesline tug-of-war. My tattered bras and undies waved in surrender.

I hurried to rescue the remaining laundry. Tundra raced by my side in his usual place. I showed him the ripped clothing and scolded, "No."

For the first time in his young life, I swatted him on the rump.

Tundra stared at me, his eyes registering betrayal. He wilted against my leg, lifted his muzzle, and poured out his distress in an eerie howl. Goose bumps rose on my arms. His unnerving howls increased in intensity and echoed through our suburban neighborhood.

Patty ran outside and stared, white-faced, at her playmate.

I dropped to my knees, wrapped my arms around his neck, and pressed my face against his. "Shh. It's okay, baby. I'm sorry."

Tundra, his eyes squeezed shut, huddled closer to my side. I tightened my grip and pulled Patty close with my free arm to quiet the tremors wracking all three of us.

From that day on, one quiet word to Tundra provided enough correction.

Despite his runt status, Tundra grew into a 100-pound housedog. Somehow, he anticipated my movements and synchronized his steps to remain by my side as I gardened or did housework.

Seven happy years passed with Tundra as my constant companion until, one day, his voracious appetite lessened. He lost weight and grew listless.

A trip to the vet confirmed the worst. "I'm sorry, but the cancer is too far advanced." The vet handed me a bottle of pain medicine. "When the time comes, I'll put him out of his suffering."

I drove home sobbing and shared the grim news.

Tundra declined at an alarming rate. We fixed him a blanket bed in the living room. The dreaded day came when he could no longer walk by my side. His eyes followed me as if apologizing.

In the evenings, I sat on the floor with his head in my lap. My tears trickled onto his dry, rough coat. He managed a weak tail thump each time I choked out, "You're my good baby."

One Sunday morning, our church held a special healing service. We drove home and found Tundra too weak to stand.

Jake took my hands. "Honey, he's suffering. We have to put him down tomorrow."

Patty shook her head and cradled Tundra's face. "Remember how God healed all those people at church today? Let's ask God to heal Tundra."

"Sweetie, that's different," I said. "God loves people and wants to help them."

"God loves Tundra, too," Patty insisted.

I knew my dog was dying, but Patty's confident faith sent me to my knees. I buried my hands in Tundra's coat. "Lord, will you please ease Tundra's suffering?"

The next morning, I awoke red-eyed from crying. I whispered, "Lord, did you answer my prayer by letting Tundra pass away last night?"

Dread filled my chest like a lead lump. I opened the bedroom door.

Tundra stood there with his eyes shining and his tail wagging exuberantly. My legs trembled, and I sagged against the wall in shock.

He squeezed in next to my side and pushed his head under my hand.

I dropped to my knees, wrapped my arms around his neck, and shouted, "Thank you, Jesus!"

Patty ran barefoot from her bedroom.

"Sweetie, God healed Tundra!"

Patty kissed the top of Tundra's head. "Of course, Mom. You asked Him to, remember?" She ruffled his fur. "C'mon, boy, let's go outside."

I watched Tundra race out the door after her and thought, *Oh, for the faith of a child.*

Miraculously, Tundra's cancer remained in remission three more years.

Three more years of love. Three more years of joy. Three more years by my side.

~Jeanie Jacobson

51

Murphy

Scratch a dog and you'll find a permanent job.
~Franklin P. Jones

One summer, hoping to be a role model for my kids, I volunteered at a local animal shelter as an assistant helper — in essence, a pooper-scooper. Starting at 6:00 a.m., I bagged poop and hosed down dog cages. I remained on poop patrol until my shift ended at 11:00 a.m.

During the training orientation, I was instructed not to feed the dogs. This task was reserved for the full-time senior staff.

I abided by these rules until a Monday morning in early July when I met Murphy. His ninety-six-year-old owner, Lila, had passed away, and Murphy was found sitting beside her on the bathroom floor, head on her shoulder.

When Lila's body was transferred to a stretcher, Murphy climbed aboard. Unable to reach next of kin, a kind EMT brought him to the shelter.

He looked exactly like a Labrador in every way, except he was a color they usually don't come in — pure white.

My morning routine at the shelter always began with a cacophony of barks, growls, yips, and yaps — the basic pandemonium. This particular morning was no exception.

My canine friends acknowledged my arrival with a standing ovation. Our newest guest didn't budge.

I introduced myself to him. The rest of the crowd went wild. Murphy didn't move.

I knew conventional wisdom says to let sleeping dogs lie. The only problem was that I didn't think Murphy was actually sleeping. I thought that, at best, he was ignoring me, and at worst, he was depressed.

At that moment, I decided to break the no-feeding rule. Grabbing a dog biscuit off the shelf, I placed it by Murphy's nose.

He wouldn't touch it. I pretended to leave the room. He devoured it. I repeated this routine at least five more times. On the sixth go-around, I decided to stay. Murphy decided he'd eat.

More than three weeks passed before Murphy decided to take part in the standing-ovation segment of the morning.

After that, he was first off his feet, and after that, I was hopelessly in love.

The end of summer was now approaching. It was time for the shelter's annual "Adopt a Furry Friend" campaign. I made posters and greeted many of the prospective adoptive families. The event was a huge success!

Fifteen dogs were in need of homes. Fourteen were adopted. No one chose Murphy, and I couldn't understand why until the shelter director explained, "All the others dogs play the part. They work hard at making themselves appear adoptable. They allow themselves to be petted. They lick hands and faces, give out their paws, and play with the kids. Murphy mopes. That is, with everyone but you."

We lived in a condo with a no-pets policy. It did not seem fair. Murphy and I belonged together. I knew that. The shelter director knew it, too. So we made an arrangement.

I would be allowed to "adopt" Murphy. The only caveat: He would sleep at the shelter. I would provide love, nurturing, food, and exercise. The shelter would provide, well, shelter. And so Murphy and I began our unorthodox partnership.

Every morning after I put the kids on the bus and before I left for work, I'd head out to feed Murphy breakfast, take him for a run and cuddle with him on a chair in the employee lounge. Dog treats and toys became staples on my weekly shopping list. Every afternoon, once the kids finished their homework, Murphy and I played Frisbee in the exercise yard, and then stretched out on the lawn for a hug-fest before I left.

It took time, but I taught him how to keep a biscuit steady on his nose and not move until I said, "Okay, buddy, chew!" He never cheated. Not even once.

Sometimes on the very best of summer days, we walked to the park down the block and ran through the sprinklers together. He chased birds and ducks and geese and squirrels and little kids in wagons. I chased him.

Our love affair lasted nearly two years. Murphy passed away in his sleep. I was just one block away when it happened. I placed a biscuit by his nose.

Murphy was the only pet I was ever privileged to have. Some would argue I really wasn't his owner because he didn't live with me.

I would argue back that he did indeed live with me in the most important place of all: my heart.

~Lisa Leshaw

Chapter 6

The Dog Really Did That?

Who Me?

52

On Walkabout

The dog wags his tail, not for you, but for your bread.
~Portuguese Proverb

We'd never had a Beagle before, but when we fostered Sugar, a fifteen-pound Beagle mix, we fell in love with her small size, sweet temperament, soulful eyes, and silly bat-like ears. It didn't hurt that she wagged her tail constantly, seeming perpetually happy.

Since she's part Beagle, Sugar loves to wander, so I have to walk her on a leash. However, despite my kids' best efforts to close the door tightly, Sugar occasionally noses her way out of the house. We live in a safe, friendly neighborhood with lots of woods around us, so she loves to get out there, happily following scents for hours. Sometimes, just sometimes, I turn a blind eye since Sugar always comes back. Eventually.

I call these little sneak-outs "walkabouts," after a fictional Australian Aboriginal crime-fighter who went on walkabout in the Outback whenever he needed time to think to help him solve a crime.

When I want Sugar to come home, I walk outside and loudly bang the top of her metal food container to the bottom, like two cymbals. That clapping sound means forthcoming kibble, and she can't help but dash right home.

One day while I was walking Sugar, I saw the housekeeper at the house next door. The people who bought it had moved in a year ago, but they worked full-time and I rarely saw them. Their house had also been under minor construction ever since they bought it.

The woman saw Sugar and said, "Oh, I know that dog. Boy, she really loves cat food!" I must have given her a strange look since she continued. "I always find her in the house. She eats all the cat food, wags her tail and then leaves." I realized that while on walkabout, Sugar didn't solve crimes, but commit them. Reluctantly, I had to make sure Sugar's walkabout days came to an end.

~Jennifer Quasha

53

The Pet Collector

There is in all animals a sense of duty
that man condescends to call instinct.
~Robert Brault, rbrault.blogspot.com

He came to us as a gangly pup, a strange mix of Pit Bull and Great Dane. He had the stocky, muscular build of a Pit, but the long legs, golden coat, and black face of a Dane. He was a very odd-looking guy, with a bump on the top of his head that looked like someone had recently "beaned" him. We named him "Knothead."

The original owner did not want him because he had no "killer instinct" whatsoever. The man wanted a big, mean "muscle dog" to show off to his friends. Knothead was a lover, not a fighter.

I had worried a bit about adding Knothead to our household as we already had a dog and some cats. I had taken the risk because his previous owner was about to have him put down. As it turned out, I shouldn't have worried, as Knothead loved other animals, and people, too!

Knothead would visit all our neighbors on a regular basis. All the houses in our neighborhood were connected by five-foot, cinder-block walls. Knowhead walked the walls at every given opportunity and dropped in to visit all the other dogs and cats in the neighborhood — and even people with no dogs or cats. Everyone for blocks around got to know him. Everyone loved him. In fact, one elderly couple loved him so much that they built him a doghouse, gave him a special lounge chair, and cooked steaks for him when they barbecued. Eventually, we gave Knothead to them, but that is a different story.

Knothead would also find his own pets and bring them home. He guarded them and cared for them as if they were his own children. He was the only dog I ever knew who would tolerate "critters" like squirrels, opossums, raccoons, rats, mice or chipmunks.

Knothead not only got along with them, he adopted them. I first noticed this when our other dog, Brandy, was barking in the back yard. When I went out to see what was happening, I saw she was barking at Knothead, who was inside the big doghouse. His head was lying on his crossed paws, and he had a very worried look in his huge brown eyes. I brought her inside and then went to see what was happening with Knothead, afraid that maybe he'd been hurt during one of his adventures.

It didn't take long to see what the commotion was about. As soon as the coast was clear, Knothead wiggled out of the doghouse with four young squirrels clinging to his back and neck. They weren't tiny babies, but not full-grown either. How he ever got them is still a mystery to me, but there they were. As the young squirrels hopped down and began exploring the porch area, Knothead started whimpering and tried to push them back into the doghouse with his nose. He looked up at me with pleading eyes, as if I could do something to help him round up his new pets.

I had a vegetable garden that was fenced off to keep the dogs from digging up the area. That was the only solution I could think of. I couldn't let him bring the squirrels into the house. They belonged in the wild. But, at the same time, when I tried to put them into one of the trees, Knothead howled as if I were killing his own puppies.

We compromised by putting a large crate in the corner of the fenced garden with a dog mat inside. We made a doggie door for Knothead in the fence. Brandy had never tried to jump the fence. All I could do was hope that she would leave him and his new "family" alone.

Knothead seemed to know what we were doing, and when the new house was done, he carefully carried each of his new friends inside and settled down. We let Brandy out and she sniffed around a minute, but then promptly lost interest in the whole affair. Once she checked and saw there were no foreign critters in "her" doghouse, she was fine.

I put Knothead's water and kibble dishes near the new lair. For weeks, he enjoyed his new furry pets. He stayed at home the whole time the squirrels were with him. The squirrels would scamper in and out and over the crate — and ride on Knothead around the garden. Slowly, they started going up the tree in the corner, staying away longer and longer each day. Eventually, they left him for good.

Knothead returned to normal life in the yard and went back to walking the walls and visiting his neighborhood friends. In the years that followed, he adopted more pets, including a baby rabbit, a young opossum, five white rats, and a few more young squirrels. To this day, I have no clue where he found any of them.

~Joyce Laird

54

Brains Versus Brawn

Dogs laugh, but they laugh with their tails.
~Max Eastman

I was the proud owner of two Basset Hounds that I got through Wyoming Basset Hound Rescue, which was located at that time in Casper, Wyoming, my hometown. Longfellow was a petite French Basset, mostly black with a white ruff. Bascombe was a raw-boned, brown American Basset with a black saddle.

Bascombe was definitely the alpha male. He lorded it over the smaller Longfellow.

There was one area, however, where Longfellow came out the victor. Every evening after being fed dinner, each dog was given a large dog biscuit. Bascombe always took his out to the back yard and hid it.

Longfellow wouldn't hide his. He would gobble it down immediately and then sit inside, watching Bascombe through the sliding glass doors that led to the back yard. As soon as the dog treat was securely hidden away, Longfellow would run down the steps to the front door and start barking frantically, as if somebody was at the door.

Bascombe never missed an opportunity to greet a visitor, and being the alpha dog, he couldn't let Longfellow handle this important task alone. He would rush back into the house and take his place barking at the front door.

As soon as Bascombe came in and started his very important barking, Longfellow would race outside and eat the dog biscuit that Bascombe had just hidden. Eventually, Bascombe would give up barking at the front door and return to the back yard to retrieve his hidden treasure. He would search the yard, returning again and again to the place where he knew he had hidden his treat. I could almost see him scratching his head and thinking to himself, *I'm sure I put it right here! Where did it go?*

I always took pity on Bascombe and gave him a second biscuit to make up for the one he lost. He always ate that one immediately, before it had a chance to escape.

At the time, I was a fifth grade teacher. Every Friday after school, I brought two students home with me. We would take the dogs to the park and walk them around the pathways, averaging about a mile and a half. After walking the dogs, we would go back to my house and order pizza. Throughout the year, I made sure that each of my students came home with me at least once. This was the best incentive I ever discovered to get the students to keep up with their assignments and engage in good behavior. If they were up to date and they had no behavior infractions they got to put their names in a basket for a random drawing to go to my house.

The students always thought it hilarious to watch Longfellow pull his nightly trick on Bascombe. I had several students over the years who found it hard to stand up for themselves and allowed themselves to be pushed around by some of the more assertive students. They were encouraged when they saw the "weaker" Longfellow outsmart the "bully" Bascombe. A few of the students learned to stand up for themselves by outsmarting the classroom bullies who made their lives uncomfortable. I got just as much enjoyment out of seeing them gain confidence as I did watching Longfellow get the better of Bascombe.

For as long as I had both Bassets, Longfellow played the same trick on Bascombe, and Bascombe never figured out what happened to his missing dessert. Bascombe was the alpha male when it came to brawn, but Longfellow definitely came out on top when it came to brains.

~Bonnie Sargent

55

What a Card!

The dog is the god of frolic.
~Henry Ward Beecher

Shalimar was the Afghan Hound my dad brought home from the shelter when he really shouldn't have. I guess Daddy was mesmerized by Shalimar's big brown eyes, silky champagne-colored coat, her whip-like tail that curled into a circle above her lower back, and her long legs, because he surely wasn't thinking about our small back yard in Lemon Grove, California.

Maybe he just didn't know about the athletic abilities of the Afghan. Bred to hunt, an Afghan Hound runs in excess of thirty-five miles per hour. It can leap seven feet straight into the air and broad-jump twenty feet from a standstill.

My family loved Shalimar. She was affectionate and entertaining. She gladly returned our love. But there was no containing her within the confines of our fence, even after Daddy added a foot to its height. So, she provided us with a summer of aerobic exercise.

"Your dog is running through the cornfield." It was the neighbor's voice on the phone. They had a small farm directly behind our property where they raised and sold corn and tomatoes.

My older sister, Amy, grabbed a leash, and she and I took off after Shalimar. I was eleven; Amy was sixteen. We had chased Shalimar many times before. She was cagey. She usually ran down streets. Amy would drive the car, and we would chase her until she decided to hop in and ride home like royalty in the front seat. But this time, we would be on foot chasing her through the farm behind our house.

We heard the rustling of the corn as she ran through the rows. We headed toward the sound and caught a glimpse of her rump as she rounded the end of a row and headed in another direction. We followed, running between rows of tall green corn, occasionally catching sight of Shalimar as she sped by, or blurred flashes of tawny fur as the sun caught its sheen and sent it reflecting back to us. Every few minutes, she would tease us with a playful bark, as if to let us know how much she was enjoying this game of chase. Shalimar may have been bred to run and hunt, but Amy and I were not. We were not enjoying this chase through the neighbor's cornfield as much as our speed demon hound dog.

Finally, we caught sight of Shalimar, seemingly waiting for us as she often did when she, and only she, decided the chase was over. We walked up to her and, of course, she sprinted away, running between the last row of corn and a hedge that separated the farm from a new subdivision built on adjacent property. Sweating, gasping, and panting, the three of us ran — a dog with sisters in pursuit. We saw Shalimar duck into the hedge and disappear into whatever hid behind those dense, protective bushes. Amy and I bent down low to the ground and crawled through on our hands and knees.

On the other side of the hedge, we sisters rose to our feet just in time to see the long-legged Shalimar leap across a card table between four stunned senior women sitting wide-eyed with their mouths agape. Stunned. Speechless. They dropped the playing cards they held in their hands, scattering them on the patio floor.

Amy, who was always in control of things, didn't ask permission or wait to be told. She just followed Shalimar through the open sliding-glass patio door of this stranger's home, where Shalimar had foolishly and unknowingly trapped herself. Amy snapped the leash on Shalimar's collar, and we led her home, back through the cornfield, but following a less circuitous route than the way we came.

We never saw any of the card players again. I don't know how long it took them to recover from their shock or if they ever forgave us and our Afghan Hound for ruining their game. As for Amy and me, it has been well over fifty years, and we're still laughing.

~Mason K. Brown

56

I Loved Lucy

We long for an affection altogether ignorant of our
faults. Heaven has accorded this to us in
the uncritical canine attachment.
~George Eliot

One of the great loves of my life was a dog, a sweet, Bearded Collie I named Lucy. She adored me as much as I did her. From the start we were inseparable, bonded at the heart.

I got her from a woman who used to breed Bearded Collies until she discovered that some of her dogs were ending up in shelters. She gave up breeding and started rescuing. I met her when I was working at a local newspaper and interviewed her for an article about people who rescue dogs, who take them into their homes and find suitable pet parents.

I had never seen, much less "met" a Beardie before that day. I was hooked in minutes and wanted to adopt one of the dogs in her home, but they were all spoken for. When I left the interview I asked the woman to call me the next time she was looking for a home for one.

A few weeks later she called and said that she had a new rescue and that I had to get to her house that day or she would call someone else. I was there in thirty minutes. I walked into her house and she pointed to her new rescue that looked nothing like the elegant dogs I'd seen at her house before. This one was scrawny, her fur dull and lifeless. She was a sorry sight.

"Why does she look so different?" I asked diplomatically.

"A bit scruffy, isn't she?" the woman smiled. "She was on the streets for a while, lost a lot of weight and her hair is badly matted. They cleaned her up at the shelter as much as they could. She will look as pretty as the other Bearded Collies you saw at my house if you give her a good bath and a brushing, that is if you want her."

I bent down and looked into the dog's milk-chocolate-brown eyes and stroked her black and gray and white fur. She stared back with a slight look of trepidation, as though she was wondering if I was "the one" who would give her a real home and a stable life. I've always had a soft spot for others in need; it was clear that this dog needed a good home and someone that would love her. In that moment I knew that I would be the best dog mom she could want and certainly one that she deserved.

I signed the paperwork and off we went. She sat on the passenger seat as though she knew she belonged there. I rolled the window down just enough to give her room to put her head outside. Within minutes she poked her head out the window, relishing the wind in her face. By the time we got home she was relaxed. I got my first lick before we exited the car.

Within days, it seemed as though Lucy had always been a part of the household. She fit right in and our Shepherd/Malamute was happy to have a friend. I began training her to stay in the fenced back yard whenever I had to go out. All was going well until I came home from a short errand to discover the back yard empty, except for my other dog. I looked everywhere, but she was gone and I panicked. I ran and got a leash and began jogging up and down every street in my neighborhood. *Had she been dognapped? Had a neighborhood kid let her out?* She didn't know my area yet; I feared the worst… that she would get hit by a car, or simply vanish.

I turned down a major street and saw her trotting toward me, her long, silky fur bouncing to the rhythm of her gait.

"Lucy!" I screamed. She broke into a gallop, clearly happy to see me. I should have yelled at her but all I could do was hug her and wipe at the tears spilling down my face. I put the leash on her and held it tight. She pranced on home, unaware that she'd given me a heart-stopping scare. I never did figure out where she went or how she got out. Perhaps she was checking out her new neighborhood. Fortunately she never escaped again.

One of her favorite treats was ice cream, though not any ice cream. A couple of blocks from my home was an old-fashioned ice cream shop. The owner made the richest, highest milk-fat ice cream I'd ever eaten. In addition to serving ice cream in cones and cups he sold mini cones for little kids and dogs. After taking both dogs there one hot summer night it became a weekly stop on our evening walks. The doggie cones were tiny and contained only a couple of tablespoons of ice cream, just enough for one big dog bite. Lucy didn't care what flavor I gave her.

Of course she always finished hers before I finished mine and would sit in front of me boring those sweet brown eyes into mine and whimper at the cruelty of it all — why I was still eating ice cream and she wasn't. I told her that if she didn't wolf hers down so quickly she would have some left. She never bought my argument, whining until I finished or until I surrendered and gave her the last of mine.

I think Lucy sensed that there wasn't anything I wouldn't do for her. One day while I was walking her and we were a half-mile from home she stopped and lay down on the sidewalk. I thought something was wrong because she'd never done that before. She stared up at me with the most despondent expression. I bent down to see what was wrong and lightning quick she wrapped her arms around my neck and her back legs slid around my waist, bear-hug style. I tried to peel her off me but it was like trying to peel bark off a tree.

Ultimately I had to carry her home like that. It was a long walk carrying her forty-five-pound body, her chin resting on my shoulder. As soon as we stepped into the house she jumped down on her own, the happiest look on her face. She pranced around doing what I could only call a dog's version of an Irish jig. I realized in that moment that she had tricked me, yes, *tricked me!* There was nothing wrong with her and I guess she knew that I would cave.

Every walk after that she attempted the same con. Sometimes I gave in, because she did have a medical condition and I was never sure if she was faking or not. I'll tell you one thing; I never again took her on long walks just in case I had to carry her home. I'd learned my lesson.

~Jeffree Wyn Itrich

57

Old Shep Becomes a Mom

My goal in life is to be as good a person
as my dog already thinks I am.
~Author Unknown

I came out of the house one spring morning, walked around the corner, and something caught my eye. It was Old Shep, the German Shepherd my wife had rescued from rush-hour traffic some years ago.

And why would he especially catch my eye? Because the sorry rascal was sneakin', that's why.

You know what a sneakin' dog looks like. Shoulders drawn up. Ears flat, tail tucked, belly low to the ground. Zero eye contact. This dog was up to something.

Why?

He had as much right to be there as any of us. Why should he need to sneak? And why did his face not turn to me as I came around the corner? Why no wag, not even a little one? What was up with all this?

"Shep."

He froze. Lay down flat on his belly. Never turned his head.

"Shep. What are you up to? Shep?"

He grinned that guilty grin that some dogs do. The catch to this one was a flash of bright yellow in the grin. What was that about?

I walked up to him. He was trying to disappear into the dirt, but it didn't work. He couldn't look at me. His belly was plastered to the ground, and his tail was just going crazy.

"Shep, look up here. What have you got in your mouth? What's going on here?"

A muffled sound. His eyes got big. You could almost see a cartoon balloon over his head with "OMG" in it.

I got down on my knees, put out my hand, palm-up, and said, "Shep, give it to me. No. Don't try to get out of it. Give it here."

He slowly opened his mouth enough for the baby duck to hop out and into my hand.

"What are you doing?" I contemplated taking the duck back to the pen from whence it came, but then decided otherwise. "Shep, come with me." I started in the direction he had been going, toward the horse pen. He followed closely, his posture a model of contrition, begging forgiveness. But his eyes were locked onto the duck with a look that said, "Please, Daddy. Please. Please let me have the baby."

We continued to the stalls, one in use and the other empty. Shep straightened up and went quickly past me, around the corner and into the empty stall.

I followed and then, as I turned to enter the stall, I saw it. My massive, big-boned, muscular German Shepherd, on his side in the soft sand in the corner, curled protectively around his little family of six baby ducks. They were all nestled into the curve of his belly, and his big eyes were looking at me, saying, "Please, Daddy? They're my babies. Please?"

I set his seventh child down among the others, wiped the dog slobber off my hand, placed my palm on Shep's head, and gently petted. "Good boy. Good Shep. What a good duck daddy." He wagged as much as he could, being pressed into the corner as he was.

I straightened up and went away quietly, leaving my happy duck-dog family in as cute a pile as I've ever seen.

Long story short, he wound up with nine. They followed him everywhere. He normally spent most of his day and all of the night pretty much with me, either at my heels or smushed together in bed, but that all stopped while he cared for his babies.

They grew, got bigger, and gradually began to leave and follow the big ducks back to the little pond in the woods behind the house.

Finally, there came a day when Old Shep was scratching at the front door, asking if he could come inside and hang together, just him and me.

He was an old dog. It wasn't long before we had to make a trip together to the vet to get that shot that hurt me so much, but gave him relief from his suffering.

But the hurting's not so bad when I recall that image — one yellow telltale feather sticking out between those powerful jaws, and those eyes saying, "Please, Daddy?"

~William C. Gibson

58

Third Home a Charm!

*You won't change the world by saving an animal. But
you will change that animal's world.*

~Author Unknown

y daughter Hilary and her husband Joey were ready for
a dog. They loved the idea of adopting a rescue. When
they heard about Leo, they drove straight over to see
him.

As a young dog, Leo had been tied up outside for long periods
of time in all kinds of weather. He was often without food and water.
Concerned neighbors finally reported his mistreatment, and Leo was
taken to a shelter.

"The second owner wasn't the right person for Leo, either," explained
the woman at the shelter. "I don't know why she adopted him. She was
an older lady, and Leo had way more energy than she could handle.

"To keep him off her furniture," the woman continued, "she put
mousetraps on everything. Needless to say, he doesn't like anyone
touching his paws."

Hilary and Joey were a young couple and had the energy to match
the now fifteen-month-old, big-pawed, broad-chested, handsome dog
before them. They adopted him and I got to meet him for the first time
when they visited us on Easter.

"If you wake up before us, Mom, you can take him out, but you
have to promise to hold the leash with two hands," warned Hilary.

I had entered my fifties by that time, but worked out regularly to maintain physical fitness and strength. "Honey, don't worry. I'm strong," I said, a bit disappointed that she thought I couldn't handle a dog.

"Mom, I'm not doubting that you're strong. It's just that Leo's *really* strong."

"Okay, I promise."

The next morning, as predicted, I woke first. I attached the leash to Leo's harness, excited to walk a dog again. "Okay, Leo, let's go."

Dutifully, I held the leash with two hands. It felt a bit awkward, but I understood now why Hilary insisted that I double my grip on the leash. Leo pulled much harder than Watson, the Springer Spaniel who was our family pet for fourteen years.

So far, so good, I thought, when we reached the first corner. Leo and I turned west and continued along a long cedar hedge. "Beep beep!" My dental hygienist drove past and waved. Automatically, I waved back, taking one of my hands off the leash.

In that instant, a gray squirrel darted from below the cedars. Leo lunged and ran after it, pulling me off my feet and dragging me, belly down, another ten feet. It's not clear whether Leo tired of the squirrel or the weight that dragged behind him, but I was relieved when my "ride" came to an end.

A few years into life at his new home, Leo showed himself to be a singer, as well. It all started the year that I gave my daughter a trumpet for Christmas. The instrument that she played in high school was corroded on the inside. She missed playing from time to time, but especially at the holidays.

"Mom, you've got to come over and see this," Hilary exclaimed on the phone one day. "When I start playing my trumpet, Leo walks to the doorway, turns his head away from me like he's shy, and starts singing. He doesn't bark, but howls kind of tunefully."

A bit of time passed before I had a chance to witness the musical side of my grand-dog. In that time, Leo had refined his taste. He didn't join in with every song, but couldn't resist "Moonlight Serenade" when Hilary played it.

"You can't look directly at him when he sings or say anything because he'll stop," advised my daughter. A few notes into the song, true to Hilary's word, Leo walked into the doorway between the kitchen and living room. He turned his back end to us and began to "sing."

It was hard not to laugh.

There was much laughter in the ten years that he lived with them, and many, many tears when he passed. I'm so glad that his third home was the charm.

~Deb Biechler

59

Chester's Bath

Many dogs will give a greeting grin
much like a human smile.
~Richard A. Clarke

C hester is one of the sweetest Golden Retrievers we've owned, but sometimes even good dogs misbehave — especially at bath time. Chester doesn't like baths. When I tell Chester it's time for a bath, he runs and hides behind a chair with his stuffed duck toy in his mouth. And when I do finally get Chester into the tub, he just looks at me with sad eyes until he's all soap-covered. Then he launches from the tub and bolts through the house trailing bubbles.

After that, it's chase, rinse, and repeat.

One day, I decided to have a mobile groomer come to the house. I thought maybe Chester would like baths better if he went to someone who actually knew how to groom dogs. Terry, the groomer, came to the front door with a bright smile and a cheerful voice. She had a blond ponytail and wore clean, blue scrubs — ready to go to work. Terry let Chester smell the back of her hand as she spoke. "I've groomed hundreds of dogs, big and small, in the van," she said easily as she summarized her background. "I bought the van three years ago, and it really works out well for everyone. Chester will do great."

I felt relieved as she spoke. Terry seemed like a professional, and Chester obviously liked her, too. He wagged his bushy tail as she talked and even gave her a toothy grin when she scratched him behind his ear. So with that, Terry took Chester gently by the collar, told him he was a good boy, and walked him out the door, down the driveway, and to her groomer's van parked in front of the house. "Come on, Chester," she said in a playful voice as she opened the van door. "Let's get you all clean!"

I smiled as the van door shut, feeling relieved. *Why didn't I think of this before? Sure, it's more expensive to have him groomed — but isn't it worth it?* I thought, patting myself on the back as I went inside the house. An hour went by, though, and there was still no Chester Bear. I peeked out the front window. With the exception of a muffled hum (like a generator), the van was still sitting quietly on the curb. After another thirty minutes, I grew a little worried and peered out the window again. The van door swung open at last. There, standing in the doorway, was a very tired-looking Terry. Her hair was disheveled, and her scrubs were covered with fur, but sitting next to her was Chester — all shiny, brushed, and clean — with a brand-new kerchief around his neck. He looked beautiful!

I threw open the front door just as Chester yanked himself from Terry's hand, leaped from the van, and bolted down the street across the neighbors' yards.

"Oh, my gosh! I've never had that happen before!" cried Terry from her van's doorway, her cheeks flushing red.

Terry clambered down from her van with a leash and started running after Chester. I didn't have the heart to tell Terry that she'd never catch him. I knew exactly where Chester was going, and for a moment, I couldn't help but feel sorry for Terry as she chased Chester down the street. I watched my shiny Golden Retriever, Terry, and a neighbor (who had just stopped his lawnmower to assist) all run around a corner and onto the greenbelt, out of sight.

With a sigh, I took a shortcut across my back yard to the greenbelt, a shaded walking path, which ran behind my house. Chester had too much of a head start. It would be too late.

I was right. Just as I opened our back gate and stepped onto the greenbelt, I saw Chester tearing down the path toward me with the groomer and neighbor running behind him. Before I could even call

Chester, he leaped from the greenbelt and flew into a creek, splashing after the ducks.

Terry looked appalled. I think I knew how she felt: All that work for nothing. I hiked down to the creek and managed to get Chester out of the water (after a few prayers for help). My "groomed" dog walked up the grassy bank with a muddy, dripping coat that smelled like fish. His soggy kerchief floated down the creek near a log. Chester shook himself, drenching the groomer and me in the process, and then gave us a happy grin.

Chester had finally found a bathtub that he liked.

~Marianne L. Davis

60

Sassy

Dogs are loyal friends, and if they could talk,
your secrets would still be safe.
~Richelle E. Goodrich, *Making Wishes*

She came from a litter of five. Her mother was a Husky and her father was a Golden Retriever who happened to visit only once at just the right time. The litter of pups and their mother were being fostered at a horse farm not too far from our house until the puppies were old enough to be adopted. We were looking for a new four-legged family member so we went to see the eight-week-old pups and she was the only one who wouldn't leave us alone. So, we decided to take her home with us. At least that's what we thought — that we could make decisions and be in control. In the thirteen years she owned us, that never happened.

We named her Sassy. And that's exactly what she was. Sassy! Come to think of it, I think she named herself since she took charge of everything else and had to have things her own way. She was very loving and wanted human contact… when she wanted it. My husband and our sons used to lie on the floor and she would lie on top of them… when she wanted to. If she didn't want to no amount of coaxing — or the promise of treats — could make her change her mind. Although she looked very much like her Golden Retriever father she took her personality traits from her Husky mother. And Huskies are known to be independent, energetic, adventuresome and, also, loving.

Sassy talked. Not with words exactly and not with barks. She made these continuous sounds with varying high and low tones that sounded as if she were having a lengthy conversation with you. So, what do you do when a dog talks to you? Obviously, you talk back. And tilt your head to one side while Sassy, sitting across from you, tilts her head to the other side. These conversations would go on for as long as Sassy had things to say. If you were done before she was, she would get annoyed and talk even louder until you came back, sat down, tilted your head, and continued talking.

Sassy didn't like us to leave the house unless she was going, too. We never left her alone in the back yard when we went out; we would leave her in the house. She had free run of the entire house so we weren't confining her to one room or a crate. But that still didn't sit well with her. When it was time for us to go someplace, I would go outside to call her in and she would turn her back on me and walk to the furthest part of the yard. There, she would burrow into the hedges that grow on the property line and lie down. No amount of calling, yelling, cajoling, or promising of treats made a difference. She didn't move. She had that "You talkin' to me?" look on her face. I would have to get a broom and go and find her.

The hedges were thick and I had to figure out where she was hiding. And each time she would hide in a different place. I would take a broom with me so that, when I would find her deep within the bushes, I could poke at her with the bristles of the broom to get her to get up and come into the house. I wouldn't have been able to reach her without using the broom. Getting her out of the hedges and into the house was not easy nor was it silent. The yowls and snarls and growls were ear-splitting. At first some of the neighbors were concerned that a massacre was happening in our yard but they soon learned it was only Sassy being vocal and protesting. I started sneaking out with the broom before I called her, hoping I could herd her into the house before she went into hiding. Sometimes it worked and sometimes it didn't. That dog had an attitude!

The worst thing she ever did happened when she was about five years old. We had gone out for lunch and to do some food shopping. We were only gone a few hours and when we came home we unloaded the car, carrying the bags of groceries into the kitchen from the car parked in the back yard. That's when we noticed that one of the leather armchairs was not where we had left it. There is a fireplace in our kitchen, with a small couch and two chairs in front of it. *Why was one of the chairs across the room and facing in a different direction than it had been when we left? And where was Sassy?* She usually greeted us at the door when we came home and wanted her treats as a reward for being left home while we were out. She was not around.

We called. We whistled. We clapped. No Sassy. We even rattled her treat jar… no Sassy. So we started searching the house. We found her lying in a corner in the living room with her back to the door. She did not make eye contact with us when we went over to her, which meant she was displeased. She didn't even talk to us, but we were finally able to coax her back into the kitchen for a treat. That's when my husband went to move the chair back into its usual position. What he discovered startled us. From the front the chair looked fine. But when Frank moved it to put it back next to the fireplace he found that one whole side of it was missing. Gone! Shredded! There were bits of leather and stuffing on the floor. It was Sassy versus the chair and Sassy was victorious. In her disgust with us for being left alone, she shredded one side of the chair and moved it to the other side of the room. That would show us!

"Sassy?" we said in that low did-you-do-this tone of voice. Sassy looked at us like we were crazy.

"Sassy?" we repeated. You could tell she was neither intimidated nor scared by the tone of voice she heard. She just looked at us with that "who me" look on her face. And then she got up and left the room.

Luckily the chairs were old and shabby and needed to be replaced. I was actually kind of glad this happened. I had wanted to replace those chairs for a while. Now, there was no question… we had to! And that was the only time in her life that Sassy was destructive, except for the time she took a large frozen standing rib roast off the kitchen counter and tried to eat it. But that's another story!

From the day we got her at eight weeks old until the day she died at thirteen, she was always the alpha "person" in our family. But we didn't mind. She more than made up for her bossiness with her love, devotion and caring and the silliness and laughter she brought to our lives. She was a treasured family member. And, in the end, she was still the alpha-in-charge. She let us know, in no uncertain terms, that she was suffering and it was time to do the humane thing and let her go. And, as we did throughout her life, we listened to her, obeyed her, and said our tearful goodbyes.

~Barbara LoMonaco

61

The Dog Thief

The truth brings with it a great measure
of absolution, always.
~R.D. Laing

Please don't judge me. I didn't lie. I didn't steal, except for dogs.

It was many years ago. I was about seven then and I'm a grown woman now. I LOVED dogs! But when I asked my mom for one she said, "No." I begged. I pleaded. I whined. She said, "No, no, no!"

"A dog is too much trouble," she argued. "Who will take care of it?"

"I will," I answered. But we both knew I wasn't responsible enough to have a dog.

It seemed like everyone in the neighborhood had a dog but us. Yet in our little town of Michalovce, Czechoslovakia, people didn't take care of them as they do in America today. Dogs were not kept on a leash and they didn't sleep in your bed, if they were even allowed in the house. People didn't talk to their dogs except to say, "Stop. Stay. Sit. Get out."

They didn't whisk the pooch off to the vet when he sneezed. Most dogs were not special breeds. Dogs were mainly one breed. Mutt.

Likewise, kitties never saw a vet, if they even had vets. I believe cats were kept for mice control. I don't remember anyone loving a cat.

After seeing the American movie, *Lassie, Come Home*, I made up my mind. I was getting a dog, one way or another. Actually, I wanted ten dogs.

We lived in a small house with a very long yard. At the back of the yard was a huge laundry room. I hoped the lengthy distance between the house and the laundry room was enough to cover up any barking sounds, because I had a plan.

One Friday after school I began rounding up dogs. I had no problem capturing them since most of them were kept in the street anyway. All it took was a little coaxing. I lured them into our yard with pieces of sausage in my little hand. Then into the laundry room we went and I shut the door.

After I had packed seven dogs into one room, I decided ten dogs were probably too many. Seven were enough.

I changed the names of the dogs, hoping they would forget their former lives and just happily remember being mine. Please don't think this was a sign that I'd grow up to be some kind of a monster kidnapper. I just did it for love.

I threw balls in the laundry room. The dogs chased them and brought them back and I threw some more. I bathed them in the big tub. I dried them off in the towels Mom had hanging on the line in the yard. I brushed them with my brother's hairbrush. He never missed it and the dogs had never had such treatment before. I sneaked spare blankets out of the house so my new buddies wouldn't have to sleep on the cold cement floor. I snuggled against their furry forms and tickled them behind their silky ears. I rubbed my nose against their cold wet ones. I hugged and kissed them. They played together and they played with me.

Scraps, leftovers, bread, potatoes, and bacon—you name it—disappeared out of Mom's pantry and the dogs gratefully devoured everything. There was no dog food; just people food. My new playmates were treated like family, because that's what they were. My family!

The only thing they didn't have was freedom. But they had love and they were safe from the dangers of the street, I reasoned.

It was pure joy! Up till then these were the best two-and-a-half days of my life!

But by Sunday evening there weren't enough leftovers to keep the residents happy. For their dinner, I had to resort to apples and pears from the garden. The Canine Club became cranky. Also, although I did my best to clean up the place, by Sunday night the laundry room began to develop a certain aroma. Okay, an odor.

By Monday night the natives grew more restless and the yapping more intense. I was at my wits' end. I began to think Mom was right. A seven-year-old was not mature enough to own a dog—much less seven of them.

That night at midnight we were awakened by our next-door neighbor's knock on our door.

"Have you seen my Mysko?" she inquired anxiously. "I hear him barking in your yard."

Mom took the worried neighbor outside and they listened through the breeze in the trees and something was heard.

"Shush. Listen!" the neighbor whispered. "It's Mysko."

I had followed them out. Mom looked at me and asked, "Do you hear that, Evka?"

"I don't hear anything." I lied. I think it was my first lie ever.

We followed the sounds to the back of the yard. Closer to the laundry room it became clear that it was not the whistling of the wind they had heard but barking. Mom tried to open the laundry room door but it was locked.

"Go get the key, Evka," she ordered. "Run."

The jig was up. I ran to the house. I ran with fear and I ran wondering how I could get away with what I had done. When I returned, Mom grabbed the key and unlocked the room. The noise that arose was like a bunch of wolves at a pig roast. Dogs of all colors and sizes squeezed through the door and rushed past us like a pack of wild animals. Mysko jumped up on our neighbor and nearly licked her to death. The rest of them escaped in all directions. I was hurt. Despite my feeding, devotion, and care, no one bothered to lick me goodbye.

Mom knew there was something I wasn't telling. Mothers know. "How did this happen? You did this!" she accused.

I lied again. "I have no idea how the dogs got here," I nervously replied.

But it didn't fly and I finally admitted, through my tears, that I was guilty but it was because I loved dogs and was only trying to make them happy.

My confession was not well received and I did get punished, but one good thing came out of my two lies and one little theft — okay, a GRAND theft.

Although Mysko went home with the neighbor, and five other dogs fled to their respective homes, one little pup clung to my legs of his own free will. He refused to leave. No one in the neighborhood claimed him or reported him missing, even though Mom inquired at school and at church. When I went to school he walked with me and when school was out, he was there waiting for me. At night he stayed in the yard and if it was cold, Mom let him sleep in the laundry room. I had lucked out! Although he had been the scruffiest, he was the most lovable of them all.

I promised Mom I would never lie or steal again. I kind of kept that promise throughout my life.

I had my dog and I named him Moj. Mine. All mine.

~Eva Carter

62

Hidden in Plain Sight

I was feeling insecure you might not love me anymore.
~John Lennon

We are a dog family. Ever since my children were toddlers we have had a dog, or more commonly, multiple dogs in the house.

For the longest time we had a standing rule: no dogs on the furniture. And for a long time we upheld that mandate.

Until Max.

Max was a 135-pound Mastiff. Brindle in color, he appeared menacing to those who did not know him. When we walked him, people would cross the street. When we took him to the local pet store, people would conveniently move to a different aisle.

He was about five years old when we adopted him from our local shelter. We were told that he had been surrendered by a man whose wife had become pregnant. The woman insisted that it was not a good idea to have a dog in the house with a baby. I never understood that but felt their loss was our gain. Max was something special. He was loyal and loving.

One day I walked into the living room and there lay Max on the couch. He had made himself at home, comfortably stretched out covering most of the seating area.

"Max!" I screamed. "Get off!"

He looked up at me with a puzzled expression. After a few seconds of eye-to-eye contact, he put his head down and covered his eyes with his paws.

"Max," I repeated a bit more sternly. "GET OFF!"

He just lay there with his eyes covered until I removed his paws from his face and pointed to the floor. Slowly he extended his front paws to the ground and slithered off the couch. This time a bit more hurt than puzzled. *I just don't get it*, he seemed to say with his deep brown eyes.

The next day my husband Jack was upstairs in the studio working with Max by his side. He went to move a monitor and dropped it on the floor. Along with the monitor Jack dropped a few loud, expressive words.

Max ran from the studio to the dining room and lay on the rug. When I approached him he immediately covered his eyes with his paws. I truly believe he thought he was in trouble.

"Max, it's all right, you are safe," I said to him softly.

He took his paws from his eyes, nuzzled my hand and then followed me into the kitchen for a treat.

Not an hour later, I returned to the living room and there he was again. This time he was curled up on the couch, deep in the corner.

"Max, get down!" I yelled.

This time he didn't flinch. He just looked back at me and covered his eyes again with those massive paws. I stood over him and he just lay there refusing to budge. As if saying to me, *I can't see you so you can't see me. I am invisible.*

Inside I was laughing. Did he really think I couldn't see him?

"Max, you are not allowed on the furniture. Get off."

After tugging on his collar, I was able to guide him onto the floor and over to his bed. He again looked hurt but lay down on his appointed bed.

After dinner, my husband sat in his recliner and I on the end of the couch. Gracie Lou, our senior dog, went to her bed and Max sat upright next to his bed assessing the situation. I turned on the TV, and within minutes there was Max up on the other end of the couch. He was extremely stealthy for such a massive dog. This time all I had to do was look in his direction and he took those gorgeous paws and covered his eyes.

Jack was laughing so hard. "I think he really believes we can't see him!"

"Off, Max!" And onto his bed he went.

One day our Internet went out so I placed a service call. About three hours later, the doorbell rang and a friendly middle-aged service man appeared at the door. When I let him in, I casually mentioned that we had a dog but that he was friendly. "Not to worry," he replied. "I love dogs."

He went to the cable box. He pushed and pulled and then went outside to check a connection. When he came back in, Max was there to greet him. The man's facial expression changed. He appeared shocked and frightened. I grabbed Max and told the man not to be afraid.

He said that he wasn't frightened and asked me where I got him. I told him that we had gotten him from the local pound. His expression immediately turned to sadness. He went toward Max, and softly called his name, "Max?"

Max looked at him, took in his scent, and then ran to the couch and covered his eyes.

It turned out that the service man was indeed his previous pet parent. When his child was close to being born his wife insisted that Max be surrendered. The man seemed genuinely upset. He left the house saying that he always felt bad about taking Max to the pound, but was happy to see that he had found such a loving home.

When Jack came home from work, Max ran right up to him and nuzzled against his leg. His tail was wagging so hard I thought it would fall off. I told Jack about the man and how Max reacted.

That night, Jack and I sat together on the couch. We called Max over. He looked at us adoringly and we fell for it.

"Okay. Come on up."

Max lay between Jack and me with his head on Jack's lap. This time his eyes were wide open and in plain sight.

~Jeanne Blandford

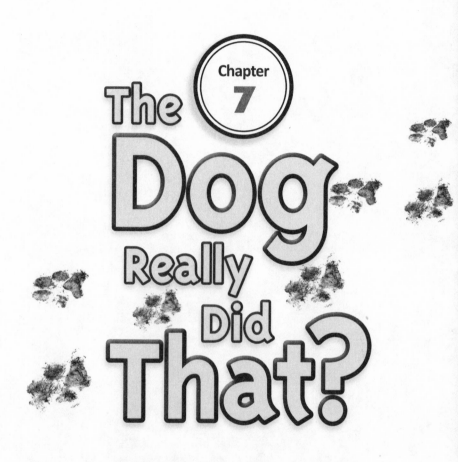

Chapter 7

The Dog Really Did That?

My Best Friend

63

Keeping Friends Together

The best kind of friend is the one you could sit on a
porch with, never saying a word, and walk
away feeling like that was the best
conversation you've ever had.
~Author Unknown

The rain started on a sleepy summer morning in June. Fat, heavy raindrops began to fall as the faint echoes of thunder rumbled and rolled across the lush hills and yawning riverbeds of West Virginia; thick sheets of hard, pelting rain erupted across the picturesque landscape, pummeling the scenic terrain as fierce winds whipped across the dark, stormy sky. Ancient trees toppled and howling gales beheaded flowers, ripping cheerful buds from long, green stems that buckled, drowning under the weight of the downpour.

The relentless rainfall rushed through rugged mountain ranges, racing down hillsides into narrow, gaping valleys, where the water started to rise. Within hours, residents in small, charming towns across West Virginia were wading through more than a foot of water. In the course of mere days, the historic floods ravaged the state, wiping out entire communities — bridges, roads, trees, cars, schools, beloved homes — and taking the lives of the innocent victims caught in the cruel, unyielding path of the water.

Frightened families fled, with many losing contact with loved ones. Those loved ones included countless innocent animals and precious pets — vulnerable, voiceless victims unable to heed the urgent weather warnings airing on every local-news channel. Among these defenseless animals was Jake, a special Golden Retriever with soulful eyes that gaze up lovingly from beneath his thick, expressive eyebrows. The floods destroyed the home the sweet dog shared with his doting family.

Only ten days after the floodwaters first started to rise, Jake fell victim to another heartbreaking disaster. The muddy rainwater had receded when Jake's owner, Robby, found him outside suffering in distress. Jake whimpered, shivering in pain, his thick golden fur slick with blood. Robby gingerly picked Jake up, holding him gently as deep-red stains continued to spread across his soft, golden coat.

Robby raced Jake to American Humane Rescue's mobile veterinary clinic, where veterinarian Dr. Lesa Staubus rushed to perform urgent, emergency surgery. Robby and his family had already lost everything in the flood; now, they feared losing Jake — their adoring, faithful companion — too. Someone had shot him.

But the canine patient, in critical condition, was in capable hands: Dr. Staubus is one of those gentle souls who emanate benevolence and warmth, with a soft Louisiana drawl that nestles in the ear and soothes the heart. Calling on almost three decades of professional veterinary experience, she performed the urgent medical procedures with grace and extraordinary ease. Jake was going to be okay.

Dr. Staubus stepped out of the humble surgical room and delivered the news to Robby, who paced as he waited right outside the door. When Robby learned that Jake, his loving companion, survived the surgery, his strained shoulders immediately collapsed, limp with relief. But suddenly, Robby's brow furrowed, a worried expression creeping back to his worn face.

"Can you tell me how much this is going to cost?" he asked. After all, this man had just lost his home and all his possessions in the flooding.

"The bill is taken care of," Dr. Staubus replied. "This will cost you nothing."

Robby stepped forward, enveloping Dr. Staubus in a long, tight embrace. "Some things require more than a handshake," he told her, wiping tears from his eyes.

Not long thereafter, Jake's anesthesia began to wear off, and the groggy — but healed — Golden Retriever started to stir. Jake strained to lift his head off the table, his nose twitching as he searched desperately for a familiar comfortable scent. Finally, he managed to open his eyes. Jake looked up at Dr. Staubus, the veterinarian who saved his life, and then his deep, hopeful eyes landed on Robby, the person he loved with all of his heart.

Robby reached down and gave his best friend a gentle scratch behind the ears; Jake's tail, still weak, thumped softly against the operating table, growing louder and louder, gaining strength with every loving nuzzle and caress. They lost their house in the flood, but to Jake, Robby and his family would always be home.

A few minutes later, still overwhelmed with emotion and joy, the two survivors walked slowly, side-by-side, out the door; Jake was bandaged and weak, but his tail was wagging. And if Robby had a tail, I know it would have been wagging, too! It was time for these two friends to go home.

~Dr. Robin Ganzert

64

Little Nike

*A really companionable and indispensable
dog is an accident of nature. You can't get it
by breeding for it, and you can't buy it
with money. It just happens along.*
~E.B. White, The Care and Training of a Dog

Nightfall had come to the Arctic and with it a temperature of minus 50 degrees. While mushing a team of dogs on a frozen river under a full moon, the ice fell out from under us without a single warning crack. I watched in horror as the dark water swallowed us like the mouth of a great whale. The dogs splashed about, clawing at the ice and swimming for their lives. My sled was sinking, and I climbed on top of its wooden frame to buy extra time.

My first winter in Alaska's Brooks Range — and my lifelong dream to become a mountain man — had gone without life-threatening predicaments up until that night. As I braced myself for the icy waters, little did I know a small sled dog would teach me that attitude is everything in the game of wilderness survival — and in life.

Whether little Nike had been named after the athletic shoe or the Greek goddess of victory, I would never know. He came into my life due to his shortcomings in a team of dogs that I had trained to run in Alaska's Iditarod Trail Sled Dog Race. Nike was a wheel dog, the last in line, running behind the other dogs just ahead of the sled. In the guise that a dog team runs only as fast as its slowest dog, Nike was holding the mass of panting Huskies at a trot about a mile an hour slower than the pace needed to win the 1,100-mile race from Anchorage to Nome.

"He's too slow."

That was the assessment of my friend, Dick, who was driving the sled a month before he entered the race. As the miles ticked by, Dick noted that Nike favored his right hind leg, and that the slight limp was caused by ice forming in the fine hair between his toes. Dick stood on the brake and brought the team to stop. Nike's hind foot shot instinctively to his mouth, and he nibbled out a bloody ice ball the size of a pea.

"Bum feet."

That was two strikes against poor Nike. I knew then that he'd never make the team. A slow dog whose feet bled in a training run had slim chances of making it halfway through the arduous race.

With his feet licked clean, Nike looked back at us with dark brown eyes that registered an eagerness to please. At around fifty pounds, he was small compared to other male sled dogs. Whenever we stopped, he'd engage us with bright eyes and wag his tail from between the gaps of his bright blue nylon harness.

Not making the cut and joining the team meant Nike would have a hard time finding a good home, if he could find a home at all. Sled dogs aren't typically sold or given away as pets. I loved that dog and begged to take him in an effort to build a team of my own.

That next autumn, Nike fell into the rhythm of pulling the sled over ninety miles of trap line. My wife Cheryl and I had acquired other dogs and headed into the mountains with provisions to live for five months. In January, we had begun pushing east toward an untraveled tributary of the Yukon River. The trapping prospects there looked promising. We returned to our main cabin and made plans for me to use Cheryl's dogs, hooking them together to form a large team. The idea was to haul supplies several miles down the river and establish a permanent camp.

That meant I'd be traveling alone and driving a sled loaded with around 300 pounds of freight, which meant extra hard work for my wheelers, Nike and Doc. The first serious challenge in our trip came where the trail descended a steep gorge that led to the river. As we started down, I stood on the brake with all of my weight in an attempt to jab its sharp cutters into the icy trail. But the heavy sled began overtaking the dogs, and they picked up their pace to stay ahead of it. Soon, we had gone from trotting to loping, leaving Nike to run for his life. His forelegs shot out ahead of him, and he flew through the air between strides like Superman. We came to a hairpin turn at the bottom of the hill. With eyes wide, I leaned to the left in hopes of counterbalancing the sled.

So much for that effort. We wound up in a massive heap. With my adrenaline pumping, I emerged from a large snowdrift and assessed the damage. I expected to find crippled dogs and a broken sled. But the sled was fine, and the dogs had jumped over each other and untangled themselves. Nike emerged from the snow, shook himself off, looked at me with those encouraging eyes and made me smile.

Now I was bracing myself for an icy death in a river. As the sled wallowed beneath me, I jumped toward the edge of the ice, but fell short and prepared myself for a swim. To my astonishment, the water was only up to my thighs, and there was very little current. The dogs bobbed frantically. I worked my way to the front of the team, grabbed my lead dogs, and threw them onto solid ice. They began pulling toward shore while I threw pairs of team dogs out until they were all out of the water. With my dogs back on solid ice, they pulled enough to extract the sled from the open water.

I fought back my fear that we would fall through again. When we finally came to the safety of the riverbank, I fell into a deep apathy. The cold was rapidly creeping deep into my muscles, and I realized that my chances of survival were no better than back when we were in the water.

I had begun to accept that this was how I was going to die, but Nike wouldn't have it. He charged into his harness and wagged his tail, and it clattered with frozen shards of ice. I looked into his eyes and could swear he was smiling. I gathered my wits and dry firewood — and started a huge blaze. As I recounted my experience in the warmth of my sleeping bag, I wondered if I'd have survived if not for Nike and his attitude. Cheryl and I put in several more winters of wilderness adventure before moving to town and starting a small family. And always, Nike was there, a model of strength and happiness.

Good dogs come, and good dogs go. Careers, college, kids, grandkids and life have taken up nearly four decades since my years with Nike, but I'll never forget those ethereal days and nights, driving dogs through Alaska's remote mountains—when problems seemed simpler. Sometimes, when life's hurdles seem insurmountable, I think back to Nike. I lean into my harness, adjust my attitude and charge down the trail ahead.

~Charlie Ess

65

A Fluffy, White Angel with Paws

Angels have no philosophy but love.
~Terri Guillemets

Two days after our first Thanksgiving as a married couple, my husband, Michael, and I welcomed a Great Pyrenees named Huck into our home. At just eight weeks old, he was charged with the prodigious job of helping unite two families into one. Yes, it was a big job, but there is nothing like puppy love. Long before we'd eaten all the turkey and stuffing leftovers, he'd won us over with his wobbly run and the steadfast devotion that shone through his dark eyes. We may have not shared the same blood, but we now shared a puppy, and that made us a family.

Now, here we were, just five years later, and Huck was gone.

"I'll never get another dog," I cried into my husband's shoulder as we sat on the couch.

It felt like heartbreak was stalking our family. Four months earlier, we'd lost our son, Ryan, my stepson, in a tragic accident. This new devastation further splintered our already broken hearts.

Michael and I opted to have Thanksgiving alone. Although it would be just us, I prepared the usual feast: turkey, dressing, broccoli casserole, the works. The tantalizing smells of Thanksgiving filled our huge old farmhouse, but instead of the usual joy-filled clatter, it echoed with silence. Grief stole our appetites for food and conversation. We spent the day staring at each other over a much-too-large turkey.

When the page on the calendar turned, instead of enjoying the hustle and bustle of the Christmas season, I wished we could skip December. I just wanted the holidays to be over.

Then my mom called. "Hey, Randy and I would like to come see you guys for Christmas."

I knew they didn't want us to spend Christmas alone, staring at an empty chair where Ryan should be. But we hadn't even bothered with holiday decorating. We didn't even have a tree.

"Oh, Mom, we'd love to see you, but holiday flights from Nebraska to Ohio are so expensive."

"That's right, they are, so we've decided to drive. It will be an adventure."

The next day, my phone pinged with an incoming text. I picked it up and saw it was from our college-aged daughter, Alexa. "Hey, found a cheap flight. I'll be there as soon as finals are over." Our younger daughter, Maddie, would be here, too. The only one who couldn't make it was our son, Ross.

Ready or not, we were going to have a full house to celebrate Christmas. We sprang into action. We found a small, living evergreen, perfect for replanting in honor of Ryan and Huck when the holiday was over. Then we faced the crowds to fill the space underneath it and to stock our barren refrigerator. Everything came together nicely, but it still didn't have that home-for-the-holidays feeling. Something was missing.

As Christmas and the arrival of our guests marched closer, I found myself sneaking in online searches for female Great Pyrenees puppies. I wasn't sure if I could take the next step, but it didn't matter; there were none to be found within 200 miles of us.

I looked at other breeds; there are so many choices out there to love. But I kept coming back to those little, white bundles of fluff with dark eyes, and pink and black feet. Finally, it hit me. I was no longer just thinking we "might" get a puppy; I wanted a puppy for our family — for Christmas.

On December fourteenth, I found a litter of Great Pyrenees puppies in our home state of Ohio. Immediately, I e-mailed the breeder. Of eight, three were left, and only one was female. I asked for a picture. Twenty minutes later, she texted me the picture, telling me that the one on the far right was the one that was available. She was all white, exactly what I had been imagining.

I was shocked when she texted her address. They were less than twenty-five miles from our house.

I called Michael. "Hey, honey, I was wondering if we might go look at something for Christmas after you get off work." I was worried about telling him we were going to look at puppies because we hadn't even discussed getting another dog. My fears were put to rest once we arrived at the farm, and he held the pink-bellied bundle. She curled right into the curve of his neck. He was ready to take her home that night, but we had to wait until she was old enough to leave her mama.

Less than two weeks later, real joy found its way into my heart for the first time that holiday season as our guests arrived and oohed and aahed over our new family member — Scarlett O'Hara — who was fast asleep in her red-and-white, polka-dotted bed under the Christmas tree.

About six months later, I looked up at a drawing done by Ryan that hangs on the wall above my desk. I started really missing him, and soon the tears were flowing. Through my sobs, I heard a low, nasal whine coming from Scarlett, who was lying on the floor next to me. I reached down to pat her, but she got up, walked over to me and laid her chin on my knee. As I rubbed her head, she just sat there looking up at me with eyes that seemed to say, "I understand everything you are going through. Here, pet me. Let me help you heal."

A couple of weeks before Scarlett's first birthday, we were walking her at our favorite park. Michael had brought along his camera and was snapping pictures of the garnet and brown leaves on the trees circling the pond. "Hey," I said, "get one of Scarlett. I'll put it on Facebook so everyone can see how much she's grown." Then I gave Scarlett the hand signal to sit.

Later that night, after I had posted the picture, my cousin, Charlotte, commented, "She's beautiful, and wow, look at her halo." I read the comment, and then looked at the picture again. I hadn't even noticed the white gauzy circle that appeared to be floating a few inches above Scarlett's head in the photo.

It really did look like a halo. Fitting, I thought, since I always call her my angel on earth. No, she isn't perfect. Occasionally, she still has an accident inside, and I've lost numerous shoes and the downstairs bathroom rug to puppy teething. Still, to us, she is so much more than a dog — she's family.

Although she's not a rescue, she rescued us. As Michael is fond of saying, "Huck came into our lives to unite our family, and Scarlett came into our lives to help our family heal."

~Amy Catlin Wozniak

66

Perimeter Girls

If your dog is fat, YOU need more exercise.
~Author Unknown

"**W**eight gain happens in middle age. If we don't drop a couple of pounds, problems could develop. We wouldn't want a blown-out knee or anything."

I swung my sights from the veterinarian over to my gray-haired dog, Daisy, whose belly was practically scraping the floor. For a moment, I thought the vet might've been referring to me. After all, I'd been facing middle-age wrestling matches getting into my jeans lately, only to be met with a muffin top whenever I managed to zip them closed.

"Cut out the treats and try a weight-management food," the vet suggested. "And up the exercise."

It was one thing for me to pack on pounds, but if my poor eating and exercise habits were now influencing a defenseless creature I adored, I decided to take the vet's words to heart — not only for Daisy's sake, but also for mine.

I'd struggled with weight issues all my life. If low-calorie Similac had existed in my infancy, I probably would've been nursed on it. Of my three siblings, I was born the heaviest at nine pounds, nine ounces. "Heavy" as an adjective of physical proportion had been a constant coloring in my life ever since. I'm plump. Chunky. Or as a generous doctor once wrote on a medical report, I'm "well nourished." How thoughtful of him not to call me the "f-word"! And while I've spent decades trying to reign in the circumference of my waist, thighs, and hips, it's been a losing battle.

When I mentioned about Daisy being put on a weight-management plan — and my own malaise — my sisters said, "Forget dieting. If you want to knock off some pounds, become a 'perimeter girl.'"

"A what?"

They explained, "When you go to the supermarket, only buy food from the perimeter of the store. Stick to fresh stuff — produce, fish, meat, and dairy. Keep out of the aisles. They're filled with booby traps of salty snacks, cookies, and frozen and baked goodies."

It wasn't easy, but Daisy and I became "perimeter girls," soon pleasantly sharing healthier meals and snacks of grilled chicken and fish, whole grains, yogurt, veggies and fruits. We motivated each other, adding extra walks and even exercising together in our aboveground backyard pool. Daisy — an excellent swimmer — did laps, while I spent thirty minutes daily treading water.

Every week, on Sundays, I'd allow myself — and Daisy — one binge meal, which mostly consisted of a slice of pizza for me and a couple of liver treats for her.

Our progress was slow, but the pounds ultimately began to come off as my wholesome eating and exercise regimen soon replaced my former concepts of dieting. Feelings of wellbeing actually caused me to start enjoying foods that were good for me. And the sense of discipline instilled by implementing a "perimeter lifestyle" allowed Daisy and me to tone up, get healthier and have a lot more energy than before. With a more confident bounce in my step, I even stopped craving the junk food that used to trip me up.

I wasn't sure I could say the same for Daisy, however. Months into our "perimeter crusade," I hosted our family's annual Saint Patrick's Day dinner. We're Italians on both sides, going generations back. But because my father's name was Patrick, we'd celebrated his namesake saint with a feast for as long as I could remember.

Our holiday menu ritual was always pasta dressed with pesto (the sauce is green, after all!), and we'd cap off the meal with an angel-food cake topped with bright green pistachio icing.

This particular year, I cooked our feast, eager to make it my weekly binge meal. While we gathered to eat in the dining room, I set the iced, green cake—proudly fashioned as a shamrock—on a cake stand. It sat like a work of art atop a pedestal on the coffee table in the living room.

It wasn't until we'd cleared the dishes that I noticed Daisy's dog food was left untouched in her bowl. I called for her, but she didn't come. Anxious, I looked for her in the yard and den. She was nowhere to be found—until I stepped into the living room and found her cowering beneath an end table.

Through the shadows, I spied her gray face. Why was her fur green? Was she ill?

I followed a trail of green paw prints that led across the floor to the coffee table, where two of the three shamrocks of my beautifully decorated, pistachio-iced St. Patrick's Day cake had been devoured.

I gasped. Daisy, tail tucked and ears flagged back, shot me a doleful, guilt-ridden gaze.

We still laugh about that cake today. And when I fall off the wagon myself, which happens very occasionally, I take comfort in the fact that my friend Daisy had her own guilty moment, too.

~Kathleen Gerard

67

A Loyal Companion

*When I look into the eyes of an animal, I do not see an
animal. I see a living being. I see a friend. I feel a soul.*
~A.D. Williams

I threw the negative pregnancy test against the wall. Tears rolled
down my cheeks as I lay curled in a fetal position on the bathroom floor.

Our fourth and final round of infertility treatments had failed.

Between my gasps for air, I heard the door get nudged open.
Through blurry eyes, I watched the door open slowly.

First, I saw her wet nose peek through the crack, and then her
head peered around the corner of the door. She cautiously opened
the rest of it with the side of her body and plopped down next to me
on the floor.

Her blue eyes stared straight into mine.

She didn't say a word — after all, dogs can't talk — but she didn't
have to. I felt her whisper straight into my soul, "I'm here. It's okay."

Maggie was our rescue mutt from the local Humane Society. She
had a presence about her that was special.

She stayed by our side through multiple moves, job changes, and
our struggles with infertility. And she was with us when we decided,
years later, to pursue adoption. We wrote all about her in our adoption
profile and paperwork. After all, she was a big part of our family.

As the weeks went by, Maggie quietly watched us prepare for
parenthood. She watched us transform the guest bedroom into a nursery,

and she saw the flurry of activity as we accumulated baby items. Six months into our wait, she was with us when we got the call.

It was a Saturday morning in August. I was groggy, slowly waking up for the day, and Maggie was sprawled out next to me in bed. She jolted with my scream when the social worker on the other end of my cell phone bubbled over with excitement that we had been chosen as parents for a baby girl in Texas. Maggie paced the house with us — upstairs and downstairs, upstairs and downstairs — and she watched as we frantically threw suitcases together and loaded up an empty car seat reserved for the six-pound miracle waiting for us hundreds of miles away.

It wasn't until we arrived in Texas that the social worker told us our daughter's birth mom had spent all night flipping through family profiles, and when she came across ours, she knew. There were three things that jumped out at her, and one of them — you guessed it — was Maggie. She loved dogs and instantly fell in love with Maggie from our family photos. *Of course, our most loyal companion would find a way to help orchestrate happiness after so much heartache,* I thought to myself.

It's been three years since we brought our daughter home. We adopted another, and then found ourselves spontaneously pregnant shortly after. Our young daughters keep Maggie on her toes, and certainly offer her a wide platter of dining choices from their high chairs and booster seats.

Most days are chaotic, crazy and loud, much different from the lazy afternoons I used to spend snuggled next to Maggie on the couch. But there are moments between changing diapers, filling sippy cups and breaking up squabbles over yellow Mega Bloks when I'll glance at Maggie lying comfortably on the floor and smile. Her eyes are still as loving and supportive as they were nine years ago when I was lying on the bathroom floor begging for these moments of motherhood.

She has been there through it all.

~Shelley Skuster

68

The Rescued One

The gift which I am sending you is called a dog,
and is in fact the most precious and valuable
possession of mankind.
~Theodorus Gaza

motorist first spotted him alongside a busy country road just east of town. The young pup was trembling as he lay curled next to his dead mother. She had been hit and killed by a car, and by the looks of it had been there for days. He was starving, dehydrated, and alone. Several passersby had stopped and attempted to help him, but he was fearful and stayed out of reach, never straying far from his mother's body. It was as if he expected her to wake up.

I had separated recently and was trying to adjust to the single life. My new house was quiet and lonely, so I had been considering getting a pet. Little did I know that my life would soon be tied to this animal who was about to make headlines around the world.

Concerns that the pup would face the same fate as his mother had residents talking, and word of his plight spread quickly. Before long, the news reached two young women who were so moved by the story that they drove to the site to see if they could help.

Upon arriving at the scene, they attempted to coax the distressed dog in close enough to get a leash on him so they would be able to transport him and provide the help he so desperately needed. Patiently, the pair gently talked to the weary animal for hours, trying to calm his fears and earn his trust. But he repeatedly shied away from them, always circling back to the only security he knew: the lifeless form on the side of the road.

Realizing the futility of the situation, but not wanting to concede defeat, the women managed to find a fenced enclosure and skillfully herded the young black Labrador toward the gate. Once he ran past them and into the makeshift jail, they slammed the gate shut. The pup became frantic when he realized that he was trapped and separated from his mother. He growled and snapped at his would-be captors.

Eventually, his sheer exhaustion slowed him down enough so that one of the young women was able to slip a collar over his head. This began a new surge of desperation, and he fought, pulling and jerking at the leash, growling and baring his teeth. They covered his head with a blanket to keep him from biting them as they picked him up and carried him to the car. Although they succeeded in his capture, they both expressed concern that he was feral and might need months of rehabilitation. But as they placed him in the crate they had brought, the fear, despair, and defiance seemed to leave him and gave way to surrender and calm. For the first time since his ordeal began, the exhausted puppy sighed, lowered his head and wagged his tail.

They had accomplished what no one else was able to do. They spent over three hours in the stifling heat of the summer sun to save an animal with no home, no mother, and no intention of letting any-one near. Good Samaritans? Guardian angels? Most of us would have walked away, telling ourselves, "We tried," and the little dog would have perished.

By the next day, the Lab was eating, drinking, and enjoying his first bath. The road to recovery seemed quick. He began playing with the other dogs and wagging his tail non-stop. What started out as a tragic story was taking a turn for the better.

The entire rescue from start to finish was videotaped and, once posted on the Internet, went viral. The puppy they named Prince captured the hearts of all who witnessed his ordeal on YouTube, and later on local and national news stations. Queries poured in, and people from across the globe reached out with love, support, funds to pay his veterinary expenses, and offers to adopt him. He became an instant poster child for animal rescues and adoptions.

I rarely watch television, so I was oblivious to the entire situation. I own a small gym in town, and I stay pretty busy with fitness boot camps, spin classes, group fitness, and personal training. The two women who rescued Prince happened to be clients of mine, and I had spoken with them months earlier about possibly adopting a Greyhound. They both have retired racing Greyhounds, and they seemed like great companions.

At some point, while pondering the fate of the puppy they had saved, they both thought of me. The phone rang, and it was one of the rescuers on the other end.

"Hi, Joe, it's Katy. Would you be interested in a black Lab puppy?"

The question caught me off guard. I had been fixated on getting a Greyhound. I hesitated, took a deep breath, and started asking questions." Is it a boy or a girl? How old is it?"

"Where have you been?" she asked. "This puppy has been all over the Internet and the news. He needs a good home, and we think you two would be perfect for each other."

My mind was racing. *A rescue dog? What was I getting myself into?* I finally told her, "Katy, I've never 'chosen' a pet. I have always let them choose me." But I wanted to be open-minded so I asked halfheartedly, "When can I meet him?"

I had a fitness boot camp that evening at the park, so Katy agreed to bring him there. I still wasn't sold on the idea, but when Prince stepped out of the van, something magical happened. All I could see were long, clumsy puppy legs, an ear-to-ear smile, a perpetually wagging tail, and the most beautiful, trusting brown eyes. How could I say no to this little boy who needed a home and someone to love him?

The very moment Katy placed the leash in my hand and Prince looked up at me, any doubt vanished.

Both of our lives were about to change. I felt like a father coming home from the hospital with a newborn baby. There was much to do. There was "puppy proofing" the house (inside and out), and there was the matter of food and water bowls, treats, toys and a bed. The all-important potty training was first on the list. Prince thrived on affection and treats, so rewards for good behavior made him very teachable. Over the next year, he mastered an assortment of commands: Come, Sit, Heel, Stay, Down, Speak, Up, Shake, and my favorite — Crate. His plush bed and pillow are in his crate (the door has been removed), and this is where he chooses to sleep, nap, or hang out when he is bored.

Initially, I wanted to change his name, but then, for all those who were following his story, I would have to refer to him as the "dog formerly known as Prince." To me, the name seemed unfitting considering his humble beginnings, but soon enough he stood thirty inches at the shoulder and weighed eighty pounds. His black coat was sleek and shiny, his chest was broad, his waist was small, and his body was muscular. From rags to riches, this majestic, regal animal has grown into his name.

I thought I was doing a good deed, being charitable and providing a better life for this unfortunate animal that was orphaned and left to fend for himself in the middle of nowhere. Like Prince, I was also suffering a sense of loss and emptiness. My house was not a home; it was devoid of comfort, love, warmth, and happiness. I have learned that without companionship, love, interaction and exchanges of good energy, life rapidly becomes a drab, dreary and desolate existence, leading to monotony and depression.

With much effort, I taught Prince a few meaningless tricks. With no effort at all, he has taught me about friendship, love and loyalty, and to joyfully embrace each day and appreciate the little things that so many take for granted. In the past five years with Prince, I have come to realize that I was as much in need of rescuing as he was.

~Joe Petersen

Editor's note: To watch Prince's rescue, go to www.youtube.com/watch?v=ok5B8oDroc4

Harry, My Firstborn

Happiness is a warm puppy.
~Charles Schulz

I suppose that a small confession is in order before I share my story. There once was a time when I held a less-than-flattering opinion of a certain kind of dog owner. I'm sure that you've seen them before, too. At first glance, they appear to be perfectly normal. But upon closer inspection, any previously held opinion pertaining to their alleged normalcy quickly disappears.

Watch the interaction between the two species for a moment, and it becomes readily apparent that the collared creature tethered to the business end of the leash is much more than just the family pet. Study them a little longer, and you may even witness this goofy dog owner walking, talking, and sometimes even wearing the same matching sweater and chapeau as Fifi, Fido, Rover, or Rex.

Now as far as I was concerned, no further evidence was needed before concluding that the two-legged, snoutless half of this fashionably matching pair somehow believed that this four-legged creature was his not-quite-human, but nevertheless very hairy, little offspring. I knew that wasn't true… until an adorable, little puppy came into my life.

Suddenly, I learned how little I knew about canine relationships.

Karen and I had the perfect recipe for our life together as husband and wife, and it went much like the old schoolyard song, "…first comes love, then comes marriage…." We'd save money, buy a house, fill it with kids, and live happily ever after. And it all went as planned, too — until we discovered that there was a problem with the kids' part of the program.

As we struggled to overcome this seemingly insurmountable roadblock, we became parents, sort of. We decided to adopt a dog, but not just any dog. We wanted a rescue dog — a real-life pound puppy — and so one afternoon we called the local shelter to see if they had any. As it turned out, they did, and he'd been waiting for us to meet him.

Abandoned, unwanted, starving and not yet six weeks old, someone had left him one night in the shelter van. The volunteers suggested that he was a mix between a Lab and a Beagle, or a Beagle and a Doberman, or a Doberman and a... Well, there were just as many possible combinations offered as opinions rendered, but in the end, whatever his puppy pedigree actually was, we couldn't have cared less. This tiny, black-and-brindle bundle of trembling puppy arrived at a time in our lives when we surely needed him as much as he needed us.

We brought him home and named him Harry, but years later I'd refer to him as our firstborn, which to the astute reader should serve as a clue as to how that previously mentioned kids' part of the program eventually turned out.

As with the arrival of any new family member, Harry's wants and needs quickly surpassed our own, and we wondered how we'd ever gotten along without him. Every day became another lesson in the adventures of puppy parenting. And like all new parents, we marveled at the physical changes that seemed to occur to our little guy almost daily. We tried to imagine how big he'd one day become when he finally grew into those massive paws, which fortuitously never happened.

We celebrated his little achievements, too, like when he finally slept through the night, and when he mastered a few simple, silly tricks. And we were thrilled when he learned to tell us when nature necessitated his visiting that special spot set aside for him behind our backyard woodpile instead of the floor beside the sliding glass door!

Our neighbors came to know the newest puppy on the block during our frequent strolls around the neighborhood. Of course, we delighted in showing off our little bundle of joy. And if someone, somehow, had missed his utter cuteness firsthand, there were always Harry photos available to keep everyone in the puppy loop — at six weeks, and then seven; wide awake or asleep; giving puppy kisses, on family vacations or just romping around our back yard; photos from last month, last week, or even last night. I was just another proud puppy pop showing off his puppy son.

I can't explain the circumstances surrounding my transformation, but somehow I'd mysteriously morphed into the very same type of dog owner that once upon a time had caused me hilarious bouts of comedic cackling. Oh, I'd become one of them all right, but once I did I couldn't imagine being anything else.

And suddenly, two years had come and gone. Harry was, of course, a full-fledged member of the family. Our lives were nothing less than perfect — or so we thought. But circumstances previously unseen were about to change our happy household forever.

When Karen shared the news, Harry didn't seem too excited. Instead, he yawned, stretched, and went right back to sleep. He couldn't have cared less about babies, whatever they were, but this would soon change when Michael was born, and two years later when Tracy came home from the hospital. In the end, Harry would prove to be an awesome big brother to his little siblings, but that's another story entirely.

And as for me? I suppose that I should offer an addendum to my original confession from all those years ago, and it is this: I'm still one of those goofy dog owners — the very same that I once found hysterical — but don't tell anyone. Instead, let's just keep this a secret between you and me and my current hairy, little, four-legged rescued son: my best friend in the world, Bailey.

~Stephen Rusiniak

70

Saint Barklee

A dog is man's best friend, and vice versa.
~Author Unknown

At forty-five, a pregnancy changed my life. I gave birth to a baby girl who weighed only one pound, nine ounces. Doctors gave her a two percent chance of survival.

We brought our miracle daughter home three months later weighing three pounds, fourteen ounces. On her second birthday, we decided that she needed a Saint to watch over her.

Barklee was the runt of the litter: tiny, like our daughter. He weighed three pounds when we brought him home at seven weeks of age. When our vet first examined him, he questioned whether he was a purebred Saint Bernard. We assured him that Barklee was AKC-registered. On the following visit for shots, our vet told us that he was indeed a Saint because he increased in size tenfold!

Barklee loved his little master. He filled her need for a constant playmate and protective caretaker. Daily escapades included our daughter's unskilled ability to dress him in bonnets, sashes, and clothes from every closet in the house. When she put her socks on his paws, he lifted his giant paws three inches off the ground, then sat down and promptly began to chew the socks into tiny pieces.

She often placed her favorite dolly, Suzi, on Barklee's back while she fed him Cheerios and fake tea (water) during playtime. Suzi sat on Barklee's back for rides through the house. Not to be outdone by

Suzi, our daughter's early rodeo career began as her little legs tried to hold on when she attempted to ride her Saint.

Barklee willingly followed our daughter into her sandbox for a "sand spa scrub." She took buckets full of sand and poured them on Barklee's back. He then followed her to her wading pool, where she gave him a luxurious bath by using the same bucket to drench him from head to toe. Truly, only a Saint would put up with this.

Sometimes, Barklee's payback for this loving treatment proved to be comical. As daughter dear chased him around our very large back yard, he circled around trees and suddenly chased her. He grabbed hold of her sagging diaper and they fell and rolled in the cool green grass. Our daughter giggled and tried to stand up. Barklee then pulled furiously and shook his head from side to side to remove her diaper entirely.

Our miracle remained rather petite and small-boned. Barklee, on the other hand, blossomed into a whopping two hundred pounds. His size never seemed to be an issue for our little girl. He made a comfortable pillow for her naps, and her purple beaded bracelets looked charming on his large paws.

We knew our daughter needed a Saint to watch over her. That is exactly what this big dog did. He showed her patience; he lay quietly next to her to be dressed and climbed on. He gave her time and commitment by never leaving her side. He showed her tolerance by allowing her to pull his ears, nap, or ride on him. Most of all, he showed her unconditionally that no matter what she did to him or asked of him, he lovingly came back with an eagerness to please, one more time.

Barklee blessed our family for nine years. He is with his friends at the Rainbow Bridge. We will see him again. Everyone knows Saints live in heaven.

~Alice Klies

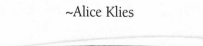

71

Saving August

*Our task must be to free ourselves... by widening our
circle of compassion to embrace all living creatures
and the whole of nature and its beauty.*
~Albert Einstein

t had been a long week, but it was finally Friday. I didn't care that it was raining. I just wanted to get my thirteen-year-old son, Jake, to school on time and get home and relax. My husband Mike and I were separated, and he had just asked me for a divorce. Emotionally, I was drained.

We had just exited the highway and caught the red light about a mile from my son's school. From a grassy field on my left, I saw a small dog run out to greet the car ahead of us. When the light turned green, the car took off, and the dog ran back into the field. Wanting Jake to be on time, I also started to drive off. Looking absolutely horrified, my son said, "I'll never forgive you if you don't go back and get it." Feeling guilty, I dropped him off and drove back there, praying all the way that someone had already rescued it.

Please don't get me wrong, I really love dogs. I grew up with them. I just couldn't handle the thought of adding anything extra to my already full emotional plate. I parked just off the road, and I didn't see anything at first. I wanted to drive away, but thinking of Jake, I got out of the car and gave a short whistle. My dumb luck, a little brown head popped up. Grabbing a rope from the trunk of my car, I ran through traffic to be greeted by a soaking wet, tail-wagging, muddy-pawed puppy that looked like a Shepherd/Lab mix. Somehow, I got the rope around her neck and got us both safely back to my car. Quickly digging an old blanket out of the trunk, I threw it on the back seat before she happily jumped in. As serendipity had it, there was a vet two blocks up the street. I couldn't get there fast enough.

I was hoping she was just lost, but the vet thought differently. They were sure she had been "dumped." I panicked. How could I keep her? I couldn't afford a dog, and besides that I was on the verge of a divorce. The vet convinced me it would be fine. So that afternoon, I picked up a happy Jake, and we drove to the vet to get our new dog. And that was the start of saving August.

August, named after the month we found her, turned out to be a six-month-old, thirty-pound beautiful mutt with calico colors and big brown eyes. She had the softest fur and the sweetest, most innocent face. I was thinking that maybe this wouldn't be so bad after all until the next day when she tried to bite me. I was sure her aggressive behavior was the reason she had been left in that field.

I bought her a crate, some chew toys and all the other necessities, and signed her up for a puppy-training class. Two weeks later, she was still biting. I was so afraid she was going to hurt my son. I knew if I gave her up, she would probably be euthanized. No one wants an aggressive dog. My son begged me to keep her and give her another chance so I had her evaluated. The trainer gave her an A+. She wasn't aggressive at all. She was diagnosed with "inappropriate play behavior." Go figure! "Totally fixable," he promised. So we began training even harder, thinking she was just a slow learner.

Sinking more and more money into a dog I wasn't sure I wanted to keep, we had her spayed and micro-chipped. Now if she got lost, whoever found her would be able to give her back to us. Honestly, once she started biting them, that really wouldn't be a problem. She became a great distraction, leaving me no time to think about the divorce or what life would be like without my husband.

August turned out to be quite smart. By "herding" us around the house with her nipping and biting, she knew we'd feed her. Food got her to sit, lie down, and even stop biting us. But once the food ran out, we were doomed! My son would hide in the kitchen pantry to get away from her, but it wasn't big enough to fit us both. We tried everything to stop her from biting — squirt guns, whistles, keeping her on a leash, crating her, bitter apple spray, shouting "No bite!" — but nothing worked.

My friends told me I was crazy for keeping her. My soon-to-be ex said I needed to get control of her, like somehow it was my fault she was biting us. What I needed was Mike's help, not his criticism.

After two months, I was desperate. She did great in the car, on neighborhood walks, and even around other people or dogs. But with us in the house, she was like a wild animal.

I knew if I gave her up, she would definitely be put down. I started to hate her. I should say, love-hate her. She reminded me of all the bad relationships I'd ever had. Here I was, spending all my money on her, trying to give her a good home, and she was biting us in return. I felt emotionally torn, abused, and very codependent.

Three months later, instead of finalizing our divorce, Mike was diagnosed with stage 4 terminal lung cancer. Jake and I were devastated. We reconciled as much as possible with Mike during the six months he had left. Somehow, through all the heartache over losing him, we kept training August. We poured the love we couldn't give him into her. And in return, she finally stopped biting and started to love us back.

It has been twelve years since that rainy Friday when I found her on the side of the road. Sometimes I think I should have named her Shadow because she follows me everywhere. My son just graduated from college, and while he was away, August was my constant companion and support.

We've been through a lot together. She stayed by my side when I had pneumonia one winter, and I stayed by hers when she had pancreatitis and then years later when she tore her ACL and needed a leg brace. She is as loving and sweet as any dog can ever be. In fact, she would have made a great therapy dog. To be honest, she already is one to me. Today, I can't picture my life without her.

~Debra Zemke

Chapter 8

The Dog Really Did That?

My Heroic Dog

72

Rescue Dog

If you have been brutally broken, but still have the
courage to be gentle to others, then you deserve
a love deeper than the ocean itself.
~Nikita Gill

The dog was a terror. He tore at the front door, crashed against windows, and threatened everyone, not just the mailman. Friends, strangers, pregnant women pushing baby carriages, a falling leaf—he growled at guests and so frightened the weekly maid that she quit. The door and frame bore deep gouges, and the windowsills were scratched. On walks, he would suddenly lunge into the street to attack FedEx trucks, school buses, and other 10,000-pound vehicles. I had to stay alert for bicyclists, motorcycles with loud mufflers, running children, strangers approaching from behind, and unleashed dogs.

His name was Monty, but I started calling him Monster Man. He had been found howling in the woods, wrapped in chains, and taken to the Auburn, Virginia shelter, which euthanized any animal not claimed within two weeks. Their policy was formed from desperation since few people neutered their cats and dogs in rural Virginia, and the shelter was small and underfunded.

The night before his scheduled death, a woman adopted him. But then she confined him to a crate at her business for three months before my husband saw his picture on a dog rescue website and fell in love.

Monty reminded him of one of his favorite dogs, Tashla, who had died the year before. They both had pointed ears, alert gold-brown eyes, fluffy black-and-gold fur, and tails that curled into a question mark. Both looked like wolves, only Tashla had weighed an appropriate seventy pounds and Monty, an underweight forty-five. Neither his ribs nor his scars showed through his thick double coat that kept falling out in chunks.

I didn't know what to do. Returning Monty to a shelter would be a death sentence. But how could I live with this impossible animal?

In desperation, I hired a trainer. "He's frightened," she said. "He's afraid of being hurt. He needs love, time, and a strong choke collar," she added. "He must know who is boss. He needs to know you will protect him."

I tried. When Monty barked, I rushed downstairs, shoved myself between the dog and the door, then turned back to him with palms extended in front of his face to signal that I was his protection, and he could go off duty. Sometimes, that worked, but sometimes, with my workday ruined, I just screamed, which left both of us feeling bad. His tail would drop. He would slink away, and I would feel angry and guilty.

To admit someone to the house, the trainer taught me to grip his collar, force him to sit, ask the terrified person on the other side of the door to come in, ignore the dog, and explain that "he is more frightened than you are." Even I didn't believe that. It became easier to meet friends at the nearby coffee shop.

After lots of trial and error, I identified the safest time to take him outside. In the late afternoon we would walk the neighborhood to the far side of the little-used city tennis courts. From there we proceeded to the safety of the woods and eventually home along sidewalks with a clear view ahead, so that I could see if anyone was coming and take Monty across the street.

For a month, Monty and I had the woods to ourselves. Then, one day, I was surprised to see children in the distance. I approached slowly, pulling in Monty's retractable leash for greater control. Four boys were whirling and waving sticks. Monty stiffened. His head jutted forward and his muscles tensed as he followed their movement.

As we walked closer, I saw a child tied to an oak tree. A ropey brown vine, the thickness of an electrical cord, looped around him, tight, neck to ankles, so that only his head and hand could move. His young captors charged and war-danced around him. Three wielded two-foot tree limbs, one a 2x4. They thrust their weapons at the child's face, stomach, and genitals, close but not touching. They retreated only to whirl and thrust again. The child attempted to protect himself with a three-inch stick, waving it back and forth, but only his wrist could rotate. His arms were lashed to his body. The threats and violence occurred in silence — no sobs or screams. No taunts or triumphal yelps.

This was the middle of the afternoon, a sunny April in Alexandria, Virginia. The woods were city-owned, adjacent to an elementary school. In the distance, about two football fields away, children scampered up monkey bars, slipped down a twisty slide, and pumped high on swings. Mothers, some holding babies on their hips, looked like they were making play dates, comparing recipes, and exchanging neighborhood gossip. Their voices were too far away to be heard in this strange and silent place. Even if they had been facing the woods, all they would have seen were four boys cavorting with sticks. The victim was tied to the side of the tree not visible from the playground. A thin rivulet of blood ran down his neck from where vine had cut into his flesh.

I had to steady myself, restrain the dog, and look again to make sure that I was really seeing what I thought I saw but couldn't believe — a boy, maybe nine or ten, immobilized and surrounded by four armed children about the same age.

Three of the children, the ones with tree branches, also froze, as surprised by me as I by them. The boy with the 2x4 could not stand still. He kept shifting his weight from side to side, hefting his fence post from hand to hand, making short swings as if the weapon were controlling him. He looked in my direction, but his eyes were strange, like they were not in the present but locked in whatever fantasy he was acting out. The captive watched me in silence. The dog strained at his leash, body alert and angled toward the children. He, too, was silent.

I couldn't drop the leash to untie the boy. I wasn't even sure, as we stood facing each other about three yards apart, that the children wouldn't turn and attack me. There was that much strangeness and uncertainty. "What are you doing?" I asked while further retracting the sixteen-foot leash so that my tense and overly stimulated dog pressed against my knee.

At first, no one answered. Reluctantly, the tallest youth, thin with a crew cut, said, "We're playing a game."

"A game?" I repeated. I looked at the bound boy, now staring at me. He said nothing. Not taking my eyes from him, I said to his tormentors, "If I were playing this game, I would be scared." The trapped child watched me silently.

"Oh, he would be," the tall one answered, "except I'm his friend." The boy with the 2x4 kept swinging his weapon like a baseball bat, warming up for the big hit. He could not stop moving.

I was scared. "Game," one had said, and I grasped at the word. "This is Rescue Dog," I announced. "Rescue Dog is angry." I directed these words to the child with the 2x4, who finally stopped moving. Monty tried to charge forward, but I held him back. "Rescue Dog likes to rescue people," I said, desperate to keep their attention. No one moved. "Rescue Dog doesn't like this game. He wants you to untie your friend." They waited, doing nothing, saying nothing, which increased my anxiety. I repeated myself, louder. "Rescue Dog wants you to untie your friend." They didn't move. "Now," I snapped.

Monty and I stepped toward them, and everyone moved. The tall boy dropped his weapon and approached the tree. The other children disappeared, but I didn't see them go. My focus was solely on the victim. I watched as his "friend" began fumbling with the knot at the victim's neck. Neither boy spoke as the vine fell in large loops around the tree. I could not take my eyes off the falling vine. I didn't dare blink. I felt like I was controlling the action, that if I looked away, anything could happen.

Once his arm was free, the boy rubbed his neck. The last loop of vine fell to the ground. The "friend" vanished.

I was alone in the woods with my difficult dog and the liberated child. I started to ask if he was okay, but before I could speak, the child rushed to Monty. He wrapped his arms tightly around his neck, nuzzled his head in deep fur, and kissed his snout.

I froze, terrified. The dog was going to rip off his face. Did I save this kid so my dog could kill him?

But nothing happened. The dog stood patiently, even kindly, and allowed himself to be hugged. The moment over, the boy jumped to his feet and ran to the playground. Monty didn't lunge, chase, or try to nip. He simply waited, relaxed but expectant. When we were alone, he looked up at me as if to say, "Let's go." And so we did.

I would love a fairytale ending—the dog that rose to the occasion, transformed by his own goodness, behavior problems no more. But that's not what happened. What changed was me, or at least I changed first. He had probably always been Rescue Dog, but I had to be shocked into seeing it.

He still barks at passersby and occasionally claws the windows and door. But I rarely look up from my work. I have stopped screaming at him, dreading our walks, and holding his leash so tight that his collar throttles his neck. I relaxed, and he relaxed. Now even strangers can pet him.

Sometimes we take our old path around the tennis courts and through the woods. I always walk up to that oak tree, part of me still not believing what happened that day. This winter, the tree was toppled by massive amounts of snow. And then I saw them: the loops of dried vine still circled its uprooted base.

~Linda Morefield

73

One Season

Dogs are always good and full of selfless love. They
are undiluted vessels of joy who never, ever deserve
anything bad that happens to them.
~Steven Rowley

I t was the first day of spring many years ago when my husband, Don, looked up over the newspaper he was reading and grinned at me. "Let's get a dog!" he said.

"We already have two cats," I pointed out, gesturing to the windowsill of our basement apartment where they were wriggling their butts excitedly, watching the antics of a squirrel outside.

"So?" he shrugged. "Cats are boring. You can do stuff with a dog."

"Yeah, like mop up after them, clean up their poop, and listen to them bark at nothing," I quipped, but I was already caving. I loved animals, so within minutes we were in the car on our way to the local shelter.

We heard the loud, yapping cacophony before we even parked. It became deafening as we entered and began our search for the perfect pet.

Though I wished I could adopt every single dog maniacally throwing itself against its cage, none stood out until I made a second tour.

In a far corner sat a small, nondescript Collie/Shepherd mix. There was nothing remarkable about him except for his pose. He sat ramrod straight in alert sphinx position staring at me.

Don called him over, but the dog didn't budge. When I crouched down, however, grasping the grating of his enclosure for balance, he came over immediately, placing his paw on the back of my hand through the small hole.

"He's scheduled for tomorrow," we heard a voice say behind us. I turned to see a female attendant standing there.

"Scheduled?" I echoed.

"Yes, he'll be euthanized. He's been here too long. He's a good dog, but too plain. No one wants him."

"I do!" I exclaimed.

I heard my husband sigh. Clearly, this was not the muscular, tough-looking, manly dog he had visualized accompanying him on his daily jogs, but he smiled and nodded at the woman.

"At least she didn't fall in love with a Chihuahua," he joked as the dog regally pranced out of his cage to plop himself at my feet in the position that would earn him his name.

Sphinx fit into our life beautifully, quickly adapting to basic commands, leash etiquette, and outdoor potty training. He did none of the chewing damage one would expect of a dog acclimatizing to new surroundings. He never barked either. Neighbors attested that he made no sound while home alone.

Rigid as his posture always was, he was loving, friendly, playful, and happy. He showed so much joy when he was chasing balls or greeting us after work. He'd go and get his leash for us in order to go on his walk sooner.

He bonded with both of us, but he seemed more partial and protective toward me, rarely leaving my side, yet careful not to get in my way while I went about my housework.

Even the cats tolerated him the way cats disdainfully endure anything they find beneath them. They would swipe at his muzzle occasionally to remind him who was boss, but his only reaction was a friendly swish of his tail and a slight adjustment in his ever-vigilant position.

Sphinx had been with us three months when he demanded a second walk. I had already given him a quick walk when I came home from work, but now I needed to go to the bank. To my surprise, Sphinx stood up and went to get his leash again.

"Not now, sweetie," I told him. "I'll be back in a bit, and I'll take you for a longer walk, okay?"

I jumped when he barked. I'd never heard him do it. I tried to pass, but he barred my way with his body, barking again — more insistently this time.

"You must need to go pretty badly," I commented, puzzled. He paced in agitation. "Okay, come on, but I'll have to tie you up outside the bank, and you have to be a good boy," I added sternly as we left the house.

Oddly, he didn't need to relieve himself. He trotted beside me, not even stopping to smell every new blade of grass, tree, or hydrant, as was his habit. Nothing interested him — not even the chipmunk that crossed our path.

My banking took longer than expected, so I decided to take an alley shortcut to get back home. Sphinx wasn't happy with that decision either. He barked again, startling me. I tugged at his leash, but he balked and kept pulling away. By then, I was tired and had enough of his odd behavior.

"Come!" I commanded, my voice sterner than he'd ever heard. Immediately, he stopped struggling and became his usual obedient self.

Halfway down the alley, a man stepped out from a recessed stairwell and approached us. His smile made me a little nervous, but I continued to walk.

"Hey, babe," he leered. I could feel goose bumps pop on my skin. He came closer, blocking my path. I heard a soft growl from Sphinx, then saw the fading sun glint against something in his hand — a knife!

"Stay quiet, and let go of the mutt. You and me are gonna have some fun," he murmured, grabbing my arm.

Frozen, I couldn't even scream. I didn't have to. In a nanosecond, Sphinx pushed forward between us. His jaws clamped around the man's wrist, and he screamed in agony, dropping to his knees. My dog continued to bite into the soft flesh, never releasing his hold.

I ran! As soon as I was far enough away, I yelled for Sphinx, who instantly let go and tore after me.

Needless to say, Sphinx got more than his fair share of treats that night. As we fawned over him, he clung protectively to my side.

Three days later, Sphinx became extremely sick. Within two hours, the seizures started. Terrified, we rushed him to the vet. By the time we got there, he was unable to walk, and we carried him in. The prognosis — advanced distemper — made me sag in disbelief. Even though he was current on all his vaccinations, somehow he was unable to fight the disease. It was recommended that he be euthanized immediately.

"No!" I bellowed at the vet. "This just started today. Fix it!"

The vet shook his head sadly. I continued arguing and screaming until something touched my fingertips. I looked down to see Sphinx nestle his paw into my hand. Our eyes locked, and his message was clear. He knew, and wanted me to know it was time to say goodbye. Within minutes, my beloved dog was gone, peacefully and painlessly.

I sobbed all the way home. When we got there, it occurred to me that it was the first day of summer. Sphinx had been with us for only one season, but thanks to his courage and loyalty, I had my whole life ahead of me.

~Marya Morin

Pitch Protection

Dogs are the best example of a being who doesn't
need to lie to protect someone's pride.
~Ammiel Josiah Monterde

'm done," I rasped, stumbling to a halt on the gravelly edge of the road. Doubling over to rest my hands on my knees, I struggled not to throw up. "Like, done done."

My mother took two more long-legged strides before slowing her pace, circling back around while our black Lab happily trotted at her hip.

"Are you sure?" Pausing in front of me, she jogged in place to keep her heart rate up. "I was planning a full five miles."

The woman was hardly out of breath. I couldn't believe we were related.

"Totally," I croaked, still gulping air like a fish on land. "You go ahead and finish your run. I can walk back," I assured her. It was that or crawl. I hadn't decided which yet.

"Okay," she agreed, cocking her head as she considered me. "But you're taking Pitch with you," she insisted.

I accepted the leash handed to me, my dog and I watching as my mother loped away.

"Sorry," I apologized to Pitch, giving her big black head a scratch. "I know you would have had more fun running with Mom."

Pitch covered her disappointment well, beaming her happy doggy smile at me.

I smiled, tugging gently on the leash as we headed back the way we'd come. "Let's go, goofy girl."

Pitch had started her life as a purebred breeder. Then, two years earlier, a fling with a neighbor's German Shepherd ruined her reputation and made her less valuable to her owners. My family couldn't have been more thrilled to take her. She was an eighty-pound softie who loved anyone who would rub her belly, but especially one lonely fifth-grade girl—me.

Enjoying the fresh spring day, and not having to run anymore, I didn't notice the car coming toward me. It was some kind of brown, four-door monster (which pretty much exhausted my automobile expertise). As it rolled to a stop, the dirt-streaked passenger's window slowly lowered.

"Hey, kid," a male voice from within called out.

"Yeah?" I answered, squinting into the gloom of the car. He seemed normal enough, with shaggy brown hair that looked like it needed washing and an unshaven face, giving him a scruffy appearance. His smile seemed genuine, though, so I wasn't immediately alarmed.

"Look, I'm trying to get to an appointment, and I'm totally lost. Can you help me?"

"Um…" I sucked at directions. Glancing around, there wasn't another soul in sight. No one else to ask. I sighed. "Where are you going?"

"It's off King Road," he replied, also looking around and shifting in his seat. Swinging back toward me, he drew a hand through his greasy hair, looking uncomfortable and intense at the same time as his dark eyes intensely fixed on me.

Things suddenly felt a whole lot weirder. I shuffled backwards a pace.

"King Road?" That one I knew, since my own street intersected it. "You're really close. It's only two blocks that way," I replied, pointing ahead of me.

"Yeah, right. I know. But I'm really lost," he insisted, putting his car in park and shooting me a crocodile smile.

"Uh, it's like, right there." I pointed again, thinking this guy must be a total idiot. I mean, I was just a kid, and I could follow the road to the next cross street.

"Sure, sure, kid, but I really could use your help." Shifting closer, he reached over and pushed open the passenger side door, barely missing me with the slab of heavy metal as it swung wide. "You think you could show me where to go?"

While not exactly worldly wise at the ripe age of ten, my mental alarm bells started going off. I realized that this guy probably wanted more from me than simple directions.

Apparently, I wasn't the only one picking up danger signals.

Throughout the entire conversation, Pitch had stood quietly by my side. What I hadn't noticed was the hackles on her neck and back slowly rising, and the soft, low growl coming from somewhere deep in her throat.

My loving and utterly harmless dog transformed into a creature I'd never seen before. With her fur standing on end and her teeth bared, Pitch let out a guttural sound of pure rage and launched herself at the man in the car. The leash practically yanked my arms out of their sockets as it tugged me forward, but she stopped just short of entering the car. Barking and snarling like a wild animal, her jaws snapped and feet clawed at the edge of the vinyl seat.

Jerking back with a strangled bellow of fear, eyes wide and terrified, Mr. Creepy threw the car into Drive and hit the gas. The open passenger door swung, not fully closing, as he sped away. He reached the intersection and turned without slowing, screeching away until he was out of sight.

I was shaking like a leaf as I realized what had almost happened. I turned to look at Pitch.

My girl stood there, panting away with a smile back on her face. Squinting up at me happily and looking very self-satisfied, the rabid monster of a moment ago had completely gone.

Dropping to my knees, oblivious to the gravel as it gouged my skin, I threw my arms around my savior. I don't know what that man had in mind for me, or what might have happened, but somewhere in my soul I knew it wouldn't have been good. Pitch, who had never been the least bit aggressive with anyone before, had saved me.

"Good girl, Pitch," I whispered, burying my face into her shiny, ebony fur. "Good girl."

~Roslyn McFarland

75

Hunting Down My Heart

If you can change your mind, you can change your life.
~William James

grew up on a farm in upstate New York where our dogs were workers, not pets. They lived outside in the barns and spent their days looking for small prey and predators, not love and affection.

The farm dogs were not allowed in our house unless the temperature fell to single digits and, even then, they were not permitted to go further than the chilly mudroom. It was nearly impossible to bond with these dogs my father referred to as "beasts" and my mother, who disliked dogs, ignored.

Once I grew up and started my own family, I never planned to have a dog. Like my mom, I didn't quite understand why people loved them so much. And, like my dad, I didn't feel they were necessary unless they had a "job."

The disinterest in having a dog changed, though, when my youngest son Brady was born with a rare neurological disorder. His disorder affects his speech, coordination, and balance, and his neurologist recommended we get him a large-breed "helper" dog.

We got a Standard Poodle puppy named Hattie. She became an amazing aide to Brady, but while I was appreciative of her, I didn't bond with her the same way he did.

When Hattie was three, she got a canine brother named Otto. Otto, a crazy Boxer, came into our lives via my second husband, Eric. My relationship with Otto was rocky from the beginning. Unlike Hattie, Otto didn't have a job, and his primary purpose seemed to be eating my shoes, counter surfing, and slobbering everywhere. Otto would not have lasted a minute inside the house I grew up in, but his presence indoors was important to Eric. I put my foot down at him being allowed in our bedroom, though, and told Eric no dog would ever be allowed to sleep in our bed ever.

Early this year, Eric said he wanted to add a third dog to our family. I thought he was out of his mind — I could barely handle two. However, when he said it would be a hunting dog that he would take care of, I agreed. We kept our eyes open for a hunting dog to adopt, and a litter of Beagle puppies appeared at our local shelter a few weeks later.

The night we went to the shelter to see the Beagle puppies, I trailed behind Eric — this was going to be *his* hunting dog. When we went into the puppy area, though, one of the tiny puppies made an effort to seek me out. He bypassed Eric and our boys' outreached arms and whimpered for me to pick him up. As soon as I did, he burrowed his head into my vest and closed his eyes. I felt my heart swell. "It looks like this puppy picked Mommy," Eric told the boys, and I didn't even disagree.

We took Wilbur Write home a few days later wrapped in the same blue receiving blanket I had used for Brady. For the first few weeks, I wore him in Brady's old baby sling — close to my heart. He loved it and, I have to admit, I did, too. I kept asking myself: *Why did this puppy choose me? Doesn't he know I have a cold heart toward dogs? Doesn't he know I have never loved a dog in my life?*

Two months after we adopted Wilbur, the reason he chose me became clear. I woke up in the middle of the night in excruciating stomach pain. I stumbled out of bed, and my little tri-colored shadow followed me. (Yes, Wilbur was allowed to sleep in our bed.)

I tried to get to the bathroom down the hall, but I fell and blacked out. When I woke up on the floor, Wilbur was licking my face. I began vomiting profusely, but was too weak to even call out to Eric. Wilbur sat with me for hours until Eric woke up and took me to the emergency room.

We would soon learn I had appendix cancer. I was thirty-nine. It was a complete shock and absolutely crushing.

When I was not in the hospital, Wilbur was a constant presence by my side — forgoing his puppy toys to lie next to me — his soulful, brown eyes watching me. There were days I could not get out of bed, but he didn't care. He would lie with me for hours. Other days, I mentally didn't want to get out of bed — I was scared to face the future, if I had one at all. Yet something about Wilbur helped get me up and moving with a smile on my face. I had to make it for my boys, my husband and… my dogs, all three of them.

As I write this, Wilbur Write is curled up on my lap sleeping, his head and big brown ears flopped next to my keyboard. Every so often, he sighs in his sleep, and it makes me smile. I am well. I am more than well. I am disease-free! My strength is returning. It is almost hunting season. Eric has decided not to use Wilbur as a hunting dog — he is just too precious to all of us to risk losing him in the woods.

Plus, Wilbur already snagged his biggest prize. He scented out a cold heart and filled it with a dog's love. In my book, he is a legendary hunter.

~Caurie Putnam

76

Rattled

You can't test courage cautiously.
~Anne Dillard

remember the first hike of that summer in 1985 — just me, my
dad and my dog Tuffy. I remember the crisp mountain air, the
abandoned mine, and the crumbling walls of the old hotel. I
remember hunting for fossils and sharing a picnic lunch. But,
most of all, I remember the snake.

We started back down the mountain after our lunch in the shade
of those tumbled-down, redbrick walls. I ran ahead of my dad, kicking
up dust from the trail and didn't see the snake until I was right on top
of it. Already coiled, it spit and rattled — the sound more terrifying
than anything I had ever heard in my life.

My dad was only three or four yards behind me, but his voice
seemed to come from a great distance. "Don't move," he said.

I couldn't have moved even if I wanted to. My feet seemed to
weigh more than all of the silver ever extracted from the abandoned
mine we had visited. I was completely immobilized by my fear.

I had never seen a live rattlesnake in all my ten years. Now, with
one only an arm's length in front of me, I could see nothing else. As it
continued to coil around and around itself, its brown and tan scales
seemed at once dry yet impossibly liquid. It met my gaze with cold,
unfeeling eyes. Standing in the heat of a bright June sun, I shivered,
chilled by those eyes.

Before my dad could reach me, Tuffy positioned herself between me and the rattlesnake. The brown and black fur on her hackles stood up, and her lips curled back, showing her teeth and spraying spittle as she barked ferociously. She had always been a calm and friendly dog, so her behavior startled me almost as much as the appearance of the snake. She lunged forward and snapped at the rattler. Faster than a bullet, it struck, sinking its fangs into Tuffy's face. Her pitiful yelp immediately replaced the snake's rattling as the most terrifying sound I had ever heard.

The snake departed as quickly as it had arrived, and Dad and I ran forward to check on Tuffy. She rolled on the ground, whimpering in pain and rubbing at her nose with her paws. Her face had already begun to swell from the snake's venom.

"We have to get her to the vet fast," Dad said as he moved to pick up Tuffy to carry her the two miles back to the truck at the bottom of the trail. Preoccupied by the pain, she was startled by Dad and nipped at him. Before he could grab her, she started to run down the trail. We tried to keep up, but soon lost sight of her. We descended the trail as fast as we could. Sagebrush seemed to pull at our pant legs, trying to slow us down. Loose rocks tripped us up, slowing our pace even more. No matter our pace, we weren't fast enough. Although Tuffy was out of sight, she filled my thoughts as we rushed down the mountain.

Tuffy was a Blue Heeler/Australian Shepherd mix. We didn't get her as a puppy. She was a gift from my uncle, given to us when she got too old to work on his cattle ranch. She was a smart dog. She didn't just know her name; she responded to dozens of commands. My parents always joked that Tuffy listened better than any of their children ever did. She was a happy dog. She loved to play. On sunny days, Tuffy and I spent hours outside. I threw a tennis ball for her to fetch until my arm got tired, then I would run and let her catch me so we could wrestle in the grass. Eventually, we would lie next to each other, and I would run my hand through her short hair, scratching behind her ears the way she liked.

She was a good dog. I loved Tuffy, but I always thought of her as just a dog. Until that day. Something changed.

My legs felt rubbery and my breath came in ragged gasps as my dad and I reached the bottom of the trail. We still had not caught up with Tuffy, and I worried about what we would find as we approached Dad's truck. Tuffy was lying by the passenger door of the truck. We approached cautiously, not wanting to spook her again. She lay still, watching us approach, a look of pure misery in her eyes. Her face had swollen even more since we saw her on the trail. I opened the door, and she tried to get to her feet to climb into the truck, but she couldn't.

"Jump in, and I'll lay her next to you." Dad lifted Tuffy and laid her on the seat with her head in my lap. He jumped in behind the steering wheel, and the old truck roared to life. The veterinarian's office was at least fifteen minutes away.

I didn't know what to do. I ran my hand softly along her back and then gently scratched behind her ears. All the time, I kept whispering, "It's okay. You're going to be okay. Everything will be okay." I think that I was trying to calm myself every bit as much as I was trying to calm Tuffy.

We reached the veterinarian's office in just under eight minutes thanks to a little horn honking and a lot of speeding. I followed as Dad carried Tuffy inside. The veterinarian poked his head above the reception counter to see what the matter was.

One look at Tuffy's swollen face was all he needed, and before we could tell him what happened, he was shouting for his assistant. "We need a gurney out front right away! And lay out a tray with some anti-venom." The doctor crossed the reception area to a set of swinging double doors just as a gurney pushed through from the other side. He took Tuffy from my dad and laid her on the padded surface. "Rattlesnake bite?"

"Yes. We were hiking above Harper Ward, by the old mine."

"What's her name?"

"Tuffy." My dad tried to cover the tremor in his voice.

"Well, let's hope she's good to her name. You two wait out here, and we'll take care of her." The doctor turned and disappeared as the doors swung closed.

We sat in the waiting area. My dad, not talkative in the best of times, sat quietly looking out the front windows. I slumped forward in my seat, elbows on my knees and my face in my hands, trying to hide my tears. My dad put his arm around my shoulders, and we waited.

I had never had a dog before Tuffy, and I never thought about what it would be like to have a dog die. I had seen a lot of TV shows in which people took a family member to the hospital and a doctor rolled them away on a gurney, leaving them to wait and wonder if they would ever see that family member again. That's when it hit me. That's what was different. Tuffy wasn't just a dog; she was a family member. I think I always knew it deep down, but I didn't realize it until the moment she put herself between that snake and me, heedless of her own safety.

Tuffy survived that snake bite and we enjoyed several more years with her as a full-fledged member of our family.

~Phillip Merrill

77

Our Two Marines

Where the battle rages, there the
loyalty of the soldier is proved.
~Martin Luther

t was homecoming day for my husband Mark after he sustained a shattered hip and broken femur in a biking accident while training for a triathlon.

"What am I going to do?" I asked our neighbor Dave, who served two tours in Afghanistan as a Marine and nearly lost his left leg from a roadside IED. "I'm not a nurse, and Mark's going to need full-time care."

"Don't worry about a thing," Dave replied calmly. "Sage and I will be by your side every step of the way." Four years prior, while Dave was recovering from his injuries at Walter Reed Medical Center in Bethesda, Maryland, he adopted a Labrador Retriever named Sage, who saw him through multiple surgeries and a year-long recovery process to regain full use of his leg.

Later that afternoon, when I brought Mark home from the hospital, Dave and Sage were waiting for us on the sidewalk. With Sage by his side, Dave was dressed in full military uniform — saluting us as we pulled into the driveway. Tears sprang to my eyes and then more tears — a veritable gushing. I jumped out of the car and gave Dave a hug while I wiped away tears.

"How am I going to get Mark out of the car?" I whimpered. "I don't even have a walker for him yet!"

"Not a problem… I'll take care of it," Dave explained, as he reached inside the car — with Sage next to him — and "threw" Mark over his shoulder like a wounded soldier. I cringed and Mark winced as Dave carried him into the house.

I set up a bed in the living room with a full view of the television. There was no way Mark could make it up to the master bedroom with two flights of stairs. Dave made sure Mark was comfortable while I played nurse — lining up all his medications, including a blood thinner to inject into his stomach every day, and pages of instructions that I could barely read. While I was setting up our medical supplies in our kitchen, Sage curled up on the floor next to Mark and didn't make a sound. I think she already sensed she was on duty!

When it was time for Dave to leave, he saluted Mark and told Sage to behave. "Stay girl… stay!" he repeated.

I didn't know what to say or think. *Was I going to take care of my patient and a Marine dog, too?* I had absolutely zero training in both.

As Dave turned on his heels and walked toward the front door, I chased after him, grabbing him by his crisp uniform and sputtered, "What am I supposed to do now?"

"Not a thing," Dave said. "Sage will sense when Mark needs his meds, when he has to use the bathroom, and I'll bring over food for Sage. You'll thank me tomorrow."

That night, I left both my "soldiers" in the living room and wearily climbed up the stairs — leaving the bedroom door open so I could hear my patient and his "comrade at arms."

Around 2:00 a.m., I heard Sage's dog tags rattling as she hoofed upstairs, sat by the edge of the bed and gave me a nudge. I grabbed my robe and trudged downstairs with Sage leading the way. Mark was trying to get up — using the walker that Dave let us borrow — to make it to the bathroom. With Sage flanking one side and me on the other, Mark accomplished his mission.

Sage went back to her "post" after I helped Mark back into bed.

Sage became commander-in-chief of bathroom duty and meal-times — even alerting me when Mark needed the television channel changed. When Mark's pain level got out of control, Sage sensed that as well and lay her head on Mark's chest. By the end of the week, when Mark took his first walk outside with his walker, Sage was right by his side leading the way. Dave checked in from time to time to see how we were doing, but Sage had her orders, and she was sticking to them. By the end of two weeks, we had a Marine farewell as Sage's services were no longer needed, but certainly not forgotten.

The day she left us, Dave dressed up in his full Marine uniform and saluted Mark once again. Of course, Sage was by his side. I cried as I watched them walk across the street — both fulfilling their sense of duty.

More than seven years have passed, and Mark has regained full use of his left leg. It was all thanks to two brave Marines — one who served his country with honor with two tours in Afghanistan and the other with four paws who stood by his side and ours.

~Connie K. Pombo

78

My Comical Security System

A dog can't think that much about what
he's doing; he just does what feels right.
~Barbara Kingsolver

Of all the dogs I have raised, not only did I feel the safest with my Irish Wolfhound, but he was also the most comical. His sheer size and cartoon-like presence were capable of cheering up anyone. Before Zeek joined our family, my husband and I had talked about owning the tallest of the dog breeds a few times, mostly because the image of two small adults walking a huge canine was very funny. One day, on a whim, we decided it was time. From the moment we first set eyes on the grey-and-black-striped, fuzzy-faced puppy, we were smitten.

Zeek grew and grew like Clifford the Big Red Dog. His larger-than-life appearance was so significant that when sitting, his head would appear above the kitchen table, and he looked like he was trying to join in on the dinner conversation. As with all our previous furry friends, Zeek was well mannered. We never fed him from the table, and he never learned to beg.

My husband, who considered Zeek a great source of amusement, enjoyed humming an elephant circus march to the rhythm of Zeek's heavy, plodding steps. When friends with small children visited, someone would inevitably hint about their child riding this majestic canine. Zeek would cordially oblige long enough for a quick photo, and then sit down placidly as if to inform everyone that the joke was over. If that wasn't confusing enough for our Wolfhound, on many walks, horses in a nearby field would approach from across the fence, giving Zeek an inquisitive "How did they let you out?" stare.

Unaware of his bulk, he would stand next to someone he liked and then lean on them as a great show of affection. We were used to his physicality, but he didn't quite understand that this was not the best way to get a person's attention. If the individual Zeek targeted politely moved away, our enormous male would move closer and then attempt the same leaning-in stance.

"Zeek, go lie down over there," one of us would instruct him and point to one of his favorite spots. With an audible sigh and a hurt expression clearly displayed across his face, Zeek would move to another area.

If anyone sat on the living room carpet, Zeek would saunter over and lie down almost on top of them, smothering them with love.

"Ugh," was the sound that usually came out of the person caught underneath Zeek's weight. My husband or I would push Zeek away, freeing the innocent victim.

"Are you okay?" I would ask.

"That was close," someone might say with relief, once out of Zeek's clutches.

Zeek would always give an "I can't help myself" stare, which would trigger a round of laughter.

For many summers, my husband and I, with our previous dogs, backpacked along scenic trails carrying all our food and supplies. It was clear that food for this small horse would be too much for us to lug. Faced with this dilemma, I racked my brain until I found the ideal solution.

"I got it!" I exclaimed excitedly, entering our home a few days before our trip.

I pulled out a brand-new, two-saddle bike pack, and then strapped it around Zeek's torso. If the horses in the field could have seen him, they would have surely believed he was being fitted for a trail ride.

During the winter when I was pregnant, Zeek was an immense help with my ever-growing body. Quite a few times, as I clutched his collar while gingerly walking over patches of unforgiving ice, his solid-as-a-rock, 180-pound frame stopped me from slipping. My heart would race with the thought of the potential fall, but Zeek's strength never wavered, so I continued with my daily walks despite the harshest weather conditions. As my son's life began, surrounded by his extra-large buddy, he was unaware that any pet could be anything other than lovable and kind. One of my baby's first words was unmistakably "doggie," and by ten months he learned to crawl over this sizable animal that filled our tiny kitchen.

The times my husband was away for work, Zeek became my security system. If a stranger knocked on our door, all I had to do was cue Zeek to stand up, and the system was turned on. Even though Zeek was actually very timid, I was sure that no one would dare try anything untoward with this impressive beast looking on.

I remember one morning, though, when I was truly scared. A forty-something, rough-looking man appeared outside my home. My baby was just a few months old, and my husband wasn't there.

"Could you give me a boost?" he asked. "My truck battery died."

"Where's your truck?" I asked suspiciously.

The guy pointed to our closest neighbor's house. Down our rural road, there was a large hayfield between our home and this residence, so I could barely make out what type of vehicle it was. I hesitated, feeling very vulnerable about getting into my van with this stranger. I hoped this man was genuine, but I was frightened. The male picked up on my nervousness and repeated, "I'd really appreciate if you could help me. I just need a boost."

I thought it too convenient that he was able to veer into the neighbor's driveway just when his truck stalled. I wanted to help this man, but would I be sorry if I allowed him into my vehicle? I decided that the only way to appease my nervousness was to bring Zeek along for safe measure.

"Okay," I said. "I'll just get my baby and be right out."

I put on my shoes, picked up my son, and opened the door.

"Come on, Zeek," I called, and let him out first.

Always glad to be included in whatever was going on, Zeek accompanied us to the van. I opened the back door, and Zeek jumped right in. There was a curious look on this man's face, but he said nothing. I had no intention of getting into a vehicle without my security system; I didn't care what this man thought. We drove over to his truck, and I stopped the van, almost touching his vehicle so the cables would reach his battery. He got out, opened the hood of his truck and connected the cables.

"Thanks," he said once his truck started up and my mission was complete.

"No problem," I said.

My adrenaline was pumping as I drove back to my home. If Zeek only knew how much he helped me by just being himself. True to the Wolfhound reputation, Zeek was a "gentle giant," but I knew in my core that he would not have hesitated to protect me.

It warms my heart to think back on those memorable years with my comical, living breathing security system. Then I usually burst out laughing.

~Dalia Gesser

79

My Little Heroine

A dog is the only thing on earth that loves
you more than he loves himself.
~Josh Billings

The day I met Icey, she was at the local shelter with her mother and three siblings. She was about nine weeks old. She galloped toward me and jumped into my arms. I was smitten, but to be fair, I considered the others, including the mama dog.

The mama, Buttons, was an AKC-registered black Cocker Spaniel with an attitude. She had mated with a white Miniature Poodle from next door. The family brought her and her four puppies to the shelter after Buttons, who had gotten ornery after giving birth, had nipped their two-year-old son.

I feared they would put her down as an aggressive dog when maybe she really wasn't. I asked if I could play with Buttons. The shelter said she wasn't up for adoption. She was going to a special-needs foster home to be socialized and eventually adopted.

So I took home baby Icey. She was the perfect puppy. Housebreaking was a little stressful, but she came around eventually. I taught her many tricks, and she loved to perform. She liked to burrow deep into the bedcovers and come out and lay her head on my pillow like a human.

Icey was black with a small white patch on her chest. She was soft and curly and a very cuddly girl — with family. Strangers were her enemy. She was like a wolf that only loved those she knew as a cub/

puppy—others beware. My love for Icey was tempered by my fear she would one day bite someone, and I would lose her.

Until that fateful day when she bit the gas man, she had only growled at strangers, never bitten anyone. So I kept her on-leash or in the house. As a young mom with my older child in preschool, an infant who slept a lot, and my husband at work, I had a lot of alone time. Icey filled that space. I doted on her. Nothing was too good for my pup. I made her poached chicken and rice, baked homemade dog biscuits, brushed her endlessly and, in return, she was my best friend.

But I found Icey's personality to be a bit testy. She would growl at my children's friends, bark at strangers, and guard her toys—and me! She had a grumpy side that came out shortly after she was spayed. Maybe it was hormonal or hereditary, but whatever it was, she was an alpha dog all the way. She wanted to rule the household, and we let her.

One day Icey went too far, when a guy in a navy-blue uniform called out, "Gas man!" at my back door. I opened the door and he started to step inside but Icey shot straight past me and sunk her teeth into the poor man's calf. He was hopping around on his left leg with my dog hanging from his right. I began shaking all over. My dog was biting someone!

"Please, sir. Stay still. I'll get her off you," I squeaked as I pried her mouth open and pulled her toward me. In my arms now, Icey stared down the man and emitted a deep growl. The next thing I knew he was running away in his torn pants. I was in trouble. My dog had bitten the gas man!

I was worried. Was the man okay? Would animal control come and take my dog away?

I called the gas company. My plan was to apologize and offer to pay for the man's emergency-room treatment and torn uniform, share that my little Cockapoo was up to date on her shots and had never bitten anyone before, and pray hard that the universe would let me keep my dog.

I was directed to a department within the gas company that dealt with complaints. I explained, "I'm not calling to complain. I'm calling to confess that my dog bit one of your employees."

"Your name, address, and account number?" she rattled off. Then she asked, "His name?"

"His name?" I hesitated. "I… I don't know. It was short, like Jim or Joe or Bob. He had a nametag on his shirt, but this all happened so fast…." My voice drifted off as I tried to explain and hold back my tears.

"Ma'am," the woman said, clicking away at her keyboard, "we didn't send anyone out to your address."

"Well, maybe my upstairs neighbor," I offered.

"No, we didn't send anyone to your street or your neighborhood today. You might have just dodged a bullet," she exclaimed.

"Dodged a bullet?" I questioned, not understanding. I was still focused on my obligation to make this situation right.

"What did you say his nametag said?" she asked.

"Um, it was white with blue letters. It matched his blue uniform. He had a short name, Jim, I think," I answered, visualizing his nametag.

"The gas company uniforms *aren't* blue, Ma'am; they're Army green. Like I said, you dodged a bullet. Who knows who that guy was or what he wanted."

Years have passed since the incident. I never did hear from that man again. No dog officer came to my door, and no lawsuit was ever filed. In fact, as I look back on that incident, I am sure Icey saved me that day from a robber or a rapist.

That afternoon, after thanking the gas-company complaints woman, I quickly bolted my back door, checked my front door lock, and then called my upstairs neighbor, relaying my tale and warning her about the "gas man." Then I sat down with Icey in my lap and said a few prayers of gratitude.

~Ellyn Horn Zarek

80

Gulliver's Heart

Saving just one dog won't change the
world, but surely it will change you.
~Author Unknown

O n a hot, humid morning in July, the bell in the front
office rang, signaling the arrival of a client. With a sigh, I
straightened up, wiped the sweat from my face, set aside
my scrubbing brush, and walked to the front to meet the
client and the dog. Sara, a girl who also worked there, was going
over the details of Gulliver's stay. Meanwhile, I moved in to gather his
things and greet Gulliver.

I had been working for about a month at the boarding kennel
when Gulliver arrived. After working for many years in retail, I had
switched to a job where I could interact with animals, especially since
I eventually wanted to work full-time in the field of animal care. Any
experience I could get was welcome.

"Hello, sweetie!" I kneeled down on the floor and met Gulliver,
who greeted me with lots of kisses. He was a small, energetic, brown
and black Pit Bull/Labrador mix with shining brown eyes that were filled
with love. I knew right then that I'd enjoy taking care of this little guy.

As I looked him over, I noticed a rather large scar along his back.
No hair grew from the spot about the size of my fist, and his skin was
darker there. I looked up at Sara, and she whispered to me, "I'll tell
you later." While she finished the paperwork with the client, I brought
Gulliver to his kennel.

Later, I opened the door to let him out for a run. With a trot, he ran outside, and then quickly returned with his ears perked up and a look that seemed to say, "I'm pleased."

By the sound of other dogs barking, I knew Sara was approaching. "So, what's his story?" I asked, looking at the happy pooch.

"He was rescued from a guy who kept him as a fight dog," Sara began. "Except he would never fight when they put him in the ring."

My mouth hung open as I kept glancing between the two of them. So many of these animals were adopted and rescued from shelters, but I had never met a rescue from a fighting ring.

"His previous owner got angry with him and decided he didn't want him if he wasn't going to fight." Sara paused. She looked down at Gulliver and finally continued. "They brought him to the side of the road, poured gas on him, and set him on fire."

The scar.

My throat tightened as I looked down at this happy, friendly dog wagging his tail at both of us. This was a dog anyone would be happy to have. His loving personality and open heart should have brought him a happy life. Instead, his reluctance to fight had brought him pain.

Sara continued: "A passerby saw him running down the road on fire and managed to save his life. He was adopted as soon as he healed."

I kneeled down in front of the kennel, and Gulliver licked my hand through the gate. I opened it quickly and held him to my chest, trying not to cry. Gulliver let me hold him as long as I wanted, and I gently patted his back, feeling the scar each time. When I finally let go, he licked my chin.

Each day he stayed at the kennel, I took some special time to go to Gulliver's kennel and give him a hug, just like I did on his first day. Each time I hugged him, I remembered his story. And each time, Gulliver showed me the sweet personality that, in his previous life, made him a victim. Knowing that, despite his horrible past, he was now in a home filled with people who loved him as much as he loved them, made me smile every time I saw him.

Gulliver was a different kind of hero dog. He didn't save my life, but he changed it. He showed me that all of the love I put out into the world would eventually come back to me. He showed me it was okay to open my heart, even if it meant I would get hurt sometimes. More importantly, he showed me that love will always find us.

~C.M. LaChance

81

Teacher in a Fur Coat

*Dogs do speak, but only to those
who know how to listen.*
~Orhan Pamuk

After Hurricane Katrina, I went to Louisiana to take care of lost, rescued animals. There I met Sarah, another volunteer. Even though we live 1,000 miles apart, we stayed in touch after we both returned home.

Sarah operates an animal rescue organization in a very poor area of rural Virginia. When I viewed her website, a picture of Fred, a Red Heeler mix, popped up. My dog Bandit, a red Australian Cattle Dog (a.k.a. Red Heeler), had recently lost his best canine pal and needed a buddy with whom to run and play, so I asked Sarah about Fred. She told me that she'd rescued Fred from an angry man who'd thrown him around, stuffed him into a tiny chicken crate, and had planned to shoot him for chasing sheep, which is instinctually what the breed is supposed to do. Fred had trembled on Sarah's lap for a couple of hours while she'd assured him he was safe and promised to find him a loving home.

Sarah and I determined that Fred and Bandit likely would be compatible, and I decided to adopt Fred. A team of volunteer drivers would bring him to me in Wisconsin, and I would drive him from there to my home in Minnesota.

Fred and Bandit became best buddies, and I renamed Fred "Chase" for his love of chasing everything.

Eventually, Chase's love for people and his gentle nature led us to earn a therapy-dog certification and start a reading program at the local library. Kids read out loud to Chase to improve their skills. Sometimes, even a kid who is struggling with reading will be comfortable reading out loud to a dog. It's magical to watch how the kids react when Chase enters the library.

I recall watching one little girl jump up and down when she met Chase. Her joyful enthusiasm made me smile. Chase greeted her with a play bow, lowering his muzzle away from her face. She clapped her hands and said, "Look, Mommy, he's bowing!" Chase remained calm while she jumped, then snuggled in next to her on a quilt and gave her his undivided attention while she read him a story. When her time was up, she signed up to read again the next month. She didn't have a dog at home.

I'm grateful for everything about Chase that made this little girl jump so happily. I hadn't taught him to bow; he'd bowed naturally. I'd known the library visits would be about helping kids learn to read. But I hadn't realized what a confidence-builder those visits would be for kids who were shy or had been bullied or just didn't fit in. Chase was also a wonderful ambassador for dogs — teaching kids to be loving and kind to animals. I noticed, too, that a few adults regularly appeared at the library for Chase's scheduled visits. He looked for them, too.

As I watched the little girl's confidence grow, I hoped she'd always have the enthusiasm for reading and for dogs that she showed with Chase. He's very intuitive; he knew just what she needed. He led me into this work because he knew just what I needed, too. I wondered who was getting the most from our visits: the little girl, Chase, or me.

Chase was also patient with other children, like the little boy who came along one day with his sister. While she read to Chase, her brother sat at a table six feet away, as close as he dared get to Chase. As the girl finished reading a story, Chase was watching the boy. Chase rolled over on his back, waving all four feet in the air, as if to say, "See, I'm not a threat!" We all laughed, and by the end of the session, the little boy was sitting next to Chase, telling him a story.

About six months after Chase and I began volunteering at the library, I found blood in his stool and took him to the vet. My fears were realized as he was diagnosed with colon cancer. I learned the ominous fact that not many dogs survive colon cancer, but we had caught it early, and the vet surgically removed the tumor. She couldn't remove all of it without making a hole in his colon, so she referred us to the oncology vet. For almost a month, Chase went to radiation therapy every weekday to target the area where the tumor had been removed. This must have been very hard on him, especially since dogs have to be anesthetized for every treatment. But each morning, Chase eagerly approached the hospital as though he were making a therapy-dog visit for others.

To help cure the cancer, I put Chase on a low-sugar (no kibble), whole-foods diet and took him to the Chinese-medicine doctor. She prescribed custom-mixed herbs and advised which foods and supplements were best for him. Along with the traditional cancer treatments, I did everything I knew to promote good health, support his immune system, and help him heal. Two months after Chase finished treatment, a CAT scan showed no evidence of disease. Six months after treatment ended, a second CAT scan also indicated that the cancer was gone. The treatments had been very expensive, but well worth the cost.

It was time to get on with life. We resumed our daily walks and monthly library visits. Three and a half years later, after homeopathy treatment, Chase was still doing well.

One night, standing by my bed with his hot breath blasting at me, Chase barked loudly in my face. I rolled away and mumbled at him in my sleep. He jumped on the bed, lay down next to me, and nudged me toward the edge. I leaned back into him and pulled the pillow over my head. He grabbed the pillow and pushed it off. This wasn't like him at all.

Soon after, I was diagnosed with sleep apnea. During a sleep study, I stopped breathing in my sleep thirty-six times per hour. The doctor told me that Chase likely had awakened me insistently to save my life!

Sarah rescued Chase from a violent man. I helped Chase survive cancer. Chase, in turn, literally rescued me. This amazingly loving dog, this teacher in a fur coat, has been a lifesaver in so many ways.

~Jenny Pavlovic

Chapter 9

The Dog Really Did That?

Meant to Be

82

Roji, the Syrian Refugee

*You can usually tell that a man is good if
he has a dog who loves him.*
~W. Bruce Cameron, A Dog's Journey

Roji, our big, beautiful Anatolian Shepherd, is lucky to be alive today. Born in Syria, his chances of surviving even a year were not high. I met Roji, along with many other local Syrian dogs, while serving in Syria as a member of the United States Army. Some of the pups my teammates and I encountered still appeared young and hopeful, but most gave off an unmistakable sadness.

Syrian dogs have a tough life. Many are malnourished and roam the countryside, seeking and begging for food. Often, they bear physical injuries and trauma from abuse or war. The first dog I met at our camp, who became a bit of a mascot to my teammates and me, earned the moniker "Tripod." Tripod was partially blind, semi-deaf and, true to his name, hobbled about on three legs. Not an easy life at all, but sadly a reality for many dogs in the war-torn country.

While I was serving, a small puppy had begun frequenting our camp, and I decided I would like to bring him home with me to the United States upon completion of my deployment. I discussed it with my wife, and we both agreed that our two young boys needed a dog.

The puppy was perfect. Playful and happy, he even seemed to give ol' Tripod new energy. And then one morning, he unexpectedly died.

The medics determined it was likely canine parvovirus, a relatively common disease.

As sad as this made us, not more than a week passed before a new puppy showed up at our camp. The new pup was just as sweet. The way she cowered, it was evident that she was used to physical abuse, even though she was only a few months old. But no matter, she warmed to us quickly. Then, perhaps not surprisingly, she disappeared. The hardships of Syria had claimed another little dog.

Roji was the third dog to show up in our unit. By this time, I did not want to get attached. I only had a month before leaving, and I'd already lost two dogs in less than a month. I didn't even have time to name them. And the same was true for this one until a friend offered an idea: "Roji." The name comes from "Rojava," the autonomous Kurdish region of northern Syria where he was born. I liked it instantly, and it seemed appropriate to impart a little of his "native country" into the soon-to-be American.

So Roji came with me. I handed him off on the side of the road to a veterinarian in Iraq, not knowing if I would ever see him again. Through the help of an organization that works with soldiers and their dogs, he received his vaccinations and endured a month-long quarantine while I returned home to the U.S. Finally, I got the call that he was ready to be sent home to me. After hours on an airplane, he was dropped off at a cargo warehouse in the middle of the night. I met him at the airport, and he was so happy to see me. I was sure he remembered who I was. It almost felt unreal that he had finally made it.

Roji had a lot of adjustments to make after his grand adventure. His first day at our house, he barked continually at his reflection in the glass. But to be honest, I've done the same thing once or twice. And he hasn't figured out how big he's gotten, so he tends to knock down the kids when they play. But to prove he's fully immersed himself in American culture, he flaunts a curious underbite, which we call his "Elvis lip." Also, to let us know he's a normal dog, he regularly chews up our things, but I'm not sure it's on purpose. After all, he always covers our stuff with his actual chew toys, so he probably just gets confused. At least, that's what I think.

But in spite of his occasional destruction, Roji brings us a lot of happiness. He's a real-life teddy bear to the boys, a scratching post for the cat, and a loyal companion to anyone who rubs his belly. When my wife and I watch from our front porch as he runs with the kids in the rain, it's hard to determine who enjoys it the most: us, the kids, or Roji.

Roji sleeps easy these days, dreaming whatever dreams a dog has. He sleeps at our door, keeping guard over the only family he's known. And after moving from one extreme to the next, our world-traveling, Syrian refugee dog is finally home where he belongs.

~Brett Roberson

83

Saving Blake

The reason a dog has so many friends is that
he wags his tail instead of his tongue.
~Author Unknown

I still can't tell you exactly what first attracted me to Blake, a black Pit Bull at the shelter where I volunteer. Certainly, he was a handsome dog, with a regal stance and a ready wag of his tail. Most importantly, there was a look in his eyes that just drew me to him.

He quickly became one of my favorite dogs to walk. He was very business-like about it, not interested in playing with balls, and when we rested under a tree, he didn't cuddle with me like most dogs. But he watched me like a hawk, and kept up with every move I made. When I would put him back in his kennel, he'd briefly rest his head against my leg as if to say "thank you." He had a dignity about him, almost an aloofness that made him different from other shelter dogs I walked.

Perhaps it was a trust issue, but as time passed, he became a lot more relaxed and even happy to see me. I knew we'd bonded when he started hugging and kissing me, and even the staff noted that he was livelier when I came to see him.

When Blake was moved to a newer building on the shelter grounds, I didn't worry much about him. He had started coming out of his shell, and he would get more attention and socializing, and thus a better chance at being adopted. So I continued working with the Pit Bulls in the other building.

But after a few weeks, I started hearing disturbing things. Blake was growling at the kennel staff. He had to be kept separate from other dogs, and showed no interest in the potential adopters who walked through. Some of the staff members were afraid of him.

I went to see him, and though he seemed glad enough to see me, he was quieter than usual. I put him back on my list of dogs to walk, determined to bring at least a little joy to his day.

But Blake only deteriorated. I never once saw the aggression the staff had reported, but what I did see was even more worrisome. When I came up to his kennel, he only looked at me from his bed, not wanting to get up. He went on walks grudgingly, not enjoying himself much.

What finally scared me was the day I took him out and saw how his eyes had changed: They were blank, with a faraway look. Until then, I'd been able to get him somewhat cheered up after a long walk, but that faraway look told me he was somewhere else.

Blake was going kennel crazy.

It was the worst possible thing to happen to Blake. Black dogs are difficult enough to get adopted, and him being a Pit Bull only made it that much harder. I'd known all along he would be hard to place in a home, but as long as he had no overt problems, there was always that chance the right person would come along.

Now what chance did he have? I even wondered if putting him down would be best. It seemed cruel to contain a dog that was losing its mind.

But I had to try. I got the shelter's permission to take him to a trainer to have him evaluated, and he spent a day with Ashley Shelburne of Shelburne Pet Center in Shelbyville, Kentucky. Ashley specializes in Pits, and I was willing to accept whatever she thought best.

I was on pins and needles all that day, and when Ashley called that night, I wasn't prepared for what she said.

"Paula, there is nothing wrong with Blake. He can be saved. He's not aggressive. He just needs training and socializing. He's a good dog. I can help him."

I happened to be having dinner at a swanky restaurant with my colleagues when Ashley called, and I admit I caused a small scene with my crying and laughing. Then we all toasted to Blake and his new beginning.

So the next day, I visited Blake, paid for a month's boarding, and thought to myself, *Now what?* Now that Blake was in a place where he could get help, my first concern was money to keep him there. I just had to figure out how to get it.

It's good to have friends. Michelle Bruner, another volunteer, was quite fond of Blake herself and wanted to do something to help him. Using her motto, "Don't judge Pit Bulls by their scars. They don't judge you by yours," she made a video of him on YouTube explaining his plight. To this day, the video reduces me to a puddle of tears. Then she set up a ChipIn fund and put the link on Facebook, telling the story of how we were trying to save a very special Pit Bull. Blake's board fee was $300 a month, and while he was paid up for the moment, we figured it would take a while to raise the money for another month.

In two days, we raised $420. I was astounded. Soon after, a lovely soul donated another month's boarding. The money came from all across the United States, and we even heard from a woman in Great Britain. Before we knew it, Blake had his own fan club cheering him on.

"Will you send me updates on Blake?" asked one donor.

"He shouldn't have to leave boarding until he gets his forever home, and I would like to keep supporting him."

"Pits deserve the same amount of loving as every other breed of dog," wrote another fan, "and I wish people would see that."

A Pit rescue group posted, "So wishing he gets what he needs. I'm going to keep doing all I can. Please keep me updated on this stud muffin!"

Thus, with the money issue amazingly taken care of, it was time for the real work to begin: rehabbing Blake.

Shelter life is extremely stressful on dogs: it's incredible to me how well most dogs handle it and maintain a cheerful attitude. Blake simply wasn't that kind of dog.

But with Ashley, he led a completely different kind of life. The atmosphere was more peaceful — with activity, but not the frenzy of a shelter. Ashley introduced Blake to other dogs she had rescued through her organization, Tyson's Chance, and taught Blake to socialize with others. He learned to love and trust the staff, and they all fell in love with him. He started opening up, even playing, and grinned at everyone who passed by.

But everyone agreed that he was at his happiest when I came to see him. He went berserk whenever I walked through the door, and I don't think I've ever had a dog love me so much. I've heard it said dogs know they've been rescued, and now I was seeing it for myself.

Every day that I could, I picked up Blake and took him to a local park. I kept him on a long line normally used for horses, so he'd have room to run. For the first time in nearly a year, Blake got to chase birds, play in a creek, and poke around in the woods. He rolled in the grass and gave my face a thorough licking at the end of every walk.

And that was the only thing that bothered me: Blake and I had become so bonded that I worried it would be a problem if and when he got adopted. I would have given anything to take him for myself, but I couldn't give him the home he needed. I already had several animals, including an alpha dog who would never accept Blake. Blake would have had to have an isolated kennel. He also could not live with cats. And he couldn't be left alone due to his severe storm phobia. I lay awake nights wondering how I was going to find a home that met all his needs.

Meanwhile, Blake was blossoming. He greeted everyone we met at the park, asked to play with other dogs, and when I took him to a feed store, his eyes bugged out at the sight of all the people to be patted by and all the wonderful things on shelves to sniff. He got treats at the bank, the liquor store, McDonald's, and the coffee shop. I enrolled him in obedience class, where he promptly became the top student. I sent regular reports to his fan club on Facebook, and people everywhere cheered his progress.

I wish I had something better to say than a cliché about this time, but it was true: Blake's transformation was nothing short of magical. To go from a kennel-crazed dog, and a Pit at that, to a loving, joyous dog was the most beautiful thing I've ever witnessed. It created a bit of a transformation in me, too. At one time, I would have agreed to have this dog put down, never dreaming what love, time, and attention could do.

So it was a life-changing time for both of us, but it was also time to get serious. Blake had been in boarding for several months, and while Ashley assured me that Blake could stay as long as he needed, I was getting anxious. I was having visions of five years from now, still taking Blake to the park and the feed store.

Ashley recommended I start taking Blake to animal-rescue events to show him to the public. So when Saving Sunny, an organization in Louisville that rescues Pits, had their annual fundraiser, it seemed a logical place to take him. It was a fairly large affair, and another good test for Blake to see if he could handle all the hustle and bustle. And he did handle it well for about three hours, when he started getting anxious.

I had just told Ashley and the other volunteers that I was leaving when I heard a voice behind me say, "Can I see your dog? Is he up for adoption?" I turned to see a young man standing there. I said he could see my dog, and he knelt down in front of Blake.

And that's when it happened.

Blake flew into the young man's arms, wrapped his front legs around the man's neck, and proceeded to kiss him. I was astounded. For all of Blake's newfound friendliness, I'd never seen him do anything like this. I looked around at the other volunteers; they were gawking, too.

The man introduced himself as Austin Sheehan, a college student who worked at a local TV production company and had lived in Louisville for about a year.

"I've been wanting a dog for a while now," he said, "but I was waiting for just the right dog. I've been watching Blake and, well, he seems like the dog I've been waiting for."

After talking to him more, I raised a questioning eyebrow at

Ashley, who gave me a small nod.

"Austin," I said, "you need to know how special this dog is to me. If you adopt him, you adopt me, too. If that doesn't scare you off, how about Blake and I come to your house and do a home inspection?"

I went through every corner of the house and yard, asked a million questions… and could find nothing wrong. Austin had had dogs in the past, so he knew about training and routine. He shared the house with two other men, who promptly fell in love with Blake, too. A miniature Pin lived there, and Blake liked him fine. Most important, there were no cats, and with three occupants, Blake would rarely be alone. Watching Blake and Austin interact, I was convinced it was a lovely match. A few people had expressed interest in Blake before, but they didn't feel right to me. This one felt right.

When Blake went home with Austin, I'm pretty sure I was in shock. All the worry, all the drama… and he just waltzes off into the sunset? Just writing these words now, it feels like a dream.

Austin and I texted each other late into that first night. Blake, he said, was going through the house like he'd always lived there, and he sent me pictures of Blake playing with his new toys. I couldn't help but cry with happiness: this dog that had imprinted himself on my heart finally had the home he so deserved.

It was with great triumph that I was able to post on Facebook that Blake had found a home. The cheering response was overwhelming. Blake had become something of a poster child for Pits, and it was fantastic news for all the Pit lovers that, yes, it can be done. There were so many people congratulating Blake and me that I asked Austin to say something to everyone. Austin posted:

I have been very blessed to have met Blake. From the moment I met him, I felt connected. If it were not for all the hard effort from Paula and Ashley, this would not have been possible for Blake. I want to give him nothing but love and happiness, and all of you made that possible. Thank you all again for everything you have done. I know Blake appreciates it, and my heart is touched. I promise to show as much care and dedication to being a suitable father for Blake. I think I need Blake as much as he needs me.

~Paula Sparrow

Author's Note: To view the YouTube video, go to www.youtube.com/watch?v=0y-MjtKU0HI

84

Made for Each Other

*In the end, it's not the years in your life that
count. It's the life in your years.*
~Abraham Lincoln

Many years ago, I worked at a very small county animal shelter. Under the state regulations, we were only allowed to keep a dog for a certain length of time to be claimed by its owner. Unfortunately, we had a limited amount of space, and when a new dog came in, we had to make room for it somehow. It wasn't always the most pleasant task.

One day, about an hour before closing time, the warden arrived with a small, elderly, red Dachshund, her coat shot through with gray. We had no space and the warden asked me what we should do. My heart broke. Technically, we were supposed to let go of one of the dogs who had been there too long, but the volunteers had been putting in extra hours, bathing the dogs, and taking their pictures to try to find them homes. We were full, but the other dogs all stood a good chance of finding a home if they just had some time.

That little old Dachshund waddled over to me and sat at my feet. She looked up with cloudy eyes, and then curled up on the floor. I bent down, lifted her to the desk, and gave her a quick exam. Her teeth were in terrible condition, but it appeared the cause was a lifetime of canned food. Someone was surely looking for this pampered princess.

The warden came back into the office and plopped an empty cardboard box on the floor. To our surprise, the dog whined and wagged her tail. I set her down on the floor, and she waddled over and climbed into the box! We talked it over, and I said I would take her home for the night, and she could spend the days in the office until her owner came. That way, we wouldn't have to euthanize another dog to open a cage.

I finished up my paperwork while the old dog snored in the box. When it was time to leave, she followed at my heels as I made rounds and locked up. Even with all the noise of the kennel, she never strayed from my heels. I carried her box out to my car, and she jumped right into the passenger seat and curled up. Clearly, she was no stranger to car rides. When I got home, we had to make some adjustments since we had two dogs and two cats of our own, but she didn't seem to mind being put in the bedroom.

In the morning, she hopped back in the car and accompanied me to work. I cut an opening in the front of the box and added a blanket. She dug at the blanket and turned half a dozen circles, but at last lay down and slept most of the day. This went on for the next four days. No one came looking for her. I had started calling her Gretchen, and she charmed our volunteers with her sweet disposition. Her time was almost up though, and both the warden and his deputy did not feel she was adoptable due to her advanced age and the condition of her teeth.

At lunchtime, one of our volunteers told me she knew a woman who would love this dog. She lived alone and was quite well off. I asked if she could come right away and see what she thought. In less than two hours, the two elderly women — one with two legs and one with four — were sitting in the grass enjoying the warmth of the sun. I explained that the dog needed dental work, and the lady said that was no problem. I explained she might not live too many more years, and she replied it was perfect as they would spend their remaining time together. Our only hurdle was getting the spay requirement waived, due to her age, but once that was done, Gretchen had a new owner. The last report I got was that her new owner happily paid some hefty medical bills for Gretchen and the two of them spent their days sitting on the sofa and watching television.

I think they connected in a special way and were perfect for each other. So many people discounted that senior dog, but she was perfect for her matching senior citizen. In my experience, there is always a good match to be made — dogs and humans who are meant for each other.

~Anna M. Lowther

85

The Love of a Little Dog

You encounter a kind soul that resembles a loved one.
Your angel knows that you need a physical
presence for comfort today.
~Author Unknown

I t was my first birthday after my dad passed away. I was picking up some party decorations from a woman named Mary who always had tons of dogs to greet whoever came to the door. Usually her Labrador Retrievers would almost knock me over with their excitement. This time, there was a little dog mixed in with the Labs.

Mary said she found the dog when she went to clean a rental property. The tenants had left three days earlier, and she saw this little dog caged up with no food or water. "They just moved out and left him there," she exclaimed.

Mary took him to the vet immediately. The poor dog was very dehydrated, but was otherwise a healthy pup. She had him updated on all his shots and took him home to foster him until she could find him a home.

As we headed inside the house to get my decorations, this little dog kept following me. He was cute as he could be, with a dappled coat filled with black, brown, and white spots. His eyes were different colors: One was blue, and the other was brown. I hoped he would find a loving home.

After loading my car with the party decorations, I said goodbye to Mary and her dogs. When I went to get into my car, the little dog hopped in as well. I laughed, picked him up, and handed him back to Mary.

"Silly Baxter, you can't go with her," said Mary.

I stopped.

"What is his name?"

"Baxter," said Mary.

In that moment, I looked at the dog as if he were a gift from heaven.

When I was nine, my dad bought me my very first pet kitten. I named him Baxter after a cat in a commercial. This beautiful cat was my best friend, and as an only child, I clung to him when things got bad. When I was sick, he was there for me. When I graduated from high school, Baxter died suddenly from a heart attack at the age of fifteen. I hadn't had a pet since.

I asked Mary where she got his name.

"It was on his collar when I found him," replied Mary.

It was almost as if this little dog had been put there just for me.

My dad had been killed in a motorcycle accident just seven months earlier. My dad was my world, and as much as I didn't want to have a birthday party, my friends were pushing me to. For me, knowing I wouldn't get to hear my dad say "happy birthday" for the first time in my life was the worst feeling in the world.

I had decided that I would be sad for the rest of my life… until I saw this small dog. He was filled with so much energy, so much light, and for me — hope. Before I even knew his name, I knew there was something special about him. And finding out that he had the same name as the first pet my dad gave me was almost like my dad was right there saying, "Happy birthday, kiddo."

"I'll take him," I said. I took Baxter from her arms and put him back in my car. We headed to the pet store to pick up some doggy toys and supplies.

That birthday just happened to be my best birthday of all. Baxter is the only thing that could put a smile on my face after my father died. He gave me hope and a reason to smile.

A year later, my mom died. Losing both parents before I was twenty-five years old was hard. Without that little dog, it would have been harder. Baxter keeps me smiling, even in the darkest of times. I've learned that our loved ones who are no longer with us are still part of our lives. Sometimes, they just appear through the love of a little dog.

~Tammi Kelly

86

Paying It Forward

Rescuing dogs will tear your heart out, stomp on it and
bury it where you never think you will find it...
Then along comes another dog, that digs it
up and gives it back to you.
~Author Unknown

rescued Sparky in 2007, right before the Fourth of July. That is how he got the name "Sparky." Per my vet, he's a Jack Russell Terrier/Pug mix. His personality is definitely Jack Russell, but his build shows the heavier muscle structure and the round, soulful eyes of a Pug. Plus, he likes to lie down like a Bulldog, with his back legs spread out behind him.

His personality is all Terrier. He is territorial and possessive of his yard and family, which originally included only me and his "rescue" kittens — all grown cats that still sleep on top of their "daddy" on the couch or on top of his doghouse outside. Unlike my old Husky — who loved absolutely every type of flying, crawling, or climbing animal on earth and welcomed them into our yard — Sparky keeps a vigilant watch over his territory. Opossums, raccoons, squirrels, and pigeons — any creatures attempting to breach his walls — are immediately met with the fury of a tiny tiger.

He is friendly with other dogs when we are out for a walk, but he ignores them for the most part unless they are running loose and come after us. Then, he won't back down, and I have to take over to keep the peace.

That's why I was surprised when he seemed to befriend a little, yapping dog that was obviously trying to start something with him when we were out walking. Nobody seemed to care about the dog. He was constantly running out in the street, rain or shine. When we walked by on our daily outing, he would come charging out of his yard, dash across the street, and try to chase us down the sidewalk, yapping and snapping at Sparky's heels. Instead of getting riled up, Sparky would start wagging his tail and just maneuver out of reach.

I took that dog back to his house more times than I can count. The young woman always apologized and took him inside, but every day he'd be back out again.

I called Animal Control several times because I knew that the worst would happen eventually, and he'd be hit by a car. When that happened, he disappeared for a month and I figured his owners were finally keeping him inside.

Sparky wasn't satisfied, however. He would look for the dog when we walked past the house, and whine and pull on his leash. I noticed there was a foreclosure sign on the house, and soon a large moving van took everything away, leaving dark windows looking out at the street. That didn't stop Sparky. He still tugged at his leash and wanted to cross the street to go to the empty house, now sporting a Realtor's sign out front. I would have to pull him away to get him to go on with our walk. "The dog is gone," I'd tell him. "He's not there anymore."

This went on for two weeks, and Sparky was getting worse every day. Then one day, we ran into two friends walking their dogs and found out why Sparky was acting so crazy. The family had lost the property and moved on, but they'd left the little dog behind in the back yard with no food or water. A new gate had been installed by the Realtor so he couldn't get out. My friends had been bringing kibble to the dog, and the neighbor next to the house had put water out for him.

Everyone had called Animal Control about it—as I did as soon as I heard what had happened—but Animal Control told us all the same thing: The dog was considered "property" and belonged to the bank that foreclosed on the house. They told us they had been out once, and seen the food and water, so there were no grounds for animal abuse — even when we told them that it was the neighborhood bringing the food and water, not the Realtor. They said, "Call the Realtor."

I did. She told me in no uncertain terms to "Take a hike. It's none of your business what I do with the dog."

So I did. I took one of my old dog collars and a leash, hiked over to the house with Sparky pulling me all the way, opened the gate, hooked up the little dog and took him home.

Then I called the Realtor and told her that if she wanted the dog, she would have to come to my house and face me. I also put it in writing and tacked the envelope to the front door of the vacant house. Needless to say, I never heard a peep out of her. That was more than five years ago.

Sparky was overjoyed with his new protégé. I named him Foxy because he looked like a big, fluffy fox once he had been bathed and groomed. I took him to Sparky's vet for a check-up, to get his shots, and have him neutered and chipped. The neighbor next door to the vacant house told me when the people got Foxy as a puppy for their kids, so I knew exactly how old he was. He was just over a year old when they dumped him and moved away.

He's as big as Sparky now, only with tons of long, fluffy black and tan hair. The vet doesn't know exactly what kind of mix he is, but thinks he has Sheltie, Pomeranian, and probably three or four other breeds in him.

The biggest difference between the two dogs is that Sparky has the heart of a soldier, while Foxy is a total chicken. He is sweet and loving, but the abuse he received in his early life left him afraid of everything. At first, he always seemed to be apologizing and ready to be kicked or hit whenever he was reprimanded in any way. It took a lot of love, understanding, and very delicate handling to reduce his fear. I don't think it will ever be completely gone. Sometimes, the cats bully him, but his big brother Sparky is always there to protect him. One hiss from a cat sends Sparky to Foxy's defense with a sharp bark and snap at the offender.

The two dogs are inseparable. When we go for our walks, Sparky is in the lead, and Foxy is at his heels. He knows who his protector is, and so do all the other animals in our household. Sparky was rescued by me in 2007. Sparky paid it forward in 2008 by rescuing five kittens, and again in 2012 by rescuing Foxy. That's just the way my Sparky rolls. He is a very special little guy with a very big heart.

~Joyce Laird

Runaway

*Running away was easy; not knowing
what to do next was the hard part.*
~Glenda Millard

took a much-needed break from my management job one Saturday afternoon, looking for a bit of fresh air. I walked the parking lot, kicking pebbles, as my mind raced with work concerns.

Before I realized it, I was standing in front of PetSmart and a large sign that said: *Adoptions Today*. I couldn't resist the urge.

The glass door slid open, and my ears were filled with the delightful sounds of puppy cries, the pattering of claws on linoleum, and the barking of larger dogs. It was music to my ears. I wanted to snatch them up and give them all the love they deserved, but the reality of my busy job, and my beautiful Labrador at home, gave me pause.

So I admired from a distance, watching children tug at their parents' sleeves in hopes of taking home a puppy, and volunteers sharing the positive attributes of their canine friends.

Suddenly, something caught my eye. A volunteer sat quietly in the center of the large circle of commotion. At her side, just as quiet, was a sleek black dog, medium-sized with paws gently crossed.

The dog never looked up, and the tail never wagged, but something compelled me to join them.

"May I?" I asked, wondering if this shy creature could be approached.

"Oh, of course. She's very sweet, but shy. Her name is Lady. She's been in my foster care for a while," she said.

I knelt and let my hand settle under Lady's nose. Her eyes moved up, briefly taking me in, and then turning away. She didn't seem interested, but I felt compelled.

Her foster and I chatted for some time. The poor thing had been abused, which explained how reticent she was. Unfortunately, the harsh reality was that a black dog with minimal personality and maximum fear was very unlikely to be adopted.

In the time we talked, my hand was softly petting Lady's head and neck.

"Would you like to take her for a walk?" her foster mother asked.

"Yes, that would be great."

Lady and I walked the same path that led me to her. I watched her ears retract at loud noises; I saw her freeze as cars drove by. But generally she walked well, occasionally looking up at me. That short walk and those few glances were all it took. Twenty-four hours later, I gently eased her out of her foster's car and into my own.

I was overjoyed at the addition to the family, but it wasn't going to be easy.

Lady was confused, reclusive, and untrained. She chose to huddle in the corners of the dining room and to make that her bathroom, too. If a stranger was near, she melted into the wall, relieved herself, and shook uncontrollably.

I wasn't sure I had the time, skill, or patience Lady needed. And just one week into our adjustment, I had to leave town for four days. Lady was left with a competent friend and pet sitter during my trip.

The phone rang at my brother's house on my second night away. Lady was gone! My friend could barely pass on the details through her distress, but Lady had been frightened by something, the leash had fallen, and she was gone. I was hundreds of miles away and two days from my flight home.

Images of Lady alone in the woods or injured on the roadside haunted me every second.

Finally, on a Monday afternoon, I went home. The flight had been rocked with storms, and it only got worse. Raleigh, North Carolina was being pummeled with torrential rain and high winds. I needed to attend a meeting at 4:00 p.m., right in the heart of the storm. I drove past downed trees, pulled into a stranger's driveway, and waited for hail and wind to subside. I cried as I thought of Lady alone in the storm.

By evening, I was able to go home and focus on my missing friend. I donned old sweatpants, rain boots, a heavy jacket, and gloves, grabbed a flashlight, and headed into the thick woods behind my apartment. My pet sitter had scoured the woods for two days with no luck, but I wasn't ready to give up.

I trudged through sopping grass and long weeds; I called her name over and over again. I walked along stone barriers and peered through binoculars for a sign. It seemed like hours, but just as night was settling in, I caught a glimpse of something red behind the darkening trees.

I thought I saw a silhouette poking up from the heavy brush. But with the dark creeping in, I was worried my eyes were playing tricks. Then I saw the red again. This time, I knew. A clear outline of a dog stood on the hill about twenty feet ahead of me, with torn red material hanging from her neck.

"Lady, Lady, it's okay!" I called.

She didn't move. She didn't run, but she didn't approach me either. Within minutes, I had a bowl of dog food and was on my stomach crawling up the hill. She never moved. I tried to shut out fears of any injuries I might find.

With food in my left hand and a flashlight between my teeth, I eased toward her. Her eyes seemed glued to my every move. I set the food within inches of her, but I remained prone. Still no movement. Finally, I took a chance in the darkness. I lifted myself up and reached for the broken leash. With just fingers on the leash, I moved forward quickly, wrapped my arms around her, and lifted her to safety.

I carried her down the hill, along the wall, through the woods and up three flights of stairs to our home. We headed straight to a warm bathtub where I gently washed her muddy, matted fur and told her how scared I'd been. There were no visible injuries.

I lifted her out of the tub and wrapped a soft towel around her back. She sat down as I patted her dry. Then, suddenly, she rose up, put her front paws on my shoulders, and licked my cheek.

Lady never had another accident in the house, she only ran for enjoyment, and she slowly warmed up to strangers. She woke me each day by gently placing a tennis shoe on my head. She greeted me every night with that double-paw hug. And if a storm approached, she found her way to the bathtub. She lived life to the fullest and spent almost nine years by my side. She died in my arms four years ago, and I am forever grateful I took that Saturday afternoon walk.

~Joanne Moore

When Hootie Met Roxie

Dogs are not our whole life, but they
make our lives whole.
~Roger A. Caras

When Hootie met Roxie, he wagged his tail. At fifteen, our small, black-and-white Terrier was friendly but reserved around other dogs, preferring to accompany my husband or me on our daily errands in our town, Half Moon Bay. Hootie and I walked along Main Street that morning and were heading for our car when Hootie stopped to sniff a favorite tree at the same moment as a chocolate-brown dog with a white blaze on her chest. She was a mix as well, about his size, and looked like a long-legged Dachshund with a skinny tail. Hootie's Yoda-like ears perked up when he saw her. They sniffed each other thoroughly, while I chatted with Roxie's person.

Brett, a divorced dad, lived in town. His ex-wife, who had the kids, didn't want the dog. The kids, who visited on weekends, adored her. "I'd give her up but for them," he confessed. "I work long hours. The neighbors say she cries when I'm gone. She's a good dog and deserves better."

"I worry that Hootie's lonely," I confided. "Lee and I have always had at least two dogs since we married in 1986. But after losing three in three years, we never did get around to finding him a friend. And now he's old and set in his ways. Maybe he's happy as he is."

I glanced at the dogs. They stood side by side, sniffing the tree trunk like they were old friends. "If you'll trust me with your house key," I said, "Roxie can walk with us starting tomorrow."

Thus began our walks with Roxie. Everyone we knew said she was the perfect dog for us.

"We're not adopting her. We're helping her out and providing Hootie with company," I insisted. "Lee's seventy. I'm not far behind. Someday, when we're dogless, we plan to travel."

Roxie, at seven, was sweet and eager to please. After we'd been walking her for a week, I saw how her eyes pleaded with me when I returned her to Brett's silent house after our walk. I felt like a criminal leaving her there alone. The following week, I brought her home to nap near Hootie while Lee read and I worked on a story. She was friendly and affectionate, but not clingy. I liked that in a dog.

"She's so happy here," Brett commented wistfully when he picked her up after work. "Would you like to keep her?"

"She's a wonderful dog and always welcome to visit," I said, "but Lee and I have travel plans."

A month later, Roxie spent a week with us while Brett was out of town. Two dogs in the bed again felt comfortably familiar. Roxie loved my cooking, the dog-door to the back yard, and the sunny back porch. By the time Brett returned, Roxie was part of the family. He looked overjoyed when we not only agreed to adopt her, but gave him visitation rights whenever his children wanted.

"But our travel plans…" I said, after Brett left.

Lee, who sat on the couch sandwiched between dogs, shrugged and smiled. Hootie wagged his tail. Roxie yawned and gazed up at me with amber-brown eyes.

Too late, I thought, and joined them.

~Lynn Sunday

89

A Ticket Home

Here, Gentlemen, a dog teaches
us a lesson in humanity.
~Napoleon Bonaparte

The Prison Greyhounds group was excitedly milling about, inching forward in anticipation. I was right there with them. Bouncing on the balls of my feet, I caught a glimpse of the shiny Dodge Ram rumbling forward with the haul in tow behind it. I wove through the group to get a closer look.

The haul was a climate-controlled trailer with fourteen numbered doors along each side. Behind them rested professional racing Greyhounds newly retired from a racetrack in Daytona, Florida.

As the truck rolled to a stop, a hush fell over the crowd. Goose bumps washed over my arms and down my legs as I realized I was about to become a part of something incredibly special. The group was a mix of volunteers ready to assist dogs off the truck, and adopters like me who had waited weeks for this truck to arrive.

We were accompanied by families that had adopted Greyhounds before. They were standing there with their dogs, which wore fitted jackets and stood obediently by their new owners. The group was diverse, but everyone had one thing in common: overwhelming love and support for the beautiful athletes that were about to embark upon the next chapters in their lives.

Don't use an umbrella, even if it begins to rain. Stand back fifteen feet from the truck as the dogs unload. No hugging… The rules of the day ran through my head as I was reminded of the challenges these athletes face when they leave their professional racing lives behind.

The dogs were fully grown adults, yet in many ways they were just puppies. Familiar only with life on the track, they were not accustomed to people hovering over them. Receiving warm hugs from strangers was stressful; they needed to develop trust first. They hadn't yet learned how to climb stairs and were not familiar with toys. Simple things that otherwise aren't given much thought, like an umbrella, were foreign to racers and could startle them to bolt. Capable of running at speeds up to 45 mph, these dogs could run to a nearby town within minutes.

Fortunately, the group had planned for everything. A grassy area near the parking lot was designated for socialization. Buckets of water were already filled in case the dogs were parched from their travel. Volunteers were already matched to each dog's arrival. Each dog had its own color collar and matching leash for easy identification. Profile sheets were written and distributed to adopters so they could learn a little about each dog available for adoption.

As the driver fumbled to open one of the doors, the families of adopted racing Greyhounds took their positions at the front of the group. Their role may be most important of all. They were there solely in loving support, standing at the front of the crowd so the racers peering through the doors could see dogs of their own kind. As they nervously peered out from their doors, uncertain of what the future would hold, they saw happy retired racers with their loving families. It was a reassuring sign that everything was going to be okay.

"Cain!" The first door swung open as the President of Prison Greyhounds, Inc. announced the name of the first arrival. A friendly face, white and fawn, popped out from his compartment. I watched as he unloaded, tail wagging, happily strutting about. Cain was one of four dogs selected to live the next eight weeks in Putnamville Correctional Facility, where specially selected non-violent inmates would foster and train the Greyhounds for life outside of a racing kennel. The program is ideal. Retired racing Greyhounds learn basic house manners prior to their adoption into permanent loving homes while inmate-handlers gain job skills, teamwork experience and an opportunity to explore a better way of living before being released into the community. Confident and friendly, it was easy to see why Cain was selected for the prison program.

"Kodak! Jitney!" It was as if we were witnessing a rebirth. In many ways, perhaps we were. One by one, the compartment doors swung open, a name was announced, and a lean Greyhound was released outside. I walked toward the grassy lawn to meet the new arrivals. White and fawn, red, dark brindle… they were a rainbow of beautiful colors and personalities. One was nervous. Her ears flattened back against her head, and she seemed uncertain of her surroundings. Another was frightened, as still as a statue, his feet planted firmly beneath him. The next seemed outright pompous. His name was Fireball, and he stood proudly as he lifted his leg to urinate directly into a water-drinking bucket! The crowd erupted in laughter.

Still chuckling, I turned to share the laugh with my husband. That's when I saw Maverick. Bundled warmly in a forest-green coat, his chiseled muscular legs stretched up toward my husband, who had knelt down beside him. Maverick was sleek and strong, with soft fur that was black as night. Calm and tranquil, Maverick was gently eating kibble from the tiny palm of my five-year-old daughter's hand.

With his 103H-62442 identification tattooed on the inside of his right ear, we could look up his stats. Maverick had raced in thirty-nine races, winning one and placing second in five others. He had suffered a racing injury, a fractured right leg, but was fully healed now. Only three years old and weighing seventy-five pounds, Maverick was the largest Greyhound in the bunch.

They say you don't really pick which Greyhound to adopt; the Greyhound often chooses you. Watching Maverick with my husband and daughter, I finally understood what they meant. Maverick chose us to be his forever family, and we could not be happier to be a part of his retirement.

~Robin L. Reynolds

90

A Boy and His Dog

A dog teaches a boy fidelity, perseverance, and to turn
around three times before lying down.
~Robert Benchley

When my son was seven years old, he wanted nothing more than to have a friend. Although he tried to make friends, the fact that he was autistic and largely non-verbal made other children his age uncomfortable. As a result, he was rarely invited to group outings at the park, frequently asked to leave community-based social groups, and almost never had another child accept an invitation for a play date.

My son handled the rejection much better than I did. He told me that he had been praying that he would get a best friend and he knew that his prayers were going to be answered because of what a man told him in a dream.

When the "nice man" in his dream asked him what he wanted in a best friend, my son said that he wanted someone who would always play with him, and who would like to run around a lot but also be calm at times. This best friend would be there and help him feel better when he was sad, would stick by him when he was sick, and would never want to get away from him. When he told the man this, the man smiled and told my son that he had picked out the perfect best friend for him.

The following morning, my son happily told me all about his dream. I honestly did not know what to think. My son was a very factual person, so I knew that he had to be telling the truth as he saw it. I chalked it up to a child's overactive imagination and dropped the subject, hoping my son wouldn't be disappointed when his best friend didn't materialize.

The next night he had the dream again. In his dream, the nice man told my son he had picked out a puppy to be his best friend. This puppy would love to play, and would love to run around, but would also want to be calm and just cuddle. When my son was sick, the puppy would stay by him, protecting him. When he was sad, the puppy would lick him, and make him feel better. This puppy would love my son more than anyone or anything else in the world, and would be the very best friend that a boy could have.

When my son told me all of this while we were out running errands the next morning, I was shocked. My son, who rarely spoke more than a few words at a time, was calmly explaining paragraphs' worth of information to me. Despite this, what my son said next shocked me even more.

"Mommy, he also told me that I am getting my puppy today. She is a girl puppy, with black on her back, and brown on her belly. She is not very big, and will run up to me when I see her, jump up on me, and lick my face while she wags her tail. Her name is going to be Zorro, and I love her already. We need to go to the building and get her. She is waiting for me. The man told me."

Immediately after telling me this, my son yelled and pointed at a building on the side of the road.

"That's the building where my best friend is, Mommy!"

At this, I slammed on the brakes and yanked the wheel hard to pull into the parking lot.

My son had never seen that particular building before. He had never asked for a pet. He also had never talked that much before, nor had he made eye contact with me when we were talking. He had a hard time reading and writing, and would not have been able to make out the words on the sign that indicated that the building happened to be a shelter.

When we walked into the building, a small dog immediately

ran to my son, jumped up, and put her front paws on him. Then she licked his face. She had black on her back, brown on her belly, and a tail wagging faster than I ever saw a tail wag before.

Ten years have passed, and Zorro and my son are still best friends. Although she does not move around as well as she did when she was a puppy, she still only has eyes for her boy, loves him with all of her heart, and sticks by him at all times. When he is away, she refuses to eat, and only lies on his bed, any dirty laundry that he might have in his room carefully tucked around her. When he is sad, she whines, and licks him incessantly. When he decides to go explore the outdoors, she sticks to him like glue.

As I write this, Zorro and her boy are hanging out together, spending time with each other like all best friends do. Although her boy now has human friends, his dog, shown to him in dreams by a "nice man," will always remain his very best friend.

~Marybeth Mitcham

Chapter 10

The Dog Really Did That?

Four-Legged Therapist

91

The Forecast Is Sunny Today

The strength of a family, like the strength of an army, is in its loyalty to each other.
~Mario Puzo

t all started one clear summer day with a comfortable breeze blowing across the gentle hills of our horse farm. Gary and I had turned the horses out to graze when our barn manager, Ann, stepped from her truck cradling an emaciated Golden Retriever mutt she had rescued from a Dumpster. She dropped a bag of dog food by a tree, and I wondered what she was thinking. I could barely cope with all of Tracey's needs. There was no way I could care for one more living creature, no matter how cute.

Gary, a dog lover, knelt down to greet Sunny, saying, "Welcome to heaven on earth." I seethed. Sunny pounced, danced, sniffed, and peed to announce his arrival. Suddenly, he stopped and cocked his head. His gaze roamed across the vast green lawn and rested on Tracey, her long, blond hair falling softly on a cushion as she lounged in her favorite spot under a magnificent oak tree.

Sunny took off in a stumbling gallop, going airborne and landing squarely on Tracey's lap. He licked her cheek with the tip of his soft, pink tongue as if to say, "Hello, my princess. Here's a precious gift for you." Tracey's blue eyes sparkled; she laughed affectionately and repaid Sunny by gently stroking his chest. Introductions complete, Sunny lay next to Tracey while Gary, Ann, and I continued with our farm chores. At sunset, I collected Tracey in her wheelchair, then pointed firmly at Sunny and said, "Remember, Gary, he's the new *barn* dog."

We named the puppy Sunny because he brought sunshine into Tracey's life. She had been left partially paralyzed by an accident and this little puppy seemed to be just what she needed.

I still wanted the puppy to stay in the barn, though. Gary made a bed for him in the tack room. Sunny tried to sleep there but he was lonely and frightened. He scratched the door and barked nonstop. Gary visited him over and over again, but the dog would resume whining and barking as soon as he left.

Finally, Gary snuck him into the house and Sunny trotted straight up the hallway to the last bedroom on the right, where Tracey invited him into her bed. So much for being the barn dog!

After a few weeks, it was clear to all of us that Sunny would be found next to Tracey every minute of the day. They spoke to each other through their eyes, his paws, or her hands. They passed their time making up silent games. The "Paw Game" was their favorite. Sunny softly swatted Tracey until she covered his paw with her hand or rewarded him with a big hug around the neck. They never tired of lolling around all day in each other's company. It wasn't long before Sunny proved that he was a natural service dog — a guardian, companion, and helper. Tracey and Sunny knew this instantly, but I needed more proof.

One October morning before sunrise, I hustled everyone to get ready for a horse show. This was a new experience for Sunny, but I saw it as a performance test. I could hear the clatter of the horse hooves hitting the floor of the trailer as Gary clicked his tongue and gently pulled the leads until each horse was safely on board. Excitement was in the air; the horses nickered and lightly stomped their hooves. Sunny circled Tracey and wagged his tail in anticipation. Then we piled into the truck and took off.

We arrived at an arena where the sweet smell of hay, polished leather saddles, and grooming oil filled the air. Gary and I, dressed in fancy riding clothes, mounted our horses and headed toward the show ring. In the audience, Sunny sat watchfully next to Tracey, while adults and children asked to pet him or made light conversation with Tracey. Sunny created a bridge for people to overcome their shyness with Tracey; it was a wonderful gift of freedom and joy for all of us.

Yes, I was tardy in my fondness for Sunny, but after that first horse show, he had my affection and respect. From then on, Sunny went to every horse show and on every other excursion. He sat quietly at Tracey's feet under the table at restaurants, next to her at the doctor's office, and escorted us to church every Sunday.

Each week, Sunny proudly wore the handmade neck scarf that matched the church seat covers. As Tracey rolled down the aisle with us, the congregation waved and smiled at Sunny like we were in a parade. One Sunday, the pastor called us to the front of the church for a special blessing. Sunny sat next to Tracey as the pastor laid his hand on Tracey's head. To my shock, Sunny immediately put his paw on the pew next to Tracey and, together, they were blessed. Everyone smiled and clapped, astounded that Sunny knew exactly where to place his paw. Perhaps Sunny thought the pastor just wanted to play the Paw Game, but to me, it felt like a miracle. From that day on, the congregation referred to Sunny as Tracey's Angel.

Seven blissful years followed for Sunny and Tracey. But then Tracey became very sick. She lay quietly for hours, and her eyes no longer spoke to Sunny. He remained next to her by the couch where Tracey could occasionally lay her hand on his head. Then one day, time stopped, and Tracey slipped away forever.

Without Tracey, Sunny lost his purpose. For two lonely years, no matter where he sniffed, dug, searched, or patiently waited, Sunny's purpose never returned. And then we found him under a bush; the veterinarian said it was his heart. I knew it was his heart; it was broken.

Sunny was an extraordinary dog from the moment he joined our family. Endlessly loyal, he lifted our burdens and gave us the gift of simple joy. He redefined our family life and rekindled our spirits.

Moreover, Sunny taught me to keep my heart open, because I was the one who was blind to the miracle of our four-legged angel when he first arrived.

~Suzanne D. Cook

92

Animal Magnetism

Imagination is the eye of the soul.
~Joseph Joubert

"I think something's wrong with Biscuit," Mollie said, as Ron and I settled on the sofa across from her. "Look at the way he's sitting."

I went over to pat Biscuit's golden head, and he didn't make his usual murmur.

Ron, my life partner and Mollie's son, knelt to examine the dog.

"Sit, Biscuit," he commanded, and the normally obedient mutt stared mutely. "Biscuit, roll over," Ron urged.

Biscuit looked at Ron with an unwavering gaze. Ron patted the dog and rubbed his tummy. Then Ron investigated a little compartment near the canine's tail.

"He needs new batteries," Ron said.

"Thank goodness," Mollie said. "I thought he was sick."

Even before Mollie turned ninety-five and began having spates of forgetfulness and confusion, she enjoyed Biscuit and a series of action-oriented toys. And we enjoyed them, too. First, Ron discovered a blaringly yellow singing duck in a cheesy mail-order catalogue. The duck jumped up and down and flapped its wings, while warbling, "If You're Happy and You Know It."

Mollie was going through a period of depression, and Ron felt the bird might tickle her dormant sense of humor and jolt her back to joy. When the duck arrived on our doorstep, we outfitted it with batteries and drove right over to Mollie's. As Duckie jumped and flapped on the elegant glass coffee table, demanding that we all "Clap Your Hands," Mollie broke into a huge smile. She clapped her hands, stomped her feet, and even raised her arms to shout, "Hooray!"

But a grown person can only listen to a happy children's song so often. Just as the duck was losing its charm, Ron discovered a small cow that rolled over and mooed. Next, he found a parrot that parroted whatever we said. A big mouth bass wiggled its way through "Don't Worry, Be Happy," and Mollie was happy, watching the ridiculous fish rhumba its tail as it crooned the tune.

The silliness and cheerfulness of these toys boosted Mollie's spirits and anchored many of our visits. But while these creatures amused Mollie, they didn't satisfy her growing longing for a pet of her own. She had lost her husband and had moved from her home into a retirement community. Though Mollie was gregarious and popular, with lots of friends and activities, she felt an ache of loneliness when she was in her small apartment.

"I need a dog," she said every time we called or visited. Pets had been a big part of her life. But we knew, with her fragile sense of balance and her walker and cane, a lively dog could be dangerous.

Then one day, Mollie received a giant box from Ron's younger brother who lived in California.

Ron helped her pry it open, and there was Biscuit, a life-sized golden mutt, complete with his own bone, brush, and remote control. Carefully, Ron extracted the puppy from its shipping crate and installed the batteries. Then we took turns pressing the switch and commanding the dog to "sit," "speak" and "lie down."

Mollie was ecstatic. She played with Biscuit, and the pup became part of the family. We all spoke of him and to him as if he were real. And he was real, something tangible to touch and to talk about, a catalyst for conversations about Mollie's past pets, and a symbol of unconditional love at a time when so much was changing.

When her health faltered and she needed to move into assisted living, she gave her menagerie of talking toys to great-grandchildren and friends. But she took Biscuit with her.

"How's Biscuit?" we'd ask when we called or visited.

"He's fine," she'd say. Or, "I think something's wrong with him. He wouldn't sit up for a treat." Or, "He's so cute. You should come see."

As Mollie struggled with anger and sorrow about her failing health, her frustration growing because no one understood her, Biscuit remained a stalwart and loyal friend, there to add quiet empathy and comfort.

One night, Mollie died peacefully in her sleep. After a time of mourning, we shared her clothes and other possessions with friends and family. But we weren't ready to let go of Biscuit, so we brought him home. Our young grandchildren were delighted. We were, too. Every time we asked the pup to "sit" or "stay," we thought of Mollie and the light in her eyes when she talked about her Biscuit.

~Deborah Shouse

93

Sadie, the Miracle Worker

I have always thought of a dog lover as a
dog that was in love with another dog.
~James Thurber

Wolfy, my yellow Labrador Retriever, had a large tumor in his abdomen. He was losing weight rapidly and had only months to live. The vet recommended I get another dog to help lift Wolfy's spirits, and to motivate him to get up and go out for his walks.

I turned to my friend who worked at a rescue organization in Virginia. She was in the habit of sending me pictures of dogs that desperately needed homes, hoping I would adopt one. When I told her I was ready to adopt, she said she had the perfect dog for me. Then I received an influx of e-mails, each containing a different picture of Sadie, a beautiful black Labrador Retriever. My friend had remembered that I loved Labs.

Sadie was almost a year old. She had been abandoned along the roadside in Smithfield, Virginia after giving birth to her puppies. She had a prolapsed uterus and was in bad shape when she was found. She was taken to a veterinarian clinic where she waited four days to have her surgery until the clinic received payment upfront. She was recovering nicely at the organization's facility and was ready to go to her new home.

I met Sadie and her caseworker in Pennsylvania, and from the moment I saw her, I knew she was a special dog. But she had some issues. During the entire ride home, Sadie lay between the back and front seats, her chest resting on the console, and her head resting on my arm. She slept on top of me every night with her head on my shoulder. Whenever I left the house, she scratched at the door until I returned. There were wood chips everywhere, but I didn't care. What Sadie was doing for Wolfy was nothing short of a miracle.

Wolfy's health had improved almost immediately when Sadie joined our family. He was getting up, eager to go out for his walks, and was playing tug of war with Sadie. We were having a very warm winter that year, and Wolfy loved the water. So he decided to teach Sadie how to swim. I stood there and cried as I watched Wolfy chase Sadie across the open field at the dog park. Wolfy was acting like Wolfy again, and I was thrilled.

A month later, I took Sadie to the SPCA to be evaluated for their pet-therapy program. She passed easily, and we began making visits to nursing homes. Sadie was wonderful with the residents, and they loved her visits. There was one man in particular whom Sadie really liked. He always coaxed her up into his lap and stroked her fur while he told me his favorite stories about "the war."

Then one day, Wolfy's health took a dramatic turn for the worse. He wouldn't eat, couldn't get up, and was in tremendous pain. I took him and Sadie to the vet in hopes that she could do something to make Wolfy feel better, but he was too sick. It was time to let him go.

We put Wolfy on a blanket in the middle of the floor. Sadie lay down opposite him, her nose touching his. When Wolfy took his last breath, Sadie cried. She then got up and went over to the corner, lay down, and watched him intently as I hugged and kissed him goodbye.

Sadie and I stayed at my mother's house for a few days. When we returned home, Sadie wouldn't eat. Over the next month, I tried many different dog foods, but she refused to eat any of them. She did, however, eat my spaghetti dinner one night. So I made spaghetti often. She would also eat at my mother's house. I was baffled by her behavior for quite some time, but then I saw the common denominator. Sadie would only eat if someone was there to eat with her. Sadie needed a friend.

I took Sadie to the Connecticut Humane Society, where they had three yellow Labs waiting to be adopted. My plan was to bring one of them home, but Sadie had a plan of her own.

While waiting to meet the three Labs, Sadie sat down in front of a glass door and looked at a dog that was sleeping soundly. I peered inside and saw a white dog with black spots curled up inside a dog bed. I couldn't tell what kind of dog it was, but the flyer on the door said it was a German Shorthaired Pointer. It wasn't a yellow Lab, so I sat back down and didn't give it another thought.

After meeting the three Labs, I was taken outside to the play area so Sadie could meet the dog I had picked out. They growled and snarled at each other. Well, that was the end of that. Reluctantly, I agreed to meet the German Shorthaired Pointer. But before the volunteer would bring her out to meet Sadie, he told me why the dog was in the waiting area and not with the other dogs. She was terrified of them. She was also afraid of loud noises. She had tried to jump out of her stall by climbing the walls, and when she couldn't get out, she cowered in the corner, shaking and crying. She was taken to the office area where she became attached to one of the volunteers who took her home with him at night.

When she was brought out to the play area, I looked at her dumbfounded. Her ears were neither up nor down; they just stuck out. She wasn't a big dog; she just had very long legs. And she had the biggest, bluest eyes I had ever seen. As strange as she looked, it all worked on her. She was adorable. And in less than three minutes, she and Sadie were playing as if they had been best buddies all their lives. It was a done deal.

I had no idea what I was about to get myself into, but I said to the volunteer, "Sign me up."

I filled out all the paperwork and took our newest addition home. Within a few short months, Sadie had helped her new friend, Oreo, gain confidence and overcome her fears. And then Sadie overcame her own fear of being left alone.

These two dogs are closer than any two dogs I have ever had. They are best friends who sleep together, eat together, and play constantly.

Sadie is truly a miracle worker, and I'm thrilled to see the happiness that results for her, too.

~Lorraine Lush

94

Therapy for the Therapist

A good dog deserves a good home.
~Proverb

I was jogging on the beach when a fluffy, black-and-white puppy ran toward me with a ball in his mouth. A little boy trailed behind the puppy, calling out, "YoYo, come here!" The adorable puppy ignored the boy and plopped down in front of me, dropping the ball at my feet. He had a cute button nose, floppy ears, and a pompom tail. He looked up at me with expressive brown eyes and tilted his head as if to say, "Come on, let's play."

I threw the ball for him, and as he turned around to go after it, I noticed an upside-down black heart of fur on his rear end. I was smitten.

Then the little boy's father caught up to me and apologized, "Sorry, ma'am. My dog could chase the ball all day if I let him."

"That's okay. I'm glad to play with him," I said. "He sure is a cute dog."

By now, my husband had joined us, and we continued to talk about YoYo, who was seven months old. The owner lived about six hours away and had stopped here at the beach to give the puppy and his son a chance to get some exercise.

And then he said something that shocked me. "YoYo seems to like you. Would you folks be interested in having this puppy?"

"Did you just ask us if we wanted your puppy? Why would you give away this adorable dog?" I inquired.

"We have two other dogs and a business to run. We can't take care of all of them right now. When we get to Los Angeles, I will have to turn YoYo into the animal shelter unless I can find a home for him," the man replied.

How bizarre! This dog was a Shih Tzu, an expensive breed.

Our seventeen-year-old dog had died six months earlier, and we had agreed that we wouldn't get another one for a while. My husband took me aside, and he was emphatic. "We agreed we'd have no more dogs right now. Yes, YoYo is adorable. No, I don't want anything bad to happen to him. But we can't take him. We know nothing about this dog."

I looked at my husband with puppy-dog eyes. "Honey, this is synchronicity. We were here for a jog. YoYo was here for a run at the same time. This was meant to be. We are in the right place at the right time to save him."

Now I was begging. "If we don't take YoYo, who knows what will happen to him. You know what animal shelters do when dogs aren't adopted after a period of time. They are euthanized!"

My husband rolled his eyes, but finally caved in. "I'm doing this against my better judgment," he insisted. "But I really like this puppy." The owner gave us his bowl, blanket, and leash — and YoYo, of course.

That night, YoYo was so content. He snuggled in, sleeping between my husband and me. I kept thinking how elated I was that we had rescued him. I shuddered to think what would have happened to YoYo had we not taken him.

The next day was a different story. We were invited to a party and would be leaving YoYo alone for a couple of hours in the bathroom since he wasn't housebroken.

Upon our return, we heard strange noises coming from the bathroom, and when my husband looked inside, he exclaimed, "Oh, my gosh! What happened in here?"

The hot and cold faucets were running full blast. Toilet paper was strewn throughout the room. The molding around the door was chewed into splinters as high as YoYo could reach.

My husband fumed. "Now I know why the previous owner was so intent on giving YoYo to us. It looks like he suffers from separation anxiety. That's why this expensive dog was free."

I chimed in, "He will be okay. We just need to work with him."

My husband decided that YoYo needed a new name. Maybe that would help change his behavior. We decided to call him Timmy. It fit his cute demeanor.

Timmy could not be left alone in the house but we didn't have a fenced-in yard. We went to our vet for advice. He said that maybe Timmy had been taken away from his mother too early and didn't get the chance to bond with her, which could have made him anxious. He suggested that we have him neutered. We did that, with little effect.

Next, we hired a dog behaviorist. Her advice was to leave the dog briefly and come back after short intervals. Not much change. We put him in the kitchen in a pen that would give him ample room to roam. Not much change. We left the TV or radio on while we were gone to give him company. He made very little progress. We recorded our voices on a CD and played it while we were gone. He continued to freak out when we left him. Barking incessantly, hyperventilating, he was a nervous wreck when left by himself.

Nothing worked! After six months of dealing with the separation anxiety, my husband was getting to the end of his rope. "I like Timmy," he said, "but we can't go anywhere without taking him with us. I think we seriously need to consider finding him a home where his owner can be with him all the time."

I had become so attached to Timmy. I knew he came into our lives for a reason. I had to do something quick to keep him. I saw an advertisement on the board at our vet's office for therapy dogs wanted at our local hospital. That gave me an idea. Maybe Timmy needed to feel more confident. After all, we really didn't know what he went through before we got him.

I decided to train Timmy to become a therapy dog. He needed to pass a test that would require him to sit and stay, leave food on command, be able to be around loud noises in a hospital, and have a calm temperament that would allow strangers to pet him.

It took about six weeks of working with Timmy before he was ready to take the test. At that time, he was a year old. He passed with flying colors. Visiting patients at the hospital proved to be just what the doctor ordered for Timmy. He did so much good for everyone. We watched blood pressures go down and patients perk up. The staff looked forward to his visits. As he pranced down the corridors of the hospital, this proud, perky guy brought smiles and accolades as he made people feel better.

Today, Timmy is eight years old. After seven years as a pet-therapy volunteer, he is a seasoned pro. And we can leave him alone now when necessary.

~Patricia Boyer

95

The Big, Black Dog that Stole My Heart

My therapist has a wagging tail.
~Author Unknown

When my boys were little, I rarely thought about what it would be like when they grew up and moved out. If I did think about it, I imagined them living across town, not halfway across the country. Then my son Ben was offered a job 2,000 miles away. In just nine short months, he would graduate from college and move clear across the country.

I understood this was good news, not bad news. This was what we raised our kids to do: to be independent and self-sufficient, and to have the skills and confidence to make a life for themselves away from home. But I felt like I was in the midst of postpartum depression, only in reverse. I didn't know this was something that sometimes happened to women when their children grew up. I was sad all the time and broke into tears for no apparent reason.

One day, I walked into the library while the therapy dogs were there. As a children's book author, it warmed my heart to see children sitting on pillows, reading aloud to dogs. It reminded me of when I took my boys to the library and we checked out huge stacks of books. We would read them on the couch with our Cocker Spaniel, Molly, wedged in beside us.

Oh, how I missed those days.

Then it hit me. Maybe what I needed to cope with my impending empty-nest syndrome was a new project. Maybe I should get involved in the Pet Partners R.E.A.D. program.

By then, our Molly was too old and arthritic to become a registered therapy animal. Our cat, Ashley, was an even less likely candidate. And my husband felt that two pets were enough for our family. Whenever I broached the idea of a second dog, he'd tease me: "Who do you want to replace... Molly or Ashley?"

But I started scanning listings on petfinder.com anyway, searching for a dog I might train to be a therapy dog. A listing for Mowgli, a nine-month-old, sixty-pound mix, with a lot of Retriever in him, caught my eye: *Mowgli never met a person or animal he didn't like.* That part sounded good. But sixty pounds? That was way too big.

Yet, I couldn't get Mowgli out of my head. I wanted to meet him. I sent the link to Mowgli's listing to my husband.

As predicted, his response was, "Who do you want to replace... Molly or Ashley?"

I said, "Ben! He's moving out. We're 'replacing' him."

Surprisingly enough, that worked! My husband supported my plan to get involved in the R.E.A.D. program and agreed we could consider another dog.

But was Mowgli the right dog? We wouldn't know until we met him.

A shelter volunteer brought him to our home. He was *big*. Bigger than we expected a sixty-pound dog to be. And he was a bundle of energy.

But he was sweet, too. And so cute! He looked like a black Golden Retriever. He made us all laugh when he caught a treat in his mouth. We'd never had a dog who could do that.

I asked why he was at the shelter.

The shelter volunteer shrugged. "He's a big, black dog. Big, black dogs are always the last to be adopted."

I didn't care about color, but I was worried about size. Could I handle a dog that big?

I took him for a walk to find out. It wasn't as easy as walking Molly. He pulled on the leash. A lot. But with training, that would get easier. We decided to adopt him.

We needed to change his name because "Mowgli" sounded too much like "Molly." We'd call one dog, and both would come. We tried out Shadow... Charley... Mouse...

"Wait... Mouse?" I said. That one was Ben's idea. "For a sixty-pound dog?"

"Yes. It's ironic," he said.

"It's weird," I countered. But irony won, and Mowgli became Mouse.

Next, we took Mouse to the vet. Mouse didn't weigh sixty pounds; he weighed eighty-seven pounds! And he was underweight! The vet wanted to see him closer to 100 pounds.

In other words, Mouse was big now, but he was going to get even bigger. I started having second thoughts. But I wasn't someone who returned a dog to the shelter.

We signed up for obedience classes.

"What a sweet boy," the teacher said on the first night. "Do you know anything about therapy dogs? He'd make a great one."

She had no idea that was my goal when she said that.

Mouse and I completed basic obedience, Canine Good Citizen, advanced obedience, and Rally, and then we started working on the skills necessary to pass Delta Society's (now Pet Partners') team evaluation.

Then Ben moved out. The days leading up to that were difficult for me, but once he was gone and settling into the new job, I was fine. Training Mouse really did help me cope with my empty nest. And now we had an evaluation to prepare for.

We passed! *A well-bonded team*, our evaluation read. *Highly recommend for service.* And we were welcomed into the local therapy dog group.

But participating in the library's R.E.A.D. program presented new challenges. Not everyone wanted to read to a big, black dog. Some children were afraid of him, just like I was hesitant to adopt him.

Mouse could always tell when someone was afraid of him. He didn't like it if a child or even another dog was afraid. He would get down on the ground and make himself as small and non-threatening as possible. And that often worked! The fearful child or dog gave him a chance. Anyone who truly gave him a chance fell in love with him.

I started taking Mouse with me when I visited my dad, who was in a nursing home. One day, a man called to me from inside one of the rooms. He wanted to know what my dog's name was.

"Mouse," I replied.

"Mouse? What kind of name is that for a dog that size?"

It turned out to be the perfect name for a therapy dog because it's a conversation starter. The man's name was Jim. He said Mouse reminded him of the dog that worked with his unit in Vietnam. For the next twenty minutes, he told me all about that dog and his time in Vietnam.

When we left, a nurse stopped us. "How did you do that?" she whispered.

"Do what?" I asked.

"Get Jim to talk?" Apparently, he'd been at the nursing home for a week, and despite the staff's best efforts, hadn't said a word to anyone. Yet I'd just had an entire conversation with him.

But I hadn't done a thing. It was all Mouse.

Mouse is retired from therapy work now, but he still makes friends wherever he goes. Every now and then, I remember how worried I was about adopting a big dog, but adopting Mouse was one of the best decisions I've ever made. He was the right dog at the right time.

~Dori Hillestad Butler

Rex to the Rescue

You see, sometimes in life, the best thing for
all that ails you has fur and four legs.
~Mark J. Asher, All That Ails You:
The Adventures of a Canine Caregiver

Once, when I was practicing clinical psychology, I had a young client named Katie. She was a typical six-year-old — cute, curious, and full of energy. Katie loved Barbies, Disney movies, and playing outside.

Her mother was seeking counseling for her because she had recently been through a traumatic experience during which she was almost abducted. Katie was grabbed by a stranger, but just as he was attempting to shove her into his car, he was scared off by her brothers.

Understandably, after the incident, Katie was terrified of going outside.

For several weeks, she and I engaged in exercises consistent with standard play therapy, as she gradually opened up to me about her life and fears.

She told me about her older brothers, who were typical boys with all their various antics and associated cooties. She told me about her room and favorite books. She told me about ice cream, which she loved, and broccoli, which she did not. And she told me about Rex, the beloved family dog and a gentle giant who didn't seem to realize he was a 120-pound Rottweiler, not a three-pound Chihuahua.

One of the activities we frequently engaged in was a simple drawing game. Katie would draw a picture of herself playing. I had to guess where she was and what she was playing with. Then, I would draw, and she would guess.

This activity was a catalyst for conversations about feelings. Gradually, I moved the play scenes to the outdoors. One day, I asked her to draw herself playing outdoors. Hesitantly, she drew herself at a swing set outside her apartment building. When I asked Katie if she liked to play on that swing set, she said she used to, but didn't anymore. When I asked her why, she shuddered and said she was afraid.

That was enough for that day's session. We were taking things nice and slow, so we hung the pictures on the wall for another time.

The next week, we looked at our pictures again. This time, I asked her to draw into the picture why she was afraid to play on the swing set. Katie added an ominous, black car with dark windows. Once again, we hung the picture up on the wall to be revisited later.

The following session, I asked her to draw another picture of herself playing on the swing set. When she completed this, I asked her to draw into this picture something that would make her not afraid anymore.

I expected she would draw in her big brothers, or perhaps her parents or other adults. From there, we could work toward developing a schedule of outdoor play, where these protectors would spend decreasing amounts of time with her until she felt comfortable without them.

Katie thought about it for a long time and then gave me a knowing look. She turned around, shielding the drawing from my sight as she worked on it. When she was finished, she spun around, clutching the drawing to her chest.

I asked her if what she drew into the picture would make it okay to play on the swing set again. With a huge smile on her face, she nodded vigorously.

I asked her if she wanted to show me what she drew. Proudly, she turned the picture over and held it up for my review. There, next to Katie by the swing set, was Rex, with a huge, toothy grin on his face, too.

Katie came back for one more session the next week to say goodbye and draw me one more picture of herself with Rex. I hung it in my office to remember her by. She had reached her therapy goal and now had other things to do with her time — like play outdoors with Rex.

As often happens, the therapy took its own course. I had a well thought-out plan of action for gradually giving Katie back her sense of safety. But in the end, Katie and Rex had a plan of their own.

It was her brothers who intervened in the initial incident and kept their sister from harm. But it was Rex who made Katie feel safe again.

~Donna L. Roberts

97

It's Mutual

He is your friend, your partner, your defender, your
dog. You are his life, his love, his leader. He
will be yours, faithful and true, to the
last beat of his heart.
~Author Unknown

When we met our German Shepherd, Kane, for the first time, we weren't sure what to expect. Kane was a rescue; his previous owners could no longer take care of him since they were downsizing to an apartment. They gave him to an organization that specialized in pairing dogs with combat veterans dealing with Post-Traumatic Stress Disorder (PTSD).

My husband is a retired Marine who was part of Operation Iraqi Freedom and Operation Enduring Freedom. After his third tour, he was diagnosed with severe PTSD. His therapist thought that a service dog would be beneficial to him so that he could have someone else besides me to help him deal with nightmares and the stress of being outside our home.

We were very excited and nervous to meet Kane. It was explained to us that the pairing might not go well since Kane had been going through a period of depression since being surrendered. The organization assured us that if this didn't work, they had another dog in mind for my husband.

When they brought Kane out into the field where we were waiting, they instructed me to step away so that my husband could meet him first. My first thought when I saw him was, *Wow! He is a big dog.* I have been around German Shepherds my entire life, but he was definitely one of the bigger ones I had seen. He topped the scales at over 100 pounds. It was a bit overwhelming at first.

I was a little nervous about this meeting not going well. As the kennel owner brought Kane over to my husband, I held my breath. My husband gingerly put his hand out so that Kane could smell him, and Kane immediately bypassed my husband's hand and jumped up to give him kisses. The people at the kennel cried because they were so relieved to see Kane acting happy instead of depressed.

After Kane finished kissing my husband, he came over to me. I was eight months pregnant at the time and I think he could tell, because he didn't jump on me. Instead, he licked my hand, and we instantly had a bond.

After six months of training, Kane was able to live with us full-time and be of invaluable assistance to my husband. He is in tune with my husband's moods and is able to help him deal with the aftereffects of war. I'm relieved because there's someone else who understands and supports my husband, and Kane is relieved to have found the right family for the rest of his life. It's a classic case of mutual "rescue."

~Lori Hufty

98

What the Little Dog Knew

Dogs have a way of finding the people who need them,
filling an emptiness we don't even know we have.
~Thom Jones

n a wheelchair beside the nurses' station, a tiny old woman sits, eyes closed, lips parted, hands folded in her lap. Her head droops to one side. Ragged wisps of white hair stray across her forehead. Her nightgown is rumpled; one slipper has dropped to the floor exposing a pale, veined foot. Maybe she's asleep, perhaps even comatose. Visitors pass. A nurse rushes by, jostles her wheelchair, and offers no apology. No one acknowledges her presence. It's as if she's invisible.

As nursing homes go, it's a good one. It's clean, almost pristine. The furnishings are expensive and tasteful, and the staff's white uniforms fairly rustle as they pass. Vivaldi plays softly in the background. A large vase of fresh-cut flowers is centered on an ornate metal table in the foyer. They try hard. But it is still a nursing home, where no one wants to be.

I've come to visit a friend, and since they allow dogs to visit, I've brought my Boston Terrier, Jake, to cheer her up. I'm annoyed that the staff has left this pitiful, old woman in the middle of the main hall, so that everyone has to walk around her. *It certainly doesn't do much for the facility's image,* I think to myself. I give her a wide berth as I pass, averting my eyes.

But Jake stops, sits down by her wheelchair, and refuses to move.

I tug at his leash. "Jake, come! Jake! Let's go!"

He's usually pretty good on the lead, but this time he's having none of it. Apparently, he thinks he has reached his destination. I'm in a hurry and more than a little frustrated. I change my mind when the old woman suddenly opens her eyes and raises her head. A smile slowly spreads across her weathered face at the unexpected sight of a little dog at her feet. Her watery eyes twinkle. A soft voice breaks the silence.

"Well, hello there! And aren't you a pretty little thing?"

To my astonishment, she is entirely lucid. Her voice carries a certain honeyed lilt, characteristic of finishing schools for proper southern ladies in her day. A bony finger reaches down and strokes the little dog's ear. He stands, reciprocates with a swift lick of her finger, and then sits again, tongue sidewise, looking up expectantly. They regard each other silently. She reaches down and gently strokes his back.

"What's his name?" she asks.

"Jake, his name's Jake."

"That's a good name for him. Just suits him. I love Boston Terriers." She smiles at me. "We used to have two of them: Maggie and Max. We got them as puppies from the same litter. They were inseparable. Two peas in a pod. They lived to be almost fourteen years old! Max died first, and within a few months, we lost Maggie, too. She died of a broken heart, poor little thing. Missed her buddy so badly, she'd hardly eat."

"I'm sorry."

"Oh, well, that was a long time ago." She straightens in her chair, pushes her hair out of her face.

"Well, goodness me, I've lost a slipper," she says, looking down, color rising in her face.

"Here, let me get it for you."

"Oh, thank you, dear. That's so kind of you."

"My pleasure. Would you like to hold Jake for a few minutes?"

"Oh, no, my skin is so fragile. But if you want to hold him up…"

"Of course! Here!" I lift him up, bending over to chair height so she can pet him.

"He's so soft. I'd forgotten how soft they are," she strokes his ears. "So soft…"

Jake's large eyes bug out in solemn appreciation.

"Does he like to play?"

"Oh, yes, he loves to play with toys, with other dogs, with anyone, really. He's very good with children."

"Our Maggie didn't like children. Don't know why…" Her voice trails off. Her attention has shifted to something else, something I can't see.

She turns to me suddenly, a bright smile on her face. "Susan? Oh, I knew you'd come. I'm so glad to see you. And you brought Maggie! It's been so long since I've seen her… She's so soft. So soft…" Her voice is fading now. Her eyes are closing.

It's time to go.

As I walk away, I see people I hadn't noticed before. People with walkers, in wheelchairs, sitting alone on sofas. Tears well in my eyes. I consider myself a caring person, and yet I had rushed past all these people as though they were scenery. I tell myself I was busy, didn't know these people, or might upset them. But the truth is, I didn't know what to do.

But Jake knows. It doesn't matter to him that the woman is elderly and disabled, that others ignore her. He isn't afraid of her. She offered him love, and he simply returned it. He wasn't in a rush; he lives in the moment. In that brief encounter, his simple gift of love worked a miracle on the woman in the wheelchair, and just as importantly, on me.

We started therapy-dog training the next week. Since then, we have visited many nursing homes. Each time, I witness a miracle. A woman who babbles incoherently suddenly speaks clearly to Jake as he looks up at her. An Alzheimer's patient who doesn't speak and "dislikes" dogs smiles as he holds Jake in his lap. A younger man, bedridden with ALS, chuckles as I place Jake on a pillow next to him.

I can't explain these little miracles; I only know they continue to happen. And when I tell the nurses, they aren't surprised.

"Oh, we see that all the time," they tell me.

Perhaps these aren't miracles at all; perhaps there is a perfectly logical explanation. It really doesn't matter. What matters is the transformation in another person's life that a simple act of kindness can bring about.

Thanks, Jake, for teaching me that.

~Louise Canfield

99

Dialysis and the Doberman

When an eighty-five-pound mammal licks your tears
away, then tries to sit on your lap, it's hard to feel sad.
~Kristan Higgins

D ialysis, the dreaded D-word. It goes hand-in-hand with denial, depression, and even death. Dialysis is something I never wanted to face, but here it was knocking at my door. I had known it was coming. The doctor had introduced me to the possibility of kidney failure years ago, but I never believed it would really happen to me.

Doing something crazy is not my usual M.O. when facing a critical point in my life, but this time I did. I got a dog, a puppy no less, and to top it off, a Doberman puppy. My friends told me I was crazy, insane even. They would say, "You're starting dialysis. How can you possibly care for a puppy?"

"Nuts," they said. "Pure nuts!"

But they hadn't seen the picture I'd seen. I knew from that photo that he was meant to be mine. After all, how hard can a puppy be? They are so little and, oh, so cute.

My first clue was traveling to North Carolina to pick him up. On the return trip, I thought perhaps my friends had been right. Due to my decreasing health, I had to pull off the road several times to be sick. I never thought once about taking him back, though. He had me at the first lick.

I named him Second Chance because I was soon to be on the transplant list. He would be with me during my dialysis and stay with me during my second chance at life.

My life soon consisted of nothing but the dialysis center, sleeping, and hoping for the call. A fog enveloped me like a wool curtain, dark, dreary, and too heavy to throw off. But a little Dobie nose poked right through the fog and let the light in. He was determined I feed him, walk him, and play with him. Because of his energy, we also went to obedience school.

Chance made me keep going. When I could stand, we trained. When we walked, it was only a few blocks down the street. I saw the sunshine in the morning because he had to be fed. With determination and four paws, Chance pulled me out of the fog of depression. In fact, he demanded I rise above it. How could I resist his wet nose, wagging tail and abundant happiness, no matter what state I was in? He pulled me through dialysis like pulling a drowning person to shore. Then, once he got me there, he licked my face as if to say, "Come on! Keep going."

When Chance was nine months old, I got the call for a transplant. He stayed with friends while I was in the hospital. When I got home, he greeted me with his abounding love and huge paws. Without him, I don't know if I would have been healthy enough for the surgery. He helped me avert death. The dreaded D-word has, for me, been replaced by a much more delightful D-word — dog. It goes hand-in-hand with devotion, determination, and Doberman.

~Caroline Brown

100

Are You in There?

*Sadness flies on the wings of the morning and out
of the heart of darkness comes the light.*
~Jean Giraudoux

Reincarnation is such a speculative subject. We hear stories all the time about feelings of déjà vu, of instant connections with strangers, of all the romantic, eerie, and surprisingly compelling moments that suggest we not only have lived before, but have loved before. But rarely, if at all, have we heard stories of loved ones coming back as a pet. And frankly, I'm not going to suggest now that my dog, Obie, is really the reincarnation of my late husband.

But boy, one could make the argument!

Let me start by explaining that my husband died suddenly and shockingly, and that his death shook the very foundation of my secure, well-ordered life. At that time, I had a very old, very weak Cocker Spaniel, Buddy, who graciously stuck around for one year (almost to the day) after Rich's death. I like to imagine he stayed beyond his time to help get me through the worst year of my life. He then passed peacefully at age thirteen, leaving me still struggling, but at least through the worst. I declared after he died that I would be dog free, and followed that directive for six months.

I hadn't reckoned with Obie.

Being a dog person without a dog, I needed my puppy fix anyway, and so I went to a local shelter to volunteer. There I was met by a chipper, goofy little red Cocker Spaniel who immediately claimed my heart. He had been found running loose in the forest preserve, and was neither neutered nor micro-chipped, but appeared well cared for. He was certainly gentle and friendly.

The workers called him Ernie, and they told me he was about two years old. I fell in love with the happy little creature, and after being neutered and chipped, Ernie came home with me with the new name of Oberon.

At first I thought that at age two, it was odd that he acted so puppyish, but as the months went on, Obie's legs became longer, his body filled out, and he grew into his overly large head. His red fur even faded and became more of a soft caramel. I realized then that he was actually much younger than we had thought — in fact, he appeared to have been born around the time of my husband's death — a thought that was remarkably comforting.

Soon after that, I began noticing some surprisingly familiar oddities. For example, his eyes were kind of googly, and he occasionally appeared a little cross-eyed — a trait shared with my late husband, whose optical nerve had been damaged by forceps delivery at his birth. I also noticed that Obie had a gurgly stomach — also something my husband had been plagued with. We fell in the habit of going to the dog park every day, and I noticed that when he ran he seemed to have some trouble with his hind leg in the knee area, occasionally hopping on it as he ran. My husband was a runner who constantly had knee problems, including a torn meniscus.

Okay, I thought, this is getting weird.

It got weirder.

Obie took to sleeping on my bed, frequently trying to crawl in on my right, which had been my husband's side, but which, after Richard died, I had claimed, in part for the comfort of sharing his space. When Obie tried to push in, I held firm, and he eventually resigned himself to the left side. But during the night, he would push against me as if trying to make more room for himself — an irritating habit of my husband's, pushing me to the edge. And he would occasionally snore his funny dog snores — sounds that were eerily familiar. The first time,

I actually mumbled, "Richard, you're snoring. Turn over."

He did.

One night, I was awakened to a disturbing sound: Obie was apparently having a nightmare, and his moans tore through the darkness. I spun around and rubbed his back, uttering soothing sounds, and he stopped, but my heart was pounding. Richard had been plagued with nightmares, and often woke me with a similar cry.

While all that was strange, I still laughed at the idea of reincarnation. Then one day, just for fun, I looked at him and laughingly said, "Richard, are you in there?"

He responded by coming over and licking my nose.

Do I really believe that my dog is the reincarnation of my late husband? No. I know all these things are simply coincidence, maybe their similarities elevated by my wish to once more be with the man I so loved for thirty-nine years.

But I do have to admit I get a bit of comfort from the thought. And in a world that offers us so much pain as well as joy, don't we all deserve to take whatever comfort we can, wherever we can?

He's not Richard, he's Obie.

But dog or human, love is love, and that's good enough for me.

~Joyce Becker Lee

Mission Accomplished

Hope is faith holding out its hand in the dark.
~George Iles

On a beautiful early spring day, the city sidewalk bustled with people thrilled to be outside again after a long, cold winter. Colorful spring jackets abounded. There were even a few T-shirts and sandals! And, then, there was me. Decked out in winter hat, scarf, warm jacket, slacks, support hose, socks, and sturdy black athletic shoes, I was dressed to assuage my physical aches and pains. Beneath those cumbersome layers, I was trapped in a pathetically frail body. At fifty-six, I wanted nothing more than to regain my health and vitality after a really rough few years.

As I walked along the sidewalk with my dear friend Pat I watched the revelers warily, fearful of being jostled and falling down. Desperate to feel normal, I plastered a smile on my face. Fake it 'til you make it, I told myself, even though deep inside I felt like crying. My body was working way too hard, and just being out in the world again crystallized for me how far I'd plunged from health and happiness.

I'd been praying all day for the courage and mobility to manage this outing with grace. Pat, a nurse, was well aware of my physical and emotional state. But she'd traveled all the way from Florida to upstate New York to visit me. The last thing I wanted to do was come off like another one of her needy patients. The truth was I was sick and tired of myself and my situation. I just wanted my old life back! So, I kept smiling my frozen smile, putting one unsteady foot in front of the other, and praying for guidance.

Please, Lord—lift me up! I need your encouragement, strength, and support now more than ever before. Please help me.

After walking a while, Pat and I spotted an empty bench on the sidewalk and dropped down to watch the people parade by. Young mothers with children. Boisterous, laughing college students. Lovers strolling arm in arm.

"Isn't this wonderful?" Pat gushed, breathing in the warm, scented air.

I said it was, even though I still felt pretty choked up. Sitting there on that teeming street, I felt so isolated, lonely, and sad. Biting down hard on my lip, I turned away from Pat. That's when I noticed a big commotion halfway down the block. I wondered what was going on.

Suddenly my gaze landed on a half-grown golden Labrador Retriever bounding along the sidewalk, straining at her leash as she frolicked. The young man holding her was getting quite a workout, to the delight of his pretty companion, and pedestrians were sidestepping right and left to avoid the Lab as she blasted her way through the crowd. Glancing back at my dog-loving friend, I could tell by Pat's grin that she, too, had spotted the pooch. Eagerly, we turned back to watch the show.

The exuberant dog was still twenty feet from us—zigzagging madly as she tried to touch, see, and sniff every person she passed—when, suddenly, she spotted me. Her head did a cartoon double take, brown eyes flitting past me, then snapping back to me as if yanked by an invisible hand. Our eyes locked and held. Seconds later, she abruptly threw herself backwards and sat down at military attention, smack dab in the middle of the crowded sidewalk.

Her eyes remained glued to my face, and mine to hers. Fully aware that something incredible was happening, my heart hammered. I felt more alive than I had in months. The dog's sudden mood swing and stillness came about so unexpectedly, even her young owner practically stumbled over his pet's inexplicably rigid, planted body.

"Did you see that?" Pat gasped.

I nodded without turning, unwilling to break from the Lab's laser gaze. In a heartbeat, she'd eerily transformed from an unruly pup to a mature dog with the focus and discipline of a very old soul. My eyes welled with tears. Intuitively, I sensed that this dog knew me. She knew my sorrow and pain, and she wanted to help.

For the longest moment, the bustling sidewalk seemed to fade away, and then, suddenly—I smiled. Instantly, as if that were the very invitation she'd been waiting for, the old soul became a frenzied pup again. Jumping to her feet, she bee-lined straight to me, threw her front paws up on my lap, and started squirming, slobbering, and smooching me like I was her long-lost mother or her very best friend on earth whom she hadn't seen in ages.

Tears streamed down my face as I savored the dog's unbridled love, hugging her silky head and gazing into those adoring brown eyes. Her beauty and boundless affection were balm to my weary soul, easing my aching body and filling my heart with joy. I felt the ice inside me start to thaw, and for the first time in far too long I felt the wondrous stirring of hope . . . hope that things could, and would, get better.

"I'm so sorry," the dog-owner faltered, stunned.

"Don't worry," I assured him, smiling warmly. "I'm loving this."

"Come on, girl!" the man called at last, giving her leash a gentle tug.

Planting one last juicy kiss on my face, the pup bounded to the ground and continued her fun-filled adventure. For a moment, Pat and I just sat there, speechless. Finally, our eyes met.

"What just happened?" she asked softly.

"I'm not sure," I murmured as Pat's earlier remark echoed in my brain: "Isn't this wonderful?" Suddenly, I knew that life was exactly that: full of wonders.

I hadn't imagined the incident. It wasn't some eerie, otherworldly event that I'd experienced alone, unwitnessed by others. Pat was there—she'd seen it clearly—and the dog's owner and his companion had seen it, too. On a beautiful day in early spring, a frisky young dog was tapped from above to connect with a brokenhearted middle-aged woman. Showering me with love and affection, this frisky earth angel brought joy back into my life and restored to me the precious gift of hope.

~Wendy Hobday Haugh

Meet Our Contributors

Monica Agnew-Kinnaman is ninety-nine years old and served in an anti-aircraft artillery regiment in the British Army during WWII. She is the author of two books and three short stories, and has a doctorate in psychology. Dr. Kinnaman has lived in Colorado for over sixty years and has a son and daughter — both authors.

Adrienne A. Aguirre is a graduate of CSU San Marcos, and has a Master of Arts in Theology from Bethel Seminary San Diego. Adrienne is a hospice chaplain and freelance journalist. She's also working on her first book. Adrienne enjoys roller skating and walking her neighbors' dogs. E-mail her at 2240521@gmail.com.

Tammy Allison loves stories. Having worked in senior care for sixteen years, she has had the opportunity to hear many of them. She writes for a local newspaper, her blog faithhopelovefood.com, poetry, and has a novel in progress. She shares her home with her high school sweetheart, their two children, and two dogs.

Maria Atlan, born September 10th, 1981 is an American writer, world traveler, veteran, yoga teacher, and entrepreneur. She is currently living in and exploring Central America.

Deb Biechler is a retired kindergarten teacher. She loves long walks with her partner Randy and their dog Jessie, and spending time with her daughter, Hilary, and the current "grand-dog" Murphy. Deb works part-time as adjunct faculty for Viterbo University teaching Meditation, Mindfulness, and Journaling.

Jeanne Blandford is a writer/editor who, along with her husband Jack, is producing documentaries and creating children's books. When not traveling the country in their Airstream looking for new material, they can be found running SafePet, a partnership between Outreach to Pets in Need and Domestic Violence Crisis Center.

Patricia Boyer has been volunteering with her husband and Timmy at hospitals, nursing homes, and the library for several years. She is a retired teacher and enjoys writing stories that are near and dear to her heart, including those for the *Chicken Soup for the Soul* series. E-mail her at pbdb0410@gmail.com.

Sally A. Breslin is a copy editor and writer whose award-winning humor column, "My Life," was published weekly from 1994–2016 in several New England newspapers. She has authored three novels, including *There's a Tick in My Underwear!,* a humorous look at camping back in the 1960s. E-mail her at sillysally@att.net.

Cynthia Briggs embraces her love of cooking and writing through her nostalgic tales and recipes. She enjoys speaking to women's groups, reviewing cookbooks, coaching budding authors and writing for family publications. Read her blog at cynthiabriggsblog.com, or e-mail her at books@porkchopsandapplesauce.net.

Carol Bromby has a degree from the University of Waterloo and a diploma in Early Childhood from Humber College. Recently retired, she now enjoys hiking, gardening and spending time at her cottage with her husband, daughter, and family dog. Carol plans to write her grandmother's story of being a British Home Child.

Caroline Brown received her bachelor's degree in German and master's degree in Elementary Education. She was a teacher for many years, and after retiring, began writing children's literature. Caroline participated in the Transplant Olympics and worked to raise awareness about organ donation. She passed away in April 2017.

Mason K. Brown is a frequently published humorist and an inspirational author/storyteller/speaker. Living in beautiful Oregon inspires her writing. This is her seventh story in the *Chicken Soup for the Soul* series. She has previously written under the name Karen R. Hessen. Learn more at masonkbrown.com.

Dori Hillestad Butler is an award-winning author of more than fifty books for young readers, including *The Haunted Library* series, *The Buddy Files* series, and the *King & Kayla* series. *The Buddy Files: Case of the Lost Boy* won the 2011 Edgar Award for best juvenile mystery. She lives in the Seattle area.

Louise Canfield writes about 20th century southern women. She enjoys reading, piano, and time with family. Her stories have appeared in *The Journal of The Writers Guild of Virginia* and several online blogs and journals. She is a retired biochemistry professor living in Spring, TX with her husband of thirty-eight years and two Boston Terriers.

Eva Carter is a freelance writer and photographer. She lives in Dallas, TX with her Canadian husband, Larry. They have three grown children and five grandchildren. E-mail her at evacarter@sbcglobal.net.

Barbara Clarke is a college professor who teaches about social, political, and mental health issues. Barbara divides her time between teaching, music and family life, which includes her partner, four small dogs, and her elderly parents who live nearby. She has a keen interest in the role of animals in mental health.

Suzanne D. Cook and Sharon C. Thompson are neighbors in Columbus, OH. Suzanne, a retired teacher and skilled equestrian, lives with her husband Gary. They have three daughters and ten grandchildren. Sharon, a retired telecommunications consultant and photographer, lives with her husband Roy and helped Suzanne write her story.

Gwen Cooper received her Bachelor of Arts in English and Secondary Education from Metropolitan State University of Denver in 2007, and completed the Publishing Institute at Denver University in 2009. Gwen taught high school English, and now enjoys traveling and spending time with her husband and Bloodhound in the mountains.

Marianne L. Davis received her BA in English at University of Idaho and has twenty years experience writing professionally in the tech industry. She's currently working full-time on her first book, a suspense-thriller trilogy. Marianne married her college sweetheart, Steve, in 1991 and they have three children.

James Michael Dorsey is an award-winning author and explorer. He has written for *Colliers*, *The Christian Science Monitor*, *Lonely Planet*, *Los Angeles Times* and United Airlines. His book is *Vanishing Tales from Ancient Trails* and he has work in *The Best Travel Writing* — volumes 10, 11, 12, plus *The Lonely Planet Travel Anthology*.

Sharon Dunn is married and has been living the dream in South Florida for twenty-eight years. She has one adult daughter who always managed to convince her to say yes to adding another pet to the family. Sharon enjoys kayaking, tennis, and Zumba. She would like to thank Ava Pennington for helping to share this story.

Janice R. Edwards received her BAT degree in 1974. She taught English and Journalism before working for Texaco. She now writes for *Image Magazine*. Her stories have appeared in four other *Chicken Soup for the Soul* books.

Charlie Ess, sixty-one, has lived in Alaska since 1978. He and his wife Cheryl have been married for thirty-six years and have worked as commercial fishermen, loggers and trappers. Ess has written for magazines for the past twenty-five years. He and Cheryl hope to begin producing films and books in the years to come.

Carole Brody Fleet is a multi-award-winning author and media contributor. Widely recognized as an expert in life-adversity recovery and a veteran of over 1,000 radio show appearances, Ms. Fleet appears on numerous television and radio programs nationally and internationally as well as in worldwide print and web media.

Gayle Fraser's writing focuses on Christian characteristics for young people. She has written guidelines for grandparents when praying for their grandchildren, a curriculum for preteen girls, promoting healthy, Christlike lifestyles, *Abba's Whispers*, a devotional and several children's stories. She lives in Arizona.

Kathleen Gerard has shared her life with Yorkshire Terriers since she was nine years old. Her love of the breed inspired *The Thing Is*, a novel about a therapy dog named Prozac who rescues a woman in grief. Kathleen's writing has been widely published and anthologized. Learn more at kathleengerard.blogspot.com.

Dalia Gesser entertained audiences for twenty years with her delightfully original one-woman theater shows. Since 2000, she has been sharing her theater experience with children and adults through her workshops and classes. She lives north of Kingston, ON in beautiful lake country and can be reached via e-mail at daliag@kingston.net.

William C. Gibson is a retired paramedic living in a rural community in Southeast Georgia with three wonderfully loving dogs and two very sweet and very old cats. His primary writing interests include Christian action/adventure novels and assorted short stories.

Sherri Goodall has been published in *TulsaPeople*, *TulsaWoman*, *TulsaPets*, and *TulsaKids* magazines. If it has two or more legs and lives in Tulsa, she writes about it. She lives in Tulsa with her husband and two Westies.

Gwen Hart teaches writing at Buena Vista University in Storm Lake, IA. She is the author of the poetry collections *The Empress of Kisses* (Texas Review Press) and *Lost and Found* (David Robert Books). Her short stories have appeared in magazines and anthologies such as *Calliope 2013*, *Litro*, and *Eclectically Vegas, Baby!*

A writer and wildlife enthusiast from upstate New York, **Wendy Hobday Haugh** loves writing stories, poems, and articles for children and adults. Her work has appeared in *Highlights for Children*, *Woman's World*, *Saratoga Living*, and *WritersWeekly.com*. This is her ninth piece to appear in the *Chicken Soup for the Soul* series.

Dawn Hendricks is a registered nurse who lives/works in Arizona each winter and spends time traveling with her husband and her Newfoundland and Keeshond dogs the remainder of the year. She has two children and four grandchildren. Dawn enjoys her family and dogs, reading, gardening, the outdoors, and her nursing career.

Susan A. Hoffert is crafting a collection of stories of faith inspired by the hens in her chicken coop about the empty nests and the often empty heart of midlife. Her work appears in *Fall: Women's Stories and Poems for the Season of Wisdom and Gratitude*, *Words & Other Worthy Endeavors*, and *The Skunk River Review Vol. 11*.

Joei Carlton Hossack is the author of fifteen adventure travel books specializing in RV travel. She is a photographer, a travel and memoir writing instructor, an entertaining and inspirational speaker, and recently turned an itty-bitty beading hobby into a raging addiction.

Lori Hufty is currently an adjunct English professor at a community college in southern New Jersey. She is married and has two children. She enjoys writing and reading historical fiction in her spare time and running races with her son.

David Hull is a retired teacher and, although he now lives with assorted cats, he still fondly remembers his youthful years as a dog owner. He enjoys reading, writing, gardening, and spending time losing at board games to his nieces and nephews. E-mail him at Davidhull59@aol.com.

Gayle M. Irwin is the author of many inspirational pet books for children and adults. She also freelances for several Rocky Mountain area newspapers and magazines. She supports various pet rescue groups through her book sales and by volunteering as a transporter. Learn more at gaylemirwin.com.

Jeffree Wyn Itrich has been writing since childhood. Trained as a journalist, she has four books in print, numerous articles and a blog, thegoodnessprinciple.com. She works in health communications and lives in San Diego with her husband and two animated felines. When not writing, she makes quilts. E-mail her at jeffreewyn@gmail.com.

Jeanie Jacobson is on the Wordsowers Christian Writers leadership team. She's published in nine *Chicken Soup for the Soul* books. Grab her fun book, *Fast Fixes for the Christian Pack-Rat*, on Amazon. Jeanie loves visiting family and friends, reading, hiking, praise dancing, and gardening. E-mail her through jeaniejacobson.com.

Leigh Anne Jasheway has been writing funny books, many about dogs and cats, for 140+ dog years. She is the author of *Bedtime Stories for Dogs*, *Bedtime Stories for Cats*, *Date Me, Date My Dog*, and many others. Her writing has been included in over two-dozen anthologies and she writes a weekly humor column for *The Register-Guard*.

Tammi Kelly was born and raised in her hometown of Okeechobee, FL. She has a career with her local newspaper as a reporter. Her love of writing started when she was a child. Tammi loves to ride motorcycles, explore museums, dance, and spend time with her little dog.

Alice Klies is president of Northern Arizona Word Weavers. She is a five-time contributor to the *Chicken Soup for the Soul* series. She lives in Arizona with her husband and two Golden Retrievers. She hopes her written words make someone smile, cry, or laugh. E-mail her at alice.klies@gmail.com.

Jeanne R. Kraus is a retired educator from the Broward County Schools in South Florida. She has previously written three children's books and has published several short stories and some poetry. She enjoys tutoring, gardening, and rescuing animals in distress.

C.M. LaChance stays busy by writing short stories, novels and a vegan cookbook. When not clicking away at her laptop, she is traveling, hiking, and volunteering with animal rights organizations. She lives with four cats, four rabbits, two guinea pigs, a dog and a ball python.

Joyce Laird is a freelance writer living in Southern California. Her features have been published in a wide range of consumer magazines and she is a regular contributor to both *Woman's World* and the *Chicken Soup for the Soul* series. Joyce is also a member of Mystery Writers of America and Sisters in Crime.

Cathi LaMarche is a novelist, essayist, and poet. Her work appears in over thirty anthologies. She resides in Missouri with her husband, two children, and two spoiled Collies.

Jennifer R. Land received her Master of Library and Information Science degree and is currently a web development manager for her local library system. She also founded and directs Monroe's Mighty Mission, a nonprofit focused on keeping pets and families together through difficult times. She enjoys traveling and writing.

Marie Latta is the mother of five, grandmother of seven. She grew up on a small Michigan farm and five of those years attended a one-room country school. She writes for newspapers, magazines and children's publications. One big interest is cooking; she was a food columnist for the city newspaper and two farm magazines.

Joyce Becker Lee earned her MFA from Northwestern University, and her work has been published throughout the U.S. and Canada. She has taught high school English and theater and enjoys directing for the stage. Joyce has two amazing sons, two wonderful daughters-in-law, and three perfect grandchildren.

Lisa Leshaw is a mental health professional specializing in blended families and women's issues. She conducts Parenting Skills workshops and Empowerment Circles for Women throughout New York. In her silly times she performs puppet shows with characters who behave very inappropriately in order to get a laugh!

Barbara LoMonaco has worked for Chicken Soup for the Soul as an editor since 1998. She has co-authored two *Chicken Soup for the Soul* book titles and has had stories published in numerous other titles. Barbara is a graduate of the University of Southern California and has a teaching credential.

Anna M. Lowther is a busy wife, mother, and writer. Her days are filled with family activity. Her hobbies include sewing and music. She has worked as a slush reader and an editor while still keeping at her own writing.

Lorraine Lush is a spiritual writer, blogger, and teacher, and is now writing her first book. She enjoys playing piano and cello, photography, and hiking with her dogs, Sadie and Oreo. She plans to open a spiritual center for healing in southern New York in the near future. E-mail her at LLush2015@gmail.com.

Richard Matturro has a Ph.D. in English specializing in Shakespeare and Greek Mythology. He spent sixteen years at the *Albany Times Union*, and another fourteen teaching literature at University at Albany. He is the author of numerous newspaper articles, six published novels, and one audio book. Learn more at richardmatturro.com.

Roslyn McFarland received her bachelor's degree in Social Sciences and Speech Communication. She's currently putting her fascination in human nature to use by writing clean young-adult coming-of-age romances. A first-generation American, Roslyn is married with two daughters and a houseful of pets, including three dogs.

Spending time with the grandkids, crocheting, and enjoying life are **Alice M. McGhee's** leisure activities. Her passion is teaching ladies' Bible studies, which motivate her to keep in God's Word. Her devotionals have appeared in the *Chicken Soup for the Soul* and *Cup of Comfort* series, various e-zines, and her book, *Peace in the Midst of Pain*.

Kathy McGovern is a well-known writer and speaker in the Denver area. She authors a popular scripture column, thestoryandyou.com, which is published in parish bulletins around the country. She is thrilled to have her fifth story published in the *Chicken Soup for the Soul* series! Kathy adores Ben, her husband of twenty-nine years.

Phillip Merrill is the husband of Shauntel and the father of Samuel, Abigail, Noah, and Emma. He lives in Honeyville, UT, where he was born and raised. He received a Bachelor of Arts and Humanities degree in English from Weber State University. Phillip enjoys reading, writing, and spending time with his family.

Raised in Africa as the child of missionaries, **Harriet E. Michael** is an author, freelance writer, speaker, wife, mother, and grandmother. When not writing or speaking, she works part-time as a substitute teacher. Her books can be found at amazon.com/author/harrietemichael. Read her blog at harrietemichael.blogspot.com.

Paula W. Millet is a retired high school educator and now, a writer of novels. Holding a BA in Communication and an MA in Humanities, she has always been fascinated by the human experience, the unique connection between people. Originally from South Louisiana, she curently lives in suburban Atlanta, GA.

Marybeth Mitcham holds a BS in Biology, an MPH in Nutrition, and is working on her Ph.D. in Education. She works as an adjunct biology professor and a nutrition, healthy living, and food sustainability educator. She is an Adirondack 46er, motorcycle rider, and pianist. E-mail her at marybeth.mitcham@gmail.com.

Joanne Moore is a professional photographer with a passion for writing. Joanne has always loved animals, and currently has two rescue dogs and a foster dog. She lives in the foothills of the Tennessee Smoky Mountains, a beautiful backdrop for inspiration.

Linda Morefield lives in Virginia with her husband, Chuck, and their current rescue dog, Luna. Her writing has appeared in *The Potomac Review*, *The Delmarva Review*, *The Northern Virginia Review*, and *The Washington Independent Review of Books*.

Marya Morin is a freelance writer. Her stories have appeared in publications such as *Woman's World* and Hallmark. Marya also penned a weekly humorous column for an online newsletter, and writes custom poetry on request. She lives in the country with her husband. E-mail her at Akushla514@hotmail.com.

Jenny Pavlovic is the author of *The Not Without My Dog Resource & Record Book* and *8 State Hurricane Kate: The Journey and Legacy of a Katrina Cattle Dog*. She lives in Middleton, WI, with dogs Chase and Cayenne and cat Junipurr. She enjoys walking her dogs, kayaking, and gardening. Her "day job" is Ph.D. biomedical engineer.

Ava Pennington is a writer, speaker, and Bible teacher. She writes for nationally circulated magazines and has contributed to thirty-one anthologies, including twenty-four *Chicken Soup for the Soul* books. She also authored *Daily Reflections on the Names of God: A Devotional*, endorsed by Kay Arthur. Learn more at AvaWrites.com.

Saralee Perel is an award-winning nationally syndicated columnist. E-mail her at sperel@saraleeperel.com or via her website SaraleePerel.com.

Joe Petersen owns Building Better Bodies Fitness and is a health and wellness coach, and motivational speaker. Joe is a ten-time Team Race Across America winner, transcontinental record holder, State Time Trial Champion and Hall of Fame endurance cyclist. Joe writes newspaper and magazine articles. E-mail him at BuildingBetterBodys@aol.com.

Connie K. Pombo is an inspirational author, speaker, and freelance writer. She is a regular contributor to the *Chicken Soup for the Soul* series and other anthologies. When not speaking, writing or traveling, Connie enjoys spending time with her fur babies and other family members. Learn more at conniepombo.com.

When **Becky Lewellen Povich** was a young girl, she always enjoyed reading, but didn't begin to write until she was almost fifty years old! This is her fifth story published in the *Chicken Soup for the Soul* series. Her motto, by George Eliot is: "It's never too late to be who you might have been." E-mail Becky at Writergal53@gmail.com.

Michelle Preen lives in Cape Town, South Africa. She is a university graduate and works in the field of environmental communications. Michelle has had short stories published in various anthologies and magazines. She is passionate about travelling, writing, dogs, and chocolate. Learn more at michellepreen.com.

Caurie Putnam lives outside Rochester, NY with her husband Eric, sons Brice and Brady, and four dogs, including her soul mate Wilbur Write and a new Beagle rescued via the Beagle Freedom Project. This is her second story in the *Chicken Soup for the Soul* series. Follow her on Twitter @CauriePutnam.

Jennifer Quasha has been published in more than twenty *Chicken*

Soup for the Soul books and has been a co-author of four *Chicken Soup for the Soul* titles about pets. She loves her Chicken Soup!

Robin L. Reynolds is a blogger and creator of the DearJalen.com guided writing community where she provides writing prompts that inspire parents to journal their stories, guidance and wisdom so that their children will have a family keepsake to share with generations to come. Follow Robin on Twitter @RobinDarling.

Mark Rickerby has written over a dozen stories for the *Chicken Soup for the Soul* series. He also co-authored his father's memoir, *The Other Belfast*, released a CD of songs (*Great Big World*) for his daughters, Marli and Emma, and is Head Writer for an upcoming western TV show, *Big Sky*. Mark invites you to visit him at markrickerby.com.

Brett Roberson has spent over fifteen years in the U.S. Army, and previously served as a Detachment Commander in 5th Special Forces Group (Airborne). He received his degree in economics from the University of Central Oklahoma, and lives in Oklahoma with his wife and two sons. E-mail him at brettroberson180th@gmail.com.

Donna L. Roberts is a native of upstate New York who lives and works in Europe. She is an Associate Professor and holds a Ph.D. in Psychology. Donna is an animal and human rights advocate. When she is researching or writing, she can be found at her computer buried in rescue animals.

Debbie Robertson is retired from gainful employment, but spends her days as a professional volunteer supporting the Cystic Fibrosis Foundation, the Indy Honor Flight, and the Ovar'coming Together foundation. She loves outdoor activities and enjoys traveling vicariously through the exploits of her adult son.

Sallie A. Rodman received her Certificate in Professional Writing at Cal State University, Long Beach. Her work has appeared in numerous

Chicken Soup for the Soul books. She lives with Mollie the dog and Brodie the cat in Los Alamitos, CA. Sallie enjoys her book and art clubs when she isn't writing.

Stephen Rusiniak is from Wayne, NJ, and was a police detective specializing in juvenile/family matters. Today he shares his thoughts through his writings, including several stories in the *Chicken Soup for the Soul* series. Contact him via Facebook, on Twitter @StephenRusiniak or by visiting stephenrusiniak.com.

Bonnie Sargent began writing following a twenty-plus-year career in elementary education. After a stroke ended her teaching career, Bonnie could no longer speak, so she began writing in order to express herself. She has had one children's book and several stories published.

Anna Scates is a mother of three, homemaker, author, and former mechanical engineer. She received her Bachelor of Science in ME from Tennessee Technological University in 1987. She enjoys crocheting, sewing, drawing, painting, traveling, zip lining, and writing. Her blog is entitled *The 7 Year Adventure*.

Doris Schoon is a retired ophthalmologist living in Anaheim, CA with her dog, Sheba. Her dog, Willy, was her confidant, encourager and dear friend for over thirteen years. Of all of the blessings God has given Doris, dogs rate among the dearest.

Deborah Shouse is a writer, speaker, editor, and dementia advocate. Deborah's newest book, *Connecting in the Land of Dementia: Creative Activities to Explore Together*, features dozens of experts in the field of creativity and dementia. For more information and ideas, please visit DementiaJourney.org or DementiaJourney on Facebook.

Debby K. Simon is a freelance writer and the former publisher of the award-winning companion animal newsletter, *Daisy's Paw Print News*, which was inspired by and named for her family's adopted Golden Retriever. She is currently working on her first novel about her first dog.

Shelley Skuster, of Des Moines, IA, is an award-winning journalist who left TV news to say at home with her young children. When she's not knee-deep in diapers or reheating her morning coffee for the fifth time, she writes freelance about her family's journey at ShelleySkuster.com.

Paula Sparrow has long been an advocate for animals, particularly shelter animals. Along with volunteering for animal shelters for many years, she is the author of the "Creature Comforts" column for *Kentucky Living* magazine, a column she has written since 2003. She lives on a Kentucky farm with her dogs, cats, and horses.

Lynn Sunday is an artist, writer, and animal advocate who lives near San Francisco, CA with her husband and senior rescue dogs. Eight of her stories appear in seven other *Chicken Soup for the Soul* books, and numerous magazines and other anthologies. E-mail her at Sunday11@aol.com.

Julie Theel lives in sunny Rancho Mirage, CA with her husband, two teenage daughters, four furry dogs and two fluffy cats. When not busy shuttling the girls to their many activities, Julie spends her time rescuing animals and running her business selling the Rippys, her patented rip-apart toys for dogs.

Dorann Weber is a freelance photographer for a county newspaper and Getty Images. She has a newfound love for writing and can now add freelance writing to her interests. She lives in Pinelands of South New Jersey with her family and pets, which include dogs, cats, chickens, snakes, and lizards.

Phyllis Wheeler is a Christian life coach, writer, and photographer who is happily married to a fantastic guy and blessed with great family, friends, and animal companions. She strives to inspire, encourage, and bring joy to people while glorifying God in all she does. She has a master's degree from Johns Hopkins University.

Leslie A. Wibberley's work is published in *Mamalode*, *Mothers Always Write*, *Literary Mama*, *The Manifest Station*, *Devolution Z*, the *Chicken Soup for the Soul* series, and *River Tales*. She has won a sixth place and an Honorable Mention in Writers Digest's Annual Competitions. E-mail her at wibberleythewordsmith@gmail.com.

Amy Catlin Wozniak shares her life with her soul mate, four children, two grandsons, and a Great Pyrenees named Scarlett O'Hara, who has absolutely no problem living up to her namesake. She resides in Northeast Ohio, where she writes inspirational fiction and nonfiction that reflects God's hope.

Linda Zallen is a psychotherapist and writer living in Northern California. She's written stories, poems, and songs, and is currently rewriting the draft of a novel. Linda's most recent poem, "Her Heart's Home," is published in *The Ibis Head Review*.

Ellyn Horn Zarek is a writer from South Florida. An alumnus of UMass Boston, she has had several short stories read on NPR radio and is a Chicken Soup for the Soul contributor. Ellyn enjoys writing beachside and spending time with her husband Jeff, daughter Mary Ellyn, son Bradley, and Miniature Schnauzer Daisy.

Debra Zemke is a songwriter and music publisher in Nashville, TN. Songwriting since 1992, she currently has over three dozen published and recorded songs. As a songwriter her dream is to move people emotionally and inspire them to never stop dreaming. She believes it is our relationships that make the magic in our lives.

Meet Amy Newmark

Amy Newmark is the bestselling author, editor-in-chief, and publisher of the *Chicken Soup for the Soul* book series. Since 2008, she has published 140 new books, most of them national bestsellers in the U.S. and Canada, more than doubling the number of Chicken Soup for the Soul titles in print today. She is also the author of *Simply Happy*, a crash course in Chicken Soup for the Soul advice and wisdom that is filled with easy-to-implement, practical tips for having a better life.

Amy is credited with revitalizing the Chicken Soup for the Soul brand, which has been a publishing industry phenomenon since the first book came out in 1993. By compiling inspirational and aspirational true stories curated from ordinary people who have had extraordinary experiences, Amy has kept the twenty-four-year-old Chicken Soup for the Soul brand fresh and relevant.

Amy graduated *magna cum laude* from Harvard University where she majored in Portuguese and minored in French. She then embarked on a three-decade career as a Wall Street analyst, a hedge fund manager, and a corporate executive in the technology field. She is a Chartered Financial Analyst.

Her return to literary pursuits was inevitable, as her honors thesis in college involved traveling throughout Brazil's impoverished northeast region, collecting stories from regular people. She is delighted to have come full circle in her writing career — from collecting stories "from the people" in Brazil as a twenty-year-old to, three decades later, collecting stories "from the people" for Chicken Soup for the Soul.

When Amy and her husband Bill, the CEO of Chicken Soup for the Soul, are not working, they are visiting their four grown children.

Follow Amy on Twitter @amynewmark. Listen to her free daily podcast, The Chicken Soup for the Soul Podcast, at www.chickensoup. podbean.com, or find it on iTunes, the Podcasts app on iPhone, or on your favorite podcast app on other devices.

About Robin Ganzert and American Humane

Robin Ganzert, Ph.D. is a bestselling author, radio host, television producer, animal lover and CEO of American Humane. American Humane is the country's first national humane organization committed to ensuring the safety, welfare, and wellbeing of all animals. For more than 140 years, American Humane has been first in promoting the welfare and safety of animals and strengthening the bond between animals and people. American Humane's cutting-edge initiatives are always first to serve, whenever and wherever animals are in need of rescue, shelter, protection, or security.

Under Dr. Ganzert's leadership, American Humane has been named a "Top-Rated Charity" by CharityWatch and achieved the prestigious "Gold Level" charity designation from GuideStar. Dr. Ganzert was recently awarded the Global CEO Excellence Award as the top CEO of an animal welfare organization, and she was recognized by Brava as a top female CEO in Washington, DC.

A familiar face to millions of Americans from her frequent TV appearances and the highly watched Hallmark Channel's *American Humane Hero Dog Awards*, she also hosts a new podcast, *Chicken Soup for the Soul Presents Loving Animals,* which mixes practical expert pet advice with guest appearances by some of America's best-known pet lovers from the movies, music and sports. She is also the author of *Animal Stars: Behind the Scenes with Your Favorite Animal Actors*, and has two new books coming out soon. Robin has appeared on NBC's *Today Show*, *ABC World News Tonight*, *Fox & Friends*, *On the Record with Greta Van Susteren*, and other local and national television programs.

American Humane is first to serve animals around the world, ensuring their safety, welfare and humane treatment — from rescuing animals in crisis to ensuring that animals are humanely treated. The best known program is the "No Animals Were Harmed®" animals-in-entertainment certification, which appears during the end credits of films and TV shows, and today monitors more than 1,000 productions yearly with over 3,400 production days with an outstanding safety record. American Humane's farm animal welfare program ensures the humane treatment of over a billion farm animals, the largest animal welfare program of its kind. And recently, American Humane launched Humane Conservation, an innovative initiative ensuring the humane treatment of animals around the globe in zoos and aquariums.

Continuing its longstanding efforts on strengthening the healing power of the human-animal bond, American Humane spearheaded a groundbreaking clinical trial that provides scientific substantiation for animal-assisted therapy (AAT) in the treatment of children with cancer and their families.

To learn more about American Humane, visit americanhumane. org and follow it on Facebook and Twitter. To subscribe to the weekly podcast, *Chicken Soup for the Soul Presents Loving Animals with Robin Ganzert*, visit iTunes and Google Play to have a new episode automatically downloaded every week.

Thank You

We owe huge thanks to all of our contributors and fans, and to their caring, crazy, comical, courageous, and clever canine companions. We loved your stories about your dogs and how they enrich your lives. We could only publish a small percentage of the stories that were submitted, but we read every single one and even the ones that do not appear in the book had an influence on what went into the final manuscript.

We owe special thanks to Jennifer Quasha, who read the thousands of stories submitted for this book and helped us narrow them down to a few hundred finalists. Susan Heim did a masterful job editing the first manuscript.

Associate Publisher D'ette Corona continued to be Amy's right-hand woman in creating the final manuscript and working with all our wonderful writers. Barbara LoMonaco and Kristiana Pastir, along with Elaine Kimbler, jumped in at the end to proof, proof, proof. And yes, there will always be typos anyway, so feel free to let us know about them at webmaster@chickensoupforthesoul.com and we will correct them in future printings.

The whole publishing team deserves a hand, including Maureen Peltier, Victor Cataldo, Mary Fisher, Ronelle Frankel and Daniel Zaccari, who turned our manuscript into this beautiful book.

Chicken Soup for the Soul

Changing the world one story at a time®
www.chickensoup.com